Of Magnolia and Mesquite

Suzanne Corder

Gay Thompson

First printing	March 1985	5,000 copies
Second printing	June 1985	5,000 copies

Library of Congress Catalogue Card Number: 84-52222
ISBN: 0-9614184-0-0

Copies may be obtained from **Su-Ga Publications**,
2103 Dimmitt Road, Plainview, Texas 79072
(Order form in back of book)

Printed by
Hart Graphics
Austin, Texas

To Jim and Gayle

Their love, encouragement and support have made this book and our lives very special

SUZANNE W. CORDER

Charm and versatility in harmony with family tradition and the experience gained from catering while living in Indianola, Mississippi, have been blended to perfection and the result is Suzanne Corder's recognized talents as an excellent cook and gracious hostess.

Suzanne, a native of Vicksburg, Mississippi, and her husband, Jim, moved from Indianola to Plainview, Texas in 1983, where he is Regional Manager for Riverside-Terra, Inc. She has three children, a son, Marshall, and daughters, Christi and Kendall.

Suzanne's interests are varied and involve her in many family and community projects but her greatest pleasure and the one she most generously shares comes from the time she spends in her kitchen.

GAY A. THOMPSON

From the Piney Woods of East Texas to the South Plains of the Texas panhandle, Gay Thompson draws her heritage. She is the wife of Gayle Thompson, a farmer and agricultural consultant, and the mother of three grown, married children.

Although this is her first cookbook, she has had vast experience in menu planning and "recipe sharing", with many requests from organizations planning a meeting to individuals needing a particular bread recipe.

Gay is active in church and community affairs, but her talent as a "culinary artist" has earned her the reputation as one of Plainview's best cooks and most gracious hostesses.

FOREWARD

"Never," we were told by all, "begin a title with a preposition!" . . . but that is really what this book is . . . "of" magnolia and "of" mesquite. It is of families and neighbors, our children and friends. It is of sharing and creating memories, bringing forth our best from them whether that is from the most lavish of effort and decor or the simple and totally relaxed.

We hope that you will find in these pages the spirit of pleasure that has been ours throughout the writing of the book. Our greatest sense of accomplishment will be in feeling that we have helped you better develop and refine your skills in cooking and entertaining. We hope to share with you the love of our families and friends in the way we have been able to best define these feelings . . . through cooking.

The most over-worked and misunderstood word that has become part of our everyday vocabulary is "gourmet". It is cloaked in a mystique that interests a few, charms some, and scares-to-death most. We fervently believe that once we have lifted the edges of the veil that surrounds that frightening word and allowed you to see for yourselves the many ways that elegance can be achieved, quality assured, and sanity preserved in the process, you, too, will begin to think of yourself as a "gourmet cook" . . . expanding your own efforts to the height of your imagination.

Too often we find that the distance between thinking of having guests and actually inviting them is so great that it is never overcome. It has been our observation that one of the major obstacles for most "I'd-love-to-but-don't" hostesses is in planning a menu. The uncertainty of the successful blending of taste, texture, and color becomes so overwhelming that it far overshadows the desire to entertain more than family or the closest of friends. Our main purpose in writing has been to suggest such varied, attractive, and delicious recipes in menu form that you will look forward to your NEXT party before the present one is over!

WE GRATEFULLY ACKNOWLEDGE

The problem that has plagued us from beginning to end is our inability to adequately express our appreciation or to even give full credit to the many, many people who have been responsible for "our" recipes. We have spent many years as avid collectors and most of the recipes in our individual files have come to us through the generosity of family, friends, strangers, aunts, dog-catchers, box-tops, cousins' cousins, and pages surreptitiously torn from waiting room magazines. Many of the best have been such long-standing favorites in our respective families that they are simply part of us . . . without a clue remaining as to their origin. We apologize for not being able to tell you why each recipe that we chose to use is special and if you are certain that it came from YOUR great-aunt Hattie, it probably did!! Please thank her for us . . . we love it and her for sharing it!

The collecting, writing, and editing that we did were a pleasure but without the talents of the people who did the mountain of typing the project would never have been finished. We will be forever grateful to Laura Branch, Delia Jones, Elaine Fowler, Melinda Thompson Hampton and Becky Hill Thompson. They shared their skills and enthusiasm so willingly, blending them with our efforts to give us the finished product we had hoped to create.

All of the artwork was done by Sarah Larson who has lived and studied in Texas all her life. She has a B.F.A. from the University of Houston and currently lives in Austin, where she teaches art and specializes in mosaics for swimming pools. We especially appreciate her beautiful designs.

The wine suggestions were provided by Sigels. We appreciate their help.

CONTENTS

Breakfast
and
Brunches
"Awake to Elegance"

Awake To Elegance
BREAKFAST AND BRUNCHES

Breakfasts For Two

Sunday Morning
Early Morning Elegance
Breakfast in Bed

Breakfasts or Brunches For Four

A Birthday Brunch
Wake Up to Winter
A Quick and Easy Breakfast
Brunch by the Pool

Breakfasts and Brunches For Six

Delight Your House Guests
Mostly Do-Ahead Brunch
An Elite Brunch
Autumn Leaves

Brunches For Eight

Meet the New Neighbor
Welcome Home!
Before the Game

Brunches For Bunches

A Farewell Brunch
Brunch for a Crowd
A Wedding Brunch
Fund Raiser Brunch
A Grand Old Fashioned Southern Brunch

SUNDAY MORNING

SERVES TWO

Chilled Fruit Medley

Avocado Egg Omelet

Marinated Ham

Pecan Popovers

Coffee

Chilled Fruit Medley

1 small banana, peeled and sliced
1 medium apple, unpeeled and sliced
¼ cup unsweetened orange juice
6 fresh strawberries, quartered
1 medium orange, peeled, seeded, and sectioned
1 grapefruit, peeled, seeded, and sectioned

Combine first 3 ingredients in a medium bowl; toss gently. Add strawberries, oranges, and grapefruit; cover and chill. To serve, arrange fruit on individual plates.

Yield: 2 servings.

Avocado-Egg Omelet

1½ cups sour cream
1 teaspoon salt
¼ teaspoon pepper
2 large tomatoes, peeled and chopped
1 avocado, peeled and diced
8 slices bacon, cooked crisp and crumbled
8 eggs, slightly beaten
⅓ cup milk
½ teaspoon salt
2 tablespoons butter

Heat sour cream, salt and pepper in double boiler. Add tomatoes and avocado. Heat another 5 minutes. Blend beaten eggs with milk and salt. Pour half of egg mixture into heated butter in skillet or omelet pan and cook gently, lifting edges occasionally to let uncooked part run underneath. When set, sprinkle with half the bacon, pour ¼ of sauce mixture over omelet, and fold over. Place on hot platter and pour on another ¼ of sauce. Repeat.

Makes 2 omelets.

Marinated Ham

2 slices cooked ham
½ cup red wine
¼ cup plum jelly

In small saucepan, melt jelly; add wine. Pour over ham slices in covered glass dish. Refrigerate overnight. Serve at room temperature.

Pecan Popovers

¼ cup pecans
1 egg
½ cup milk
½ cup flour, sifted
Dash salt

Chop pecans in blender container; empty blender and set nuts aside. Put eggs and milk in blender container; cover and blend 2 seconds. Add flour and salt; cover and blend 10 seconds. Stir in pecans and blend again. Fill 4 well-greased custard cups ½ full. Place cups on baking sheet and bake at 475° for 15 minutes. Reduce heat to 350° and bake 25 to 30 minutes longer or until brown and firm. A few minutes before removing from oven, prick each popover with a fork to let steam escape. If you prefer popovers dry and crisp, turn oven off and leave in oven 30 minutes with door ajar. Serve hot.

Yield: 4 popovers.

ALWAYS, ALWAYS read through a recipe BEFORE you begin! You will usually know from past experience how a recipe is going to develop, but even "old-timers" occasionally get surprised!

EARLY MORNING ELEGANCE

SERVES TWO

Apricot Gold

Ham and Eggs Elite

Quick Hot Biscuits and Jam

Coffee

Apricot Gold

- ¾ cup apricot nectar
- ½ cup milk
- ½ teaspoon lemon juice
- ½ pint vanilla ice cream

Put all ingredients in blender. Cover and blend until smooth.
Yield: 2 servings.

Ham and Eggs Elite

- 1 12-ounce can chopped ham
- 1 4-ounce can mushroom pieces and stems, drained
- ¼ teaspoon onion salt
- 4 eggs
- Salt and pepper to taste

Cut ham into strips 1¼×¼ inches. Heat ham strips and drained mushrooms in skillet; stir in onion salt. Spread ham mixture evenly over bottom of skillet. Break eggs on top of ham; season with salt and pepper. Cover and cook, without stirring, until eggs are done.
Yield: 2 servings.

Quick Hot Biscuits

Equal parts of self-rising flour and whipping cream. Put desired amount of flour in bowl; make a well in the center; add same amount of whipping cream (may need to add slightly more cream to form a slightly sticky dough). Stir with a fork just until flour is all dampened. Turn out onto floured surface and knead just until smooth. Pat out dough to about ⅓ inch thickness and cut with floured biscuit cutter. Place biscuits in greased pan, brush tops with salad oil or melted butter. Bake at 400° for 10 to 12 minutes or until brown. This is a wonderful biscuit to make in a hurry. The flavor is great and you can make one or fifty!

Pre-heating the oven seems so obvious a step that we haven't stated it in each recipe. Unless your recipe calls for a cold oven, by all means, develop the good habit of turning on the oven to the required temperature before you begin.

BREAKFAST IN BED

SERVES TWO

Breakfast Drink

Eggs with Herbed Cheese

Toasted English Muffin

Coffee or Tea

Breakfast Drink

2 very ripe bananas, cut into large chunks
4 tablespoons frozen orange juice concentrate
1 cup milk
1 cup plain yogurt

In a blender, combine the banana, orange juice concentrate, milk and yogurt. Blend until smooth and frothy, about 30 seconds. Pour into a large glass.

Eggs with Herbed Cheese

4 eggs
¼ cup heavy cream
1¼ ounces herbed fresh cream cheese, such as Alouette, cut into small pieces
1½ tablespoons chopped parsley
Salt and freshly ground pepper

In a large heavy skillet, place the eggs and cream over very low heat. Stir gently to break the egg yolks and to combine with the cream. Cook, scraping the bottom of the skillet frequently, until about half the eggs form soft curds, about 10 minutes. Add the cheese and parsley to the eggs. Continue to cook, stirring frequently, until the eggs form large soft curds, 8 to 10 minutes. Remove from the heat and season with salt and pepper to taste.

The secret to making this delicious breakfast dish is to cook the eggs slowly over very low heat. Serve spooned over or alongside toasted English muffins.

A BIRTHDAY BRUNCH

SERVES FOUR

Two Fruits Cup

Shrimp Omelet

Special Orange Muffins

Coffee

Two Fruits Cup

Cut one peeled, cored fresh pineapple into chunks. Place in glass dish and cover chunks with vermouth (or any kind of dry white wine); refrigerate covered. When ready to serve, arrange chunks in pretty bowls, divide the juice between bowls. Add several fresh strawberries and garnish each bowl with sprigs of mint.

Shrimp Omelet

- ½ pound unpeeled small fresh shrimp
- 3 green onions, finely chopped
- 2 tablespoons butter, melted
- 8 eggs
- 4 tablespoons milk
- 1 teaspoon salt
- ¼ teaspoon pepper
- 2 tablespoons butter
- 1 cup shredded Cheddar cheese

Peel and devein shrimp. Sauté shrimp and scallions in 2 tablespoons butter in a heavy skillet until the shrimp turn pink; set aside. Combine eggs, milk, salt, and pepper; beat well. Heat a 10-inch omelet pan or heavy skillet until it is hot enough to sizzle a drop of water. Add 2 tablespoons butter; rotate pan to coat bottom. Pour egg mixture into pan. As mixture starts to cook gently lift edges of omelet with a spatula and tilt pan so uncooked portion flows underneath. Spoon shrimp mixture and cheese over half of omelet when eggs are set and top is still moist and creamy. Loosen omelet with a spatula, and fold unfilled side over filling; remove from heat. Cover and let stand 1 to 2 minutes or until cheese melts. Gently slide omelet onto a serving plate; serve omelet immediately. Serves 4.

Don't be afraid to try new dishes. We hope to have removed much of the risk for you by offering you recipes that we know work well—both in taste combinations and in appearance—so try some of the things that are new to you.

Special Orange Muffins

- 2 cups biscuit mix
- ¼ cup sugar
- 1 egg, beaten
- ½ cup orange juice
- 2 tablespoons vegetable oil
- ½ cup orange marmalade
- ½ cup chopped pecans
- 3 tablespoons sugar
- 1 tablespoon all-purpose flour
- ½ teaspoon ground cinnamon
- ¼ teaspoon ground nutmeg
- Orange-Pecan Butter (recipe below)

Combine biscuit mix and ¼ cup sugar, make a well in center of mixture. Combine egg, orange juice, and oil; add to dry ingredients, stirring just until moistened. Gently stir in marmalade and pecans.

Spoon into paper-lined muffin pans, filling two-thirds full. Combine 3 tablespoons sugar, flour, and spices; sprinkle 1 teaspoon over each muffin. Bake at 400° for 18 to 20 minutes. Serve with Orange-Pecan Butter. Yield: 1 dozen.

Orange-Pecan Butter

- ½ cup butter, softened
- 1 tablespoon sifted powdered sugar
- 1 tablespoon orange juice
- 3 tablespoons finely chopped pecans, toasted

Cream butter until light and fluffy; blend in sugar and orange juice. Stir in pecans. Cover and store in refrigerator.

Yield: ½ cup.

WAKE UP TO WINTER

SERVES FOUR

Winter Fruit Compote

Baked Eggs

Sunny Coffee Cake

Ham Puffs

Hot Mocha

Winter Fruit Compote

- 2 Golden Delicious apples, peeled and cut into eighths
- 1 Anjou pear, peeled and cut into eighths
- 3 tablespoons fresh lemon juice
- 3 tablespoons unsalted butter
- ¼ cup bitter orange marmalade
- 3 navel oranges, peel, pit, and membranes discarded and the fruit cut into sections

In a bowl toss the apples and the pear with the lemon juice, in a large skillet sauté the mixture in 2 tablespoons of the butter over moderately high heat, turning the fruit gently until the apple is tender, and transfer it with a slotted spoon to a bowl. Add to the skillet the remaining 1 tablespoon butter and the marmalade and cook the mixture over moderate heat, stirring, until the marmalade is melted. Pour the mixture over the fruit, add the orange sections, and toss the mixture gently. Spoon the compote into serving bowls.

Serves 4.

Baked Eggs

- 4 eggs, hard-cooked
- ¼ cup butter
- ¼ cup flour
- 1 cup milk
- 1 cup heavy cream
- ½ teaspoon salt
- ¼ teaspoon white pepper
- ¼ teaspoon dry mustard
- 1 cup Gruyère cheese, grated
- ½ cup Parmesan cheese, grated

Place eggs which have been halved, cut side down in a buttered baking dish. Make sauce by melting butter, add flour and cook, stirring constantly for 2 to 3 minutes. Add milk gradually, stirring until thickened. Add cream and seasonings. Melt in Gruyère cheese and pour sauce over eggs. Sprinkle top with Parmesan cheese. Bake at 450° for 25 minutes or until heated through, bubbling and browned lightly on top.

Sunny Coffee Cake

- 1½ cups all-purpose flour
- ¾ cup sugar
- 2 teaspoons baking powder
- ¾ teaspoon salt
- 1 teaspoon grated orange rind
- ¾ cup milk
- 1 egg, beaten
- ⅓ cup butter, melted
- 1¼ cups powdered sugar
- 2 tablespoons milk
- 2 tablespoons chopped nuts

Combine flour, sugar, baking powder, and salt. Stir in orange rind. Combine ¾ cup milk, egg, and butter; add to dry ingredients, stirring only until well blended. Pour into a well-greased 5½ cup ring mold. Bake at 375° for 30 to 35 minutes. Cool on rack about 5 minutes. Loosen edges with spatula and remove from pan. Combine powdered sugar and 2 tablespoons milk; mix well. Drizzle icing on cooled coffee cake. Decorate with nuts.

Yield: one coffee ring.

Ham Puffs

- 4 eggs
- ½ cup milk
- ½ teaspoon dry mustard
- ⅛ teaspoon pepper
- 4 ounces brick cheese, cut up
- 2 3-ounce packages cream cheese, cut up
- 1 cup finely diced fully cooked ham (5 ounces)
- ½ teaspoon dried parsley flakes

In blender container or food processor bowl combine first 4 ingredients. Cover; process till smooth. With blender or food processor running and lid ajar (or through opening in lid), add cheeses. Process till nearly smooth. Stir in ham and parsley. Pour into four ungreased 1-cup soufflé dishes. Bake in 375° oven for 25 to 30 minutes.

Serves 4.

Hot Mocha

- 1¾ cups strong hot coffee
- ¼ teaspoon ground cinnamon
- ⅛ teaspoon ground nutmeg
- 2 tablespoons sugar
- 3 tablespoons cocoa
- ¼ cup water
- 2 cups milk or half-and-half
- ½ teaspoon vanilla extract

Combine coffee, cinnamon, and nutmeg; stir well. Set aside. Combine sugar and cocoa in a saucepan; add water, stirring well. Bring mixture to a boil. Boil 3 minutes, stirring constantly. Stir in milk; heat to boiling point (212°). Remove saucepan from heat, and stir in vanilla and coffee mixture. Serve immediately.

Yield: 4 cups.

A QUICK AND EASY BREAKFAST

SERVES FOUR

Fruit Kabobs

Breakfast Burritos

Royal Mocha

Fruit Kabobs

Alternate fruit of your choice on wooden skewers. Fresh fruit of the season such as whole strawberries, chunks of honeydew, seedless grapes, pineapple, etc. are an attractive combination; however, well-drained canned fruits may also be used.

Breakfast Burritos

½ pound bulk pork sausage
2 large potatoes, peeled and grated
1 medium-size green pepper, chopped
½ cup chopped onion
8 eggs, beaten
8 8-inch flour tortillas
¼ cup butter or margarine, melted
2½ cups (10 ounces) shredded Cheddar cheese
Taco sauce

Cook sausage until browned; drain, reserving drippings in skillet. Set sausage aside. Add vegetables to skillet, and cook until potatoes are browned. Add eggs; cook, stirring occasionally, until eggs are firm but still moist. Wrap tortillas tightly in foil; bake at 350° for 15 minutes. Spoon an equal amount of egg mixture in center of each tortilla; roll up. Place filled tortillas in a lightly greased 13×9×2-inch baking dish; brush with butter, and cover with foil. Bake at 375° for 10 minutes; sprinkle burritos with cheese. Cover and bake 5 minutes or until cheese melts. Serve with taco sauce. Serves 4.

Royal Mocha

1 pint whipping cream
1 5.5-ounce can chocolate syrup
⅓ cup brandy
1 quart coffee ice cream, softened
1 6-ounce package semisweet chocolate morsels
¾ cup chopped almonds, toasted
Whipped cream
Maraschino cherries

Combine whipping cream, chocolate syrup, and brandy; beat until thickened. Place ice cream in a large plastic or metal freezer container; fold chocolate mixture into ice cream. Stir in chocolate morsels and almonds. Freeze, uncovered, about 3 hours. Remove from freezer, and stir well. Cover and freeze. Spoon into parfait glasses, and garnish with whipped cream and maraschino cherries.

MOSTLY DO-AHEAD BRUNCH

SERVES SIX

Flipped Orange Juice
Special Scrambled Eggs
Ham and Cheddar Pudding
Cranberry Freeze
Honey-Bran Muffins

Flipped Orange Juice

1 12-ounce can frozen orange juice
4 cans ice water
2 cups crushed ice
4 eggs
2 tablespoons sugar

Put all ingredients into blender, blend on high speed about 1 minute. Serve immediately in small glasses.

Special Scrambled Eggs

Vegetable cooking spray
¼ cup chopped green pepper
¼ cup finely chopped green onions with tops
6 eggs
¼ cup milk
⅛ teaspoon pepper
⅓ teaspoon hot sauce
½ cup chopped tomato
¼ cup (1 ounce) Monterey Jack cheese
Pimiento strips (optional)
Fresh parsley (optional)

Coat a large skillet with cooking spray; place over medium-low heat until hot. Add green pepper and onions; cook until vegetables are tender, stirring occasionally. Drain and set aside. Combine eggs, milk, pepper, and hot sauce; beat well, and pour into skillet. Cook over low heat, stirring gently to allow uncooked portions to flow underneath. Cook until eggs are set but still moist. Stir in vegetables and tomato, and cook until thoroughly heated. Sprinkle with cheese. Garnish with pimiento strips and parsley, if desired. Serves 6.

Ham and Cheddar Pudding

½ pound sharp Cheddar, grated
2½ cups milk
12 slices of homemade-type white bread, crusts removed
½ stick (¼cup) butter, softened
¼ pound baked ham, chopped fine
3 large eggs, beaten lightly
1 teaspoon dry mustard
Tabasco to taste

In a heavy saucepan melt the Cheddar in the milk over moderate heat, stirring, and let the mixture cool. Spread the bread with the butter and arrange 4 slices buttered side down in one layer in a buttered 8-inch-square baking pan. Top the bread with half the ham and make layers with the remaining bread and ham in the same manner, ending with a layer of bread. In a bowl combine the eggs, the mustard, the Tabasco, and a pinch of salt, whisk in the Cheddar mixture, and ladle the mixture through a fine sieve over the bread. Let the mixture stand, covered loosely, at room temperature for at least 1 hour or chilled overnight. Put the baking pan in a larger pan, add enough hot water to the larger pan to reach halfway up the sides of the baking pan, and bake the pudding in the middle of a preheated moderate oven (350° F.) for 40 minutes. Serve the pudding warm. Serves 6.

Cranberry Freeze

1 16-ounce can whole cranberry sauce
1 8-ounce can crushed pineapple, drained
1 cup dairy sour cream
¾ cup chopped nuts
¼ cup sugar

In large bowl, combine all ingredients; blend well. Spoon into 6-cup fluted tube pan. Freeze. Let soften slightly before serving. 6 servings.

Honey Bran Muffins

1 cup honey
2 sticks (1 cup) butter, melted and cooled
¾ cup milk
2 apples, peeled and grated
2 large eggs, beaten lightly
¼ cup vegetable oil
3 cups whole-wheat flour sifted with 1 tablespoon double-acting baking powder and ½ teaspoon baking soda
3 cups bran
1 cup raisins

In a large bowl combine the honey, the butter, the milk, the apples, the eggs, and the oil. In another large bowl combine the flour mixture with the bran and the raisins. Make a well in the center of the flour mixture, add the honey mixture, and stir the batter until it is just combined. (Do not overmix the batter.) Using an ice-cream scoop or spoon fill 12 paper-lined ⅔-cup muffin tins with the batter, mounding it about ½ inch above the rim of each tin. Bake the muffins in a preheated moderately hot oven (375°) F.) for 25 to 30 minutes, or until they are browned lightly. Makes 12 muffins. Will freeze.

BRUNCH BY THE POOL

SERVES FOUR

Strawberry Bisque
Eggs Verdi
Marmalade Pancake
Coffee

Strawberry Bisque

2 10-ounce packages frozen strawberries, thawed
1 cup milk or light cream
½ cup sour cream

Purée all ingredients in blender until smooth. Serve cold.

Eggs Verdi

1 package 10 ounces frozen peas, thawed
1 package 10 ounces frozen spinach, thawed and well drained
4 tablespoons butter, melted
¼ cup beef broth
1 tablespoon fresh lemon juice
1 teaspoon salt
½ teaspoon freshly ground pepper
8 thin slices Canadian bacon
4 poached eggs
½ cup sour cream
½ cup 2 ounces freshly grated Parmesan cheese

Preheat the oven to 350°. In a medium saucepan, combine the peas and spinach with 2 tablespoons of the butter. Cover and cook over low heat for 10 minutes. Transfer to a blender or food processor. Add the broth, lemon juice, salt and pepper to the spinach and peas and purée until smooth. In a round ovenproof dish, spread a thin layer of the purée. Arrange the bacon in a circle over the puree, spacing evenly. Place a poached egg on top of bacon. (Since the eggs will be hidden by more sauce, place a toothpick at the edge of the dish next to each egg to indicate position for serving.) Spread the remaining puree in a layer over the eggs. Cover each egg with sour cream, dividing evenly. Top with a sprinkling of Parmesan cheese and drizzle with remaining 2 tablespoons melted butter. Bake for 10 minutes, until heated through. Serve hot.

Marmalade Pancake

2 eggs
½ cup all-purpose flour
½ cup milk
¼ teaspoon almond or vanilla extract
½ cup (1 stick) butter
6 tablespoons orange marmalade or any other citrus marmalade
2 tablespoons confectioners' sugar

Preheat the oven to 400°. In a medium bowl, whisk the eggs, flour, milk and almond extract until blended. Melt the butter in a large ovenproof skillet over moderate heat. Remove the skillet from the heat and pour in the batter, tilting to cover the bottom of the pan evenly. Immediately place in the oven and bake for 15 minutes, or until puffed and golden brown. Transfer to a serving plate, spread with the marmalade and dust with the sugar; serve immediately.

Use this cookbook! Make notes in the margins and by the recipes—both good and bad (we hope there won't be many of those!) which should be noted. You may remember what changes you thought you would like to make, but you will have much better luck making this YOUR book if you jot down your thoughts as you are cooking.

DELIGHT YOUR HOUSE GUESTS

SERVES SIX

Divine Ham 'N Eggs
Fruit Salad Surprise
Whole Wheat Biscuits
Coffee
Banana Cake

Divine Ham 'N Eggs

1 10-ounce package frozen broccoli, cooked and drained
6 hard-boiled eggs, peeled
3 tablespoons mayonnaise
1 tablespoon green onion, tops and bottoms, chopped
1 teaspoon prepared mustard
½ teaspoon Worcestershire sauce
1 4½-ounce can deviled ham
Salt and pepper to taste
2 tablespoon butter
2 tablespoons flour
1 cup milk
½ teaspoon salt
½ pound Cheddar cheese, grated

Arrange broccoli in a 13×9 greased Pyrex dish. Cut eggs in half lengthwise; remove yolks and mash. Add mayonnaise, onion, mustard, Worcestershire sauce and ham to mashed yolks. Mix well. Add salt and pepper. Fill each egg white with mixture. Arrange eggs over broccoli. In saucepan, melt butter, blend in flour, and gradually add milk. Cook, stirring constantly, until thick. Remove from heat, add salt and cheese, stirring until cheese is melted. Pour over eggs and bake 20 to 25 minutes at 350°.

Fruit Salad Surprise

1 can apricot halves, drain, reserve juice
1 can pineapple chunks, drain, reserve juice
3 large bananas, sliced thick
1 package vanilla pudding mix (not instant)

Add just enough apricot juice to pineapple juice to make one cup. Mix this cup of juice with pudding mix in saucepan. Cook over low heat until thickened. Beat well. Cool. Pour over fruit. Chill until served.

Whole Wheat Biscuits

1¼ cups all-purpose flour
¾ cup whole wheat flour
1 tablespoon sugar
1 teaspoon baking powder
½ teaspoon baking soda
¼ teaspoon salt
3 tablespoons butter, softened
1 package dry yeast
¼ cup warm water (105° to 115°)
⅔ cup buttermilk
Vegetable cooking spray

Combine first 6 ingredients in a medium bowl; cut in butter using a pastry blender until mixture resembles coarse meal. Dissolve yeast in warm water. Combine yeast mixture and buttermilk; add to flour mixture, stirring until moistened. Cover and refrigerate overnight. Turn dough out onto a lightly floured surface, and knead 1 minute. Roll dough to ½-inch thickness; cut with a 2-inch biscuit cutter. Place biscuits on a baking sheet coated with cooking spray. Bake at 425° for 12 minutes or until golden.
Yield: 1½ dozen.

Note: Biscuit dough may be stored in refrigerator for 3 to 4 days.

Banana Cake

¼ cup butter
1⅓ cups sugar
2 eggs
1 teaspoon vanilla
2 cups flour
1 teaspoon baking powder
1 teaspoon soda
¾ teaspoon salt
1 cup sour cream
1 cup mashed ripe banana
½ cup chopped pecans

Preheat oven to 350°. Cream butter and sugar until fluffy and light. Add eggs and vanilla; blend thoroughly. Combine dry ingredients; add to creamed mixture alternately with sour cream, beginning and ending with dry ingredients. Add bananas and pecans, mixing just until blended. Spoon batter into greased and floured 13×9×2 inch pan. Bake 40 to 45 minutes. Cool and frost with Cream Cheese Frosting, if desired.

This is the favorite cake of Stephen Thompson, my oldest son. The recipe is from my Aunt, Alma Miller.

AN ELITE BRUNCH

SERVES SIX

Bloody Marys
Creole Steaks
Easy Rice Casserole
Fresh Fruit with Honey-Lime Dressing
Lemon Muffins
Toffee Pound Cake
Coffee

Bloody Marys

46 ounces V-8 juice
¼ cup lemon juice
¼ cup Worcestershire sauce
1 teaspoon Tabasco sauce
1½ teaspoons salt
1 teaspoon white pepper
1 tablespoon celery salt
2 cups vodka

Mix all ingredients except vodka; refrigerate, covered. When ready to serve, stir in vodka. May be made several days ahead.

Honey-Lime Dressing

1 cup sugar
½ cup honey
2 teaspoons dry mustard
⅓ cup lime juice
⅓ cup pineapple juice
2 cups salad oil

In blender or food processor, mix sugar, honey, mustard, lime and pineapple juices. Mix briefly and slowly add oil, continuing to mix until all oil is added and well blended. Pour into a quart container with tight fitting lid. Store in refrigerator. Will keep indefinitely.

I have used this dressing for many years, partly because it is so good and it also reminds me of Gloria Tunnell, who gave me the recipe.

Creole Steaks

- 1/4 pound thick-cut bacon, diced
- 2 tablespoons vegetable oil
- 2 cups thinly sliced onion
- 2 6-ounce bunches green onions, trimmed and sliced into 1/4-inch rounds
- 4 medium celery stalks, cut into 1/4-inch slices
- 1/4 pound smoked ham, diced
- 1 green bell pepper, seeded, and cut into 1/4-inch strips
- 1 red bell pepper, seeded and cut into 1/4-inch strips
- 4 large, firm, ripe tomatoes, peeled, seeded and coarsely diced
- 2 teaspoons brown sugar
- 1 10-ounce package frozen sliced okra, thawed and drained
- 2 large garlic cloves, minced
- 2 teaspoons red wine vinegar
- 1 teaspoon dried thyme, crumbled
- 1 teaspoon salt
- 1/4 teaspoon allspice
- 1/8 teaspoon ground red pepper
- Freshly ground pepper
- 6 6-ounce rib eye steaks

Sauté bacon in heavy large skillet over medium-high heat until fat is rendered and bacon begins to turn golden brown. Discard all but 2 tablespoons fat. Add vegetable oil to skillet and reheat over medium-high heat. Mix in onions, celery, ham and peppers and stir with wooden spoon until vegetables soften and begin to color, 8 to 10 minutes. Increase heat to high. Add tomatoes and brown sugar and simmer until tomato juices evaporate, stirring occasionally, about 5 minutes. Blend in remaining ingredients except steaks and cook until mixture bubbles. Reduce heat to medium-low, cover partially and simmer until sauce is thick and rich, 25 to 30 minutes. Adjust seasoning. Remove from heat. (Sauce can be prepared 1 day ahead and refrigerated. Reheat thoroughly before serving.) Prepare charcoal grill or preheat broiler. Season steaks with salt and pepper. Cook to desired doneness. Transfer steaks to platter. Top with sauce and serve immediately.

Easy Rice Casserole

- 1/2 stick butter
- 1 medium onion, chopped
- 1 cup uncooked rice
- 1 10 1/2-ounce can consommé
- 1 10 3/4-ounce can beef bouillon

Melt butter in skillet; add onion and sauté. In a greased 1 1/2-quart casserole add uncooked rice. Over this pour the consommé and bouillon; stir in onion and butter. Bake, covered, at 350° about 30 minutes or longer. Uncover last few minutes for rice to brown.

Lemon Muffins

1 cup butter
1 cup sugar
4 eggs, separated
½ teaspoon lemon extract
2 cups flour
2 teaspoons baking powder
1 teaspoon salt
½ cup lemon juice
2 teaspoons lemon peel, grated

Cream butter and sugar until smooth. Beat egg yolks and add to butter/sugar mixture; beat until light and fluffy. Add lemon extract. Sift dry ingredients and add alternately with lemon juice, mixing thoroughly after each addition. Fold in stiffly beaten egg whites and lemon peel. Blend thoroughly. Fill buttered muffin tins ¾ full and bake at 375° for 20 minutes.

Toffee Pound Cake

Cake

2½ cups flour
1½ cups sugar
1 teaspoon soda
½ teaspoon salt
½ cup butter, softened
¼ cup shortening
1½ cups buttermilk
1½ teaspoons vanilla
3 eggs
1 7.8-ounce package almond brickle baking chips

Frosting

⅓ cup butter
2 cups powdered sugar, sifted
1 teaspoon vanilla
2 to 3 tablespoons water

Heat oven to 350°. Grease and flour 12-cup fluted tube or 10-inch tube pan. In large bowl, blend all cake ingredients except brickle chips at low speed until moistened. Beat 3 minutes at medium speed. By hand, stir in brickle chips. Pour into prepared pan. Bake at 350° for 50 to 60 minutes or until toothpick inserted in center comes out clean. Cool upright in pan 10 minutes; invert onto serving plate. Cool completely. In medium saucepan, heat ⅓ cup butter until light golden brown; remove from heat. Blend in powdered sugar and 1 teaspoon vanilla; add water, 1 tablespoon at a time, as needed to make frosting. Immediately spoon over top of cake, allowing some to run down sides. Freezes well.

AUTUMN LEAVES

SERVES SIX

Creamy Fruit Dip with
Apple and Pear Wedges
Sparkling Orange Juice
Chocolate Waffles
with Cinnamon Butter
Platter of Bacon and Ham
Coffee

Creamy Fruit Dip

1 cup commercial sour cream
1 to 2 tablespoons sweetened strawberry-flavored drink mix

Combine sour cream and drink mix, mixing well. Chill. Serve with fresh fruit.
Yield: 1 cup.

Sparkling Orange Juice

1 bottle champagne, chilled
4 cups orange juice, chilled

Just before serving, combine champagne and orange juice. Serve in hollow stemmed champagne glasses if desired.

Chocolate Waffles with Cinnamon Butter

Cinnamon Butter

1 stick (½ cup) butter, softened
½ teaspoon cinnamon
1 tablespoon honey

Waffles

⅔ cup all-purpose flour
½ teaspoon double-acting baking powder
¼ teaspoon salt
1½ tablespoons unsweetened cocoa powder
⅓ cup sugar
¼ cup sour cream
3 tablespoons butter, melted and cooled
2 large egg yolks
a pinch of cream of tartar

Make the cinnamon honey butter: In a small serving bowl cream the butter, beat in the cinnamon and the honey and let the butter stand at room temperature for 30 minutes. Make the waffles: Into a bowl sift together the flour, the baking powder, the salt, the cocoa powder, and the sugar. In a small bowl combine the sour cream, the melted butter, and the egg yolks. In another bowl beat the egg whites with the cream of tartar and a pinch of salt until they hold stiff peaks. Add the sour cream mixture to the flour mixture, stir the mixture until it is just combined, and fold in the egg whites gently but thoroughly. Pour the batter, using ¼ cup of it for each 4-inch-square waffle, into a preheated well seasoned or non-stick waffle iron and cook the waffles according to the manufacturer's instructions. Remove the waffles from the waffle iron as they are cooked and keep them warm, wrapped in foil. Transfer the waffles to a doily or a napkin-lined basket and serve them with the cinnamon honey butter.

Makes 6 waffles.

MEET THE NEW NEIGHBOR

SERVES EIGHT

Orange-Nog

Ham Soufflé

Fruited Rice

Lime-Cottage Cheese Salad

Apple Puff

Orange-Nog

6 eggs
2 cups sherry
1 cup orange juice
1 cup milk
4 to 6 tablespoons sugar
¼ teaspoon cinnamon
½ teaspoon nutmeg

Beat eggs until light and fluffy. Beat in remaining ingredients until blended. Add sugar. Serve well chilled.

Lime-Cottage Cheese Salad

1 3-ounce package lemon gelatin
1 3-ounce package lime gelatin
2 cups boiling water
½ cup mayonnaise
1 cup cottage cheese
1 small can crushed pineapple, undrained
⅓ cup milk
½ cup chopped nuts

In large bowl, dissolve gelatin in boiling water. Chill until thickened but not set. Add mayonnaise, blending well. Stir in remaining ingredients. Spoon into ring mold or 6-cup bundt pan. Chill until firm. Unmold on lettuce lined platter. Garnish with clusters of red grapes, if desired.

Ham Soufflé

- 10 slices bread, cubed
- 4 eggs, beaten
- 3 cups milk
- 2½ cups ground ham
- 1 cup chopped celery
- ½ cup mayonnaise
- ½ cup green onion, tops and bottoms, chopped
- ½ cup sour cream
- 1 can cream of mushroom soup
- 1½ cups sharp Cheddar cheese, grated

Place half of the cubed bread in a well greased 9×13 inch baking dish. Mix eggs and milk; set aside. Combine ham, celery, mayonnaise, onion, and sour cream. Mix until well blended. Spread over bread cubes and cover filling with remainder of bread. Pour egg mixture over bread. Cover and refrigerate overnight. When ready to bake, remove cover and bake at 325° for 15 minutes. Remove from oven. Whip soup with a fork until smooth and spread over casserole. Sprinkle with cheese and return to oven for 1 hour. Let sit several minutes before cutting in squares to serve. Seafood or chicken may be used instead of ham.

Fruited Rice

- 4 tablespoons raisins
- 8 tablespoons butter
- ½ cup dried apricots, cut into strips
- ½ cup chopped almonds
- 2 tablespoons honey
- 2 cups raw rice
- 2 teaspoons salt
- 4½ cups water

Soak raisins in warm water to cover for 15 minutes; drain and pat dry. Melt butter in large pan and add apricots, almonds and raisins. Cook over low heat, stirring until almonds are lightly browned. Stir in honey, rice and salt; add water, bring to boil, cover pan and cook over low heat 40 to 50 minutes or until all liquid has been absorbed.

Apple Puff

- ½ cup plus 2 tablespoons all-purpose flour
- 3 eggs
- ¾ cup milk
- ¼ teaspoon salt
- 5½ tablespoons butter
- 3 large tart apples, such as Granny Smith, thinly sliced
- 2 tablespoons sugar
- Cinnamon and freshly grated nutmeg

Preheat the oven to 400°. Place the flour in a large bowl. In a medium bowl, beat together the eggs and milk until blended. Pour into the center of the flour and stir until smooth. Stir in the salt. In a large, heavy, ovenproof skillet, melt 1½ tablespoons of the butter over low heat; remove from the heat. Pour the batter into the skillet and place in the oven. Bake for 20 minutes. Reduce the oven temperature to 350° and continue to bake for 10 minutes, until the edges are puffed and slightly brown. Meanwhile, in a medium skillet, melt the remaining 4 tablespoons butter over moderately high heat. Add the apples and sugar and cook, stirring, until the apples are slightly softened but still crisp, 3 to 4 minutes. Remove from the heat. To assemble, scrape the apple mixture into the center of the cooked puff, spreading the slices evenly. Sprinkle lightly with cinnamon and nutmeg. Serve hot, cut into wedges.

Nancy Spaulding, a dear friend in Austin, gave me this recipe. Our girls grew up on it!

WELCOME HOME!

SERVES EIGHT

Fruited Rosé
Herbed Brunch Casserole
Broiled Tomato Halves
Almond Loaf
Caramelized Fruit Cakes
Coffee

Fruited Rosé

1 bottle rosé wine
1 6-ounce can frozen pink lemonade
¼ cup sugar
1 6-ounce can pineapple juice

Heat all ingredients over low heat. Remove from heat. Serve hot or refrigerate until chilled thoroughly and serve over ice.

Herbed Brunch Casserole

2½ cups herb-seasoned croutons
2 cups shredded sharp Cheddar cheese (about 5½ ounces)
¼ pound sliced mushrooms (about 1½ cups)
2 pounds bulk sausage
6 eggs
2½ cups milk
1 10¾-ounce can cream of mushroom soup
¾ teaspoon dry mustard

Preheat oven to 300°. Grease 8×8-inch baking dish. Arrange croutons in single layer in bottom of dish. Sprinkle cheese and mushrooms evenly over croutons. Cook sausage in large skillet, breaking into chunks, until browned, about 15 minutes. Drain thoroughly on paper towels. Place sausage over cheese and mushrooms. Beat eggs, milk, mushroom soup and mustard in medium bowl. Pour over sausage. (Can be prepared ahead to this point and refrigerated overnight.) Bake until set, about 1½ hours. Serve hot.

Broiled Tomato Halves

½ cup sour cream
½ cup mayonnaise
½ teaspoon cayenne pepper
¼ cup Parmesan cheese
(Dash of salt and pepper, if desired)

Slice 4 large firm tomatoes in half; sprinkle each half lightly with salt and pepper. Place on baking sheet. Mix ingredients and spread on top of tomato halves. Broil until bubbly. Serve immediately.

Almond Loaf

⅓ cup butter
1 cup chopped almonds
3¼ cups all-purpose or unbleached flour
½ cup sugar
½ cup mashed potato flakes
1 to 2 teaspoons anise seed or 1 teaspoon cinnamon
1 teaspoon salt
1 package active dry yeast
1 cup lemon yogurt or dairy sour cream
½ cup water
2 eggs (reserve 1 teaspoon egg white)
2 tablespoons coarse sugar or crushed sugar cubes

Glaze

½ cup powdered sugar, sifted
Reserved almond mixture
¼ teaspoon almond extract
3 to 4 teaspoons milk

Generously grease 2 or 2½-quart casserole. In small skillet, over medium heat, heat butter and almonds until light golden brown, stirring constantly. Set aside. Lightly spoon flour into measuring cup; level off. In large bowl, combine 1 cup flour, sugar, potato flakes, anise seed, salt and dry yeast; blend well. In small saucepan, heat yogurt and water until very warm (120 to 130°). Add warm liquid and eggs to flour mixture. Blend at low speed until moistened; beat 3 minutes at medium speed. By hand, stir in remaining flour and 1 cup of the almond mixture; reserve remaining almond mixture for glaze. Stir until mixture forms a soft dough. Cover loosely with plastic wrap and cloth towel. Let rise in warm place (80 to 85°) until light and doubled in size, about 1 hour. Stir down dough; spoon into prepared pan. Cover; let rise in warm place until light and doubled in size, about 1 hour. Beat reserved teaspoon egg white; brush over top of loaf. Sprinkle with coarse sugar. Heat oven to 350°. Bake 35 to 45 minutes or until loaf sounds hollow when lightly tapped. Remove from pan immediately. Cool 30 minutes. In small bowl, blend all glaze ingredients until smooth. Drizzle over warm loaf.

1 loaf.

Caramelized Fruit Cakes

- 4 tablespoons butter at room temperature
- 8 slices pound cake, broiche, or sponge cake, cut ½ inch thick
- 2 ripe medium peaches, peeled and sliced
- 2 large plums, sliced
- 1 banana, sliced
- 2 tablespoons plus 2 teaspoons sugar
- Sour cream (optional)

Spread about ½ teaspoon of butter on one side of each cake slice. Arrange the slices, buttered-side up, on a baking sheet. Starting from the edges and working toward the center, arrange the peaches and plums on the cake slices to simulate a flower. Place the banana slices in the center. Be sure to cover the cake completely to prevent burning. Sprinkle 1 teaspoon of sugar over the fruit on each slice and dot each with 1 teaspoon of the remaining butter, cut into little bits. Broil about 6 inches from the heat or bake in a 500° oven for about 10 minutes, until the top is slightly caramelized. Serve hot or warm, with sour cream if desired.

BEFORE THE GAME

SERVES EIGHT

Sherried Ham Slices

Cheese Casserole (See Index)

Sweet Fruit Slaw

Cinnamon Bars

Monnie's Hot Chocolate

Sherried Ham Slices

2 center ham slices, cut 1 inch thick
½ cup soy sauce
½ cup sherry
½ cup water
1 cup green onions and tops, chopped
½ teaspoon powdered ginger
2 tablespoons salad oil

In a baking dish soak ham slices in a marinade of the remaining ingredients (except oil) for 1 hour. Remove, dry with paper towels and brown on both sides in oil in a heavy frying pan. Pour marinade over the ham, cover and simmer for 20 minutes.

Sweet Fruit Slaw

1 small head cabbage, cored and shredded
1 medium apple, cored and chopped
1 11-ounce can mandarin orange sections, chilled and drained
½ cup grapes, halved and seeded
¼ cup raisins or chopped nuts
⅓ cup honey
3 tablespoons lemon juice
1 teaspoon celery seed, poppy seed, or toasted sesame seed
½ teaspoon dry mustard
½ teaspoon paprika
½ cup salad oil
Raisins or chopped nuts (optional)

In a medium bowl combine shredded cabbage, chopped apple, orange sections, grapes, and ¼ cup raisins or chopped nuts. Cover and chill. For dressing, in blender container or food processor bowl combine honey, lemon juice, desired seed, dry mustard, paprika, and ¼ teaspoon salt. Cover and process till ingredients are blended. With blender or food processor running and with the lid ajar (or through opening in lid) gradually add oil in a steady stream. Process till slightly thickened. Transfer to small bowl. Cover and chill. Just before serving, pour dressing over cabbage and fruit mixture; toss gently to coat cabbage and fruit. If desired, sprinkle with additional raisins or chopped nuts. Serve immediately.

Makes 10 servings.

Cinnamon Bars

1 cup (2 sticks) butter, room temperature
1 cup sugar
1 teaspoon vanilla
1 egg, separated
Pinch of salt
2 cups all-purpose flour
2 teaspoons cinnamon

Preheat oven to 350°. Grease 10×15-inch jelly roll pan. Cream butter with sugar in large bowl. Add vanilla. Mix in yolk and salt. Combine flour and cinnamon and stir into butter mixture. Pat evenly into prepared pan. Brush top with egg white to glaze. Bake until lightly browned, about 20 minutes. Cool slightly. Cut into bars. Store Cinnamon Bars in airtight container.

Monnie's Chocolate Syrup for Christi

1 cup Hershey's cocoa
1½ cup sugar
1 cup hot water
Pinch of salt
2 teaspoons vanilla

Boil all ingredients together for 6 to 7 minutes. Pour into a jar. Keeps in the refrigerator for weeks. Use to make chocolate milk, hot chocolate, or sundaes.

My daughter, Christi, loves this syrup. When we were living in Indianola, Mississippi, her grandmother, "Monnie", kept her well supplied with it!

A FAREWELL BRUNCH

SERVES TWENTY

Chablis Cooler or Pineapple Punch

Cheese Biscuits

Sweet and Spicy Ham Muffins

Scrambled Eggs for a Brunch

Fruit Towers

Blueberry-Orange Nut Bread

Chablis Cooler

10 cups dry Chablis, chilled
10 teaspoons Cream de Cassis
Lemon twists

Pour the Chablis into a large wine glass. Pour in the Cream de Cassis and stir. Garnish each glass with a lemon twist.

Pineapple Punch

1 cup sugar
1 cup water
1 42-ounce can pineapple juice
2 6-ounce cans frozen lemonade
2 quarts ginger ale, chilled

Bring sugar and water to a boil; stir until sugar melts; cool. Mix with pineapple juice and lemonade concentrate. Chill at least 12 hours. When ready to serve, add ginger ale.

Cheese Biscuits

2 cups flour
2 teaspoons salt
Dash cayenne pepper
Dash freshly ground black pepper
1 teaspoon dry mustard
1 cup butter, softened
2 cups very sharp Cheddar cheese, grated and firmly packed

Mix flour, salt, peppers and mustard. Add butter and cheese. Blend until dough is smooth. Form dough into rolls about 1 inch in diameter. Refrigerate or freeze until ready to use. To bake, cut rolls into thin slices and put onto ungreased baking sheets. Bake at 375° for 12 to 15 minutes. Cool before removing from baking sheets.

Makes 75 to 100 cheese biscuits.

Sweet and Spicy Ham Muffins

- 2 8-ounce cans pineapple tidbits (reserve syrup)
- 20 maraschino cherries
- 8 eggs
- 6 pounds (10 cups) ground cooked ham
- 8 cups soft bread crumbs
- 1 cup firmly packed brown sugar
- ½ cup chopped green pepper
- ½ cup chopped onion
- 1 cup liquid (pineapple syrup plus enough milk)
- 4 tablespoons prepared mustard

Glaze

- 6 tablespoons butter
- 2 tablespoons water
- ⅔ cup firmly packed brown sugar

Preheat oven to 350°. Generously grease 40 muffin cups. Arrange pineapple tidbits and cherries in cups. In large bowl, lightly beat eggs; stir in remaining ingredients. Spoon over pineapple and cherries; pack lightly. Bake 30 to 40 minutes. Cool in pans for 5 minutes; invert onto serving plate. In small saucepan, melt butter in water. Remove from heat; stir in ⅔ cup brown sugar until dissolved. Brush over ham muffins. Allow 2 per person.

Scrambled Eggs for a Brunch

- ½ pound butter
- 2 cups minced green onions
- ½ cup flour
- 2½ cups evaporated milk
- 2½ cups homogenized milk
- 2 cups grated sharp cheese
- 1 cup sherry
- 1 teaspoon seasoned salt
- ½ teaspoon curry powder
- ½ teaspoon white pepper
- ½ teaspoon cayenne
- ½ teaspoon dry mustard
- 3 dozen eggs
- 2 cups water
- Salt and pepper to taste

Melt half the butter in a large saucepan. Sauté onions lightly and stir in flour. Gradually add milk and cook, stirring constantly, until thickened. Blend in cheese; remove from heat and stir in sherry and next 5 ingredients. Measure and set aside to cool. Beat 1½ dozen eggs with 1 cup water and season lightly with salt and pepper. Melt 4 tablespoons butter in skillet. Scramble eggs until they barely hold together. Set aside to cool. Repeat with remaining eggs. Grease 2 3-quart casseroles lightly and pour ¼ of the white sauce into the bottom of each casserole dish. Place scrambled eggs evenly on top of sauce and cover with remainder of sauce. Entire top and bottom of eggs must be covered. Cover tightly and refrigerate (up to 2 days). Bring casseroles to room temperature. Bake covered at 275° for about 1 hour. Keep warm over hot water until ready to serve.

Note: Do not overcook eggs or casserole will be too firm when baked.

Fruit Towers

Begin with a pineapple slice
Top with a peach half
Top with an apricot half
Top with a whole seeded prune

Sauce

1 cup melted butter
½ cup brown sugar
4 tablespoons dark rum

Mix together sauce ingredients and spoon over fruit towers, bake at 350° for 10 minutes.

Blueberry-Orange Nut Bread

3 eggs
1 tablespoon grated orange rind
⅔ cup orange juice
½ cup milk
½ cup butter, melted
3 cups flour
¾ cup sugar
1 tablespoon baking powder
¼ teaspoon soda
½ teaspoon salt
1 cup fresh blueberries (or 1 cup frozen, thawed and well-drained)
½ cup chopped walnuts

Combine first 5 ingredients; beat on medium speed of mixer just until well blended. Sift flour, sugar, baking powder, soda and salt into large bowl; make a well in center of mixture. Add egg mixture, stirring just until moistened. Fold in blueberries and walnuts.

Pour batter into a greased and floured 9×5×3-inch loaf pan; bake at 350° for 1 hour or until wooden pick inserted in the center comes out clean.

Yield: 1 loaf. Make 3 to serve 20.

BRUNCH FOR A CROWD

SERVES TWENTY TO FORTY

Bloody Bulls
Golden Tea Punch
A Compote of Fresh Fruit
Vanity Fare Eggs
Ham Mimosa
Avocado-Cranberry Salad
Pineapple Muffins
Brandy Alexander Brownies
Yeast Butterfingers
Salted Nuts
Coffee

Bloody Bulls

2 46-ounce cans V-8 juice
4 ounces lemon juice
1 teaspoon salt
5 shakes Tabasco
1 can beef broth
4 ounces Worcestershire sauce
20 ounces Vodka

Mix all ingredients and refrigerate. Keeps one week.
Yield: 1 gallon. Double for 40 people.

Golden Tea Punch

3 cups boiling water
10 tea bags or 10 teaspoons tea leaves
24 whole cloves
1 3-inch stick cinnamon, crumbled
2¼ cups fresh lemon juice
1¼ cups fresh orange juice
3 cups sugar
4 quarts cold water
Orange and lemon slices

Pour boiling water over tea bags, whole cloves, and crumbled stick cinnamon. Cover; steep 5 minutes. Strain and cool. Add lemon juice, orange juice, and sugar, stirring until sugar is dissolved. Add cold water. Pour into ice-filled punch bowl. Garnish with orange and lemon slices.
Yield: 50 punch-cup servings.

A Compote of Fresh Fruit

4 cups sliced oranges
6 cups pineapple chunks
4 cups sliced apples
1 cup grated lemon peel
2 cups brandy
6 cups strawberries
6 cups sliced bananas
4 cups grapes
4 cups sliced pears
6 cups sliced peaches

Mix first 3 fruits. Sprinkle with lemon peel and brandy; refrigerate. On day of party, add other fruits. Serve very cold.

May be started several days ahead of serving.

Vanity Fare Eggs

1 cup butter
8 large shallots, sliced
2 pounds fresh mushrooms, sliced
1⅓ cups flour
6 cups chicken stock, hot
3 cups cream, hot
8 tablespoons white wine
8 egg yolks, beaten
4 tablespoons lemon juice
2 teaspoons salt
1 teaspoon pepper
36 eggs, hard-boiled and sectioned
8 tablespoons minced parsley
2 cups buttered bread crumbs

In a heavy, large saucepan, sauté mushrooms and shallots in butter. Add flour and cook, stirring about 3 minutes. Add heated stock, cream and wine, stirring constantly until thickened. Remove from heat. Stir in egg yolks, beat well, add lemon juice, salt and pepper. Pour over sectioned eggs in a casserole dish. Top with bread crumbs and parsley. Bake at 350° for 15 minutes. Serve from casserole dish, over toast points or in pastry shells.

Pineapple Muffins

½ cup butter
1 cup sugar
2 eggs
1 teaspoon vanilla
2 cups flour
2 teaspoons baking powder
½ teaspoon salt
1 8¼-ounce can undrained pineapple

Cream together butter and sugar. Add eggs and vanilla. Stir in flour, baking powder and salt. Stir in undrained pineapple. Spoon into 12 well-greased muffin tins. Bake at 375° for 20 minutes. Will freeze. Triple this recipe to serve twenty.

Ham Mimosa

- 1½ teaspoons unflavored gelatin
- ¼ cup port or Madeira
- 2 cups chicken stock or canned broth
- 2 tablespoons butter
- 2 medium onions, minced
- 1 medium celery rib, minced
- 2 teaspoons minced garlic
- 1½ pounds boiled ham, coarsely chopped
- 2 tablespoons tomato paste
- 1 tablespoon minced fresh dill or 1½ teaspoons dried dillweed
- 2 tablespoons Dijon-style mustard
- Salt and freshly ground pepper
- 1 cup heavy cream, well chilled
- 2 hard-cooked egg yolks

In a small bowl, sprinkle the gelatin over the wine and set aside until softened, about 10 minutes. In a small saucepan, bring the stock to a boil. Add the softened gelatin mixture and simmer, stirring for 2 minutes. Set aside to cool. In a large skillet, melt the butter over low heat. Add the onions, celery and garlic; cover and cook until the vegetables are soft but not brown, about 10 minutes. In two batches, grind the ham and cooked vegetables in a food processor until a smooth paste forms. In a large bowl, combine the ham paste with the tomato paste, dill and mustard. Mix well until blended. In a bowl set over ice, stir the stock until it begins to gel. Add the ham mixture and salt and pepper to taste. Beat the heavy cream until soft peaks form. Fold into the ham mixture and turn into a well-oiled 6 to 8 cup mold. Refrigerate overnight. To serve, unmold onto a platter. Press the egg yolk through a fine sieve, sprinkling it all over the ham mold. Serve chilled. Make twice for more than 20 people.

Avocado-Cranberry Salad

- 1 6-ounce package lemon gelatin
- 6 tablespoons sugar
- 4 cups boiling water
- 2 cups fresh cranberries, ground
- 1 tablespoon prepared horseradish
- 1 6-ounce package lime gelatin
- 1 teaspoon salt
- 2 tablespoons lemon juice
- 2 ripe avocados, peeled and mashed
- 6 tablespoons sour cream

Dissolve lemon gelatin and sugar in 2 cups boiling water. Add 1 cup cold water. Chill until thickened. Fold in cranberries and horseradish; pour into 13×9-inch Pyrex dish. Chill until set but not firm. Dissolve lime gelatin and salt in 2 cups boiling water. Add 1 cup cold water. Blend in avocado, lemon juice and sour cream. Chill until slightly thickened; spoon over cranberry layer. Chill until firm. Cut into small squares to serve. A very rich salad. Make twice if serving more than 20 people.

Lightly grease your grater with salad oil to keep cheese from sticking to it.

Yeast Butterfingers

- 1 pound butter, softened
- 1 cup sugar
- 1 package dry yeast
- ¼ cup very warm water
- 2 eggs, separated
- 4 cups sifted flour
- ½ cup finely chopped nuts
- ½ cup chocolate shot or toasted coconut

Cream butter and sugar until fluffy. Dissolve yeast in water and add with egg yolks to creamed mixture. Gradually beat in flour, mixing thoroughly. Chill dough for easier handling. To form cookies, roll about 1 tablespoon dough into a finger shape. Dip in egg whites, then roll in nuts and chocolate or coconut. Place on greased cookie sheet and bake at 375° for 10 to 12 minutes. Cool and store in covered container. The cookies keep well. They may be frozen, or the dough may be frozen.

Brandy Alexander Brownies

- 6 tablespoons butter, softened
- ¾ cup sugar
- 2 eggs
- 1 square (1 ounce) unsweetened chocolate, melted and cooled
- 2 tablespoons crème de cacao
- 2 tablespoons brandy
- ⅔ cup all-purpose flour
- ½ teaspoon baking powder
- ¼ teaspoon salt
- ⅓ cup chopped walnuts
- Sweet Brandy Frosting

In a small mixer bowl cream together butter and sugar till fluffy. Add the eggs; beat well. Blend in cooled chocolate, crème de cacao, and brandy. In small bowl stir together flour, baking powder, and salt. Stir into creamed mixture. Fold in chopped walnuts. Spread in a greased 9×9×2-inch baking pan. Bake in a 350° oven for 20 to 25 minutes. Cool. Frost with Sweet Brandy Frosting; cut into bars.

Makes about 2 dozen bars.

Sweet Brandy Frosting

- 2 tablespoons butter, softened
- 1 cup sifted powdered sugar
- 1 tablespoon crème de cacao
- 1 tablespoon brandy

Cream together butter and powdered sugar. Blend in crème de cacao and brandy to make of spreading consistency. Makes enough for Brandy Alexander Brownies.

A WEDDING BRUNCH

SERVES FIFTY

Champagne Punch
or
Strawberry Spritzers
Rave Eggs
Asparagus Salad with
Herbed Dressing
Curried Fruit or Fresh Melon Balls
Tossed with Lime Juice and Chopped Mint Leaves
Assorted Breads
Elegant French Tart
(Make Four)
or
Grasshopper Parfaits

Champagne Punch

¾ cup sugar
Juice of 3 lemons
2 quarts fresh strawberries, sliced or
3 10-ounce packages frozen sliced strawberries, thawed
1½ cups orange juice
1½ cups Cointreau
3 bottles (4/5 quart) champagne, chilled
1½ quarts sparkling water, chilled

Dissolve sugar in lemon juice. Add strawberries. Add orange juice and Cointreau. Chill at least 2 hours (overnight or 2 to 3 days before serving). Pour into large punch bowl. Add champagne and sparkling water just before serving.

Strawberry Spritzer

6 10-ounce packages frozen strawberries, thawed
4 24-ounce bottles white grape juice, chilled
2 28-ounce bottles carbonated water, chilled

Place two of the packages of the thawed strawberries and their syrup in the blender container. Cover and blend till the strawberries are puréed. In a large pitcher combine the blended strawberries, the grape juice, and the remaining packages of berries. To serve, carefully pour the carbonated water down side of pitcher; stir.
Serves 50.

Rave Eggs

- 2 cups butter
- 4 medium onions, finely chopped
- 2 cups sliced mushrooms
- 2 cups flour
- 16 cups half-and-half
- 4 cups Swiss cheese, grated
- 1 cup dry white wine
- 4 tablespoons Worcestershire sauce
- 1 teaspoon salt, more to taste
- 1 teaspoon white pepper, more to taste
- 4 pounds ham, cubed
- 4 pounds shrimp, cooked and drained
- 4 14-ounce cans artichoke hearts, drained and cut into fourths
- 4 8½-ounce cans English peas, drained
- 4 dozen hard-boiled eggs, peeled and quartered
- Paprika
- Buttered bread crumbs

In very large saucepan, melt butter, add onions and cook until soft. Stir in mushrooms, sauté. Sprinkle flour over vegetables, stirring in well. Cook over low heat 5 to 6 minutes, stirring constantly. Slowly add cream, stirring constantly until mixture is smooth. Add cheese, wine, Worcestershire and pepper. Blend well. Correct seasonings. In four greased 13×9 inch Pyrex dishes arrange ham, shrimp, artichokes, peas, and eggs. Pour cheese sauce over, cover and bake at 275° for 1 hour. Remove cover, sprinkle with bread crumbs and paprika. Bake at 350° for 10 to 15 minutes. May be made day ahead. Return to room temperature before baking if made day ahead and refrigerated.

Asparagus Salad

- 8 cups asparagus spears, drained, reserve liquid
- 2 tablespoons unflavored gelatin
- ½ cup cold water
- Liquid from asparagus plus enough water to make 4 cups
- 2 teaspoons sugar
- ¾ cup lemon juice
- 2 teaspoons salt
- 1 cup chopped celery
- 1 cup stuffed olives, chopped
- 1 cup slivered almonds
- ½ cup chopped parsley

Soften gelatin in the cold water. Heat drained liquid and water; add the softened gelatin to it, stirring to dissolve completely. Add sugar, lemon juice and salt. Chill until partially set. Add celery, olives, almonds and parsley. Arrange asparagus spears standing around sides of a large ring mold (a bundt pan works very well for this). Cut asparagus not used and add to gelatin mixture. Pour into mold and refrigerate several hours. Unmold on platter of lettuce leaves. Serve with Herb Dressing. (I often make this salad for a large group in 2 13×9-inch Pyrex dishes but use cut asparagus instead of spears.) Make this recipe twice to serve 50.

Coffee beans frozen will keep indefinitely and can be ground for use while frozen.

Herb Dressing

- 1 cup fresh parsley
- 1 cup finely shredded watercress leaves, lettuce or spinach
- ¾ cup finely chopped green onions, tops and bottoms
- 4 teaspoons dry mustard
- 2 teaspoons horseradish
- 2 teaspoons Worcestershire sauce
- 4 egg yolks
- 2 cups salad oil
- ⅔ cup tarragon vinegar (or white wine vinegar plus 1 teaspoon dried tarragon)
- 2 teaspoons mixed dried herbs

Put all ingredients in blender or food processor bowl. Mix until thick. Chill. (This is also excellent on cold sliced tomatoes or as a dipping sauce for fresh artichokes.) Make recipe twice to serve 50.

Curried Fruit

- 4 29-ounce cans pear halves
- 4 29-ounce cans peach halves
- 4 17-ounce cans Royal Anne cherries, pitted
- 4 20-ounce cans pineapple chunks
- 4 11-ounce cans Mandarin oranges
- 4 17-ounce cans peeled apricots
- 2 cups white raisins, soaked in hot water to cover for 10 minutes then drained
- 3 cups sugar
- 1 teaspoon salt
- 12 tablespoons butter, melted
- 12 tablespoons flour
- 4 teaspoons curry powder
- 2 cups sherry

Drain all fruit, reserving juice. Mix all juice together and measure out 3 cups. Set aside. Mix measured juice with sugar, salt and melted butter. Stir into flour using a whisk. Heat, but do not allow to boil. Stir until thick. Fold sauce into drained fruit and raisins. Add curry powder and sherry. Let stand 3 hours or overnight refrigerated. Return to room temperature. Bake 30 minutes at 350°.

Dilly Cheese Bread

- 3 cups biscuit mix
- 1½ cups grated sharp Cheddar cheese
- 1 tablespoon sugar
- 1¼ cups milk
- 1 egg, lightly beaten
- 1 tablespoon vegetable oil
- ½ teaspoon dillweed
- ½ teaspoon dry mustard

Preheat oven to 350°. Generously grease 9×5-inch loaf pan or 6-cup bundt pan. Combine biscuit mix, cheese and sugar in large bowl. Combine remaining ingredients in second bowl and mix well. Stir into dry mixture, blending thoroughly, then beat slightly to remove lumps. Turn into pan and bake until golden, 45 to 50 minutes.

Fruited Nut Bread

- ¾ cup sugar
- ½ cup butter
- 2 eggs
- 2½ cups flour
- 1½ teaspoons baking powder
- ½ teaspoon soda
- ½ teaspoon salt
- ½ cup milk
- ½ jar (28-ounce) mincemeat
- ½ cup nuts

Beat sugar and butter, add eggs one at a time. Stir in dry ingredients alternately with milk. Stir in mincemeat and nuts. Pour into loaf pan. Bake at 350° for 60 to 70 minutes.

This bread keeps well, freezes beautifully and makes a wonderful Christmas gift.

Apricot Bread

- 1 cup dried apricots
- ½ cup hot water
- 1 cup sugar
- 1 cup brown sugar
- 3 cups flour
- ½ teaspoon soda
- 2 teaspoons baking powder
- ½ teaspoon salt
- 3 eggs, beaten
- 1 cup sour cream
- 1 cup pecans, chopped

Cut apricots in pieces and put in hot water to soak. Sift dry ingredients and add eggs. Stir in sour cream and pecans; then add soaked apricots, undrained. Put in 2 greased loaf pans. Bake in preheated 350° oven for 1 hour. Check for doneness in 45 minutes.

Banana Nut Bread

- 1 cup sugar
- 1 cup nuts (pecans or walnuts)
- 2 eggs
- ½ cup butter
- 3 ripe bananas (medium size)
- 2 cups flour
- 1 teaspoon soda

Cream butter and sugar. Add eggs and mix well. Add flour and crushed bananas alternately. Add soda last. Cook in a greased and sugared loaf pan for 45 minutes to 1 hour till done at 375°.

If you want to use the small loaf pans, this will make two. You may only need to cook them 30 minutes.

My children love this recipe as much as I do. It is from my mother, Sue Wilson, in Vicksburg, MS.

Elegant French Tart

1¼ cups flour
¼ cup sugar
3 tablespoons cornstarch
½ cup butter

Mix flour, sugar and cornstarch. Cut in butter until crumbly. A food processor may be used or cut in softened butter with a pastry blender or two knives. Press mixture into a 9-inch springform pan. Bake at 375° for 25 minutes. Cool in pan 5 minutes. Spread orange marmalade or raspberry jam over the top. Let cool completely and remove from pan. Cut into wedges to serve. Will freeze.

Grasshopper Parfaits

To each 2 cups of thawed non-dairy dessert topping, add 2 tablespoons crème de menthe and 1 tablespoon crème de cacao. Alternate layers of coarsely crumbled oreo or chocolate chip cookes with liqueur mixture into parfait glasses. Top with crushed cookies. Place in freezer. Remove from freezer 15 to 20 minutes before serving. Garnish with mint leaves, if desired.

FUND-RAISER BREAKFAST

SERVES ONE HUNDRED

Brighter Tomato Juice

or

Pineapple Juleps

Scrambled Eggs for a Group (20 dozen)

or

Western Egg Casserole

Sliced Ham

Crisp Bacon (16 pounds)

Sausage Grits

Hot Biscuits

Butter (10 pounds)

Assorted Jellies (24 jars)

Coffee (2 pounds)

Brighter Tomato Juice

4 gallons tomato juice
2 cups bottled hot sauce
4 cups Worcestershire sauce
5½ tablespoons sugar
1 cup salt
1½ cups lemon juice
1 tablespoon Tabasco

Stir all ingredients together in glass or plastic containers. Refrigerate until ready to serve.

Pineapple Juleps

8 46-ounce cans pineapple juice
8 fifths dry sherry
4 cups orange juice
4 28-ounce bottles Collins mix, chilled
Sprigs of mint

Combine pineapple juice, sherry and orange juice. Refrigerate at least 24 hours ahead of serving. When ready to serve, mix in Collins mix. Garnish with mint, if desired.

Scrambled Eggs for a Group

Cook eggs 1 to 1½ dozen at a time. To each dozen eggs add:

1 teaspoon salt
½ teaspoon pepper
½ cup milk

Beat eggs with whisk or fork until blended. Stir in seasoning and milk. Pour mixture into large skillet and cook over medium heat, stirring constantly. Remove eggs from skillet while still creamy. Keep hot in 150° oven until ready to serve.

Western Egg Casserole

2¼ pounds butter
9 cups chopped green onions, tops and bottoms
6 cups chopped green pepper
9 cups chopped celery
9 cups sliced mushrooms
9 10¾-ounce cans cream of tomato soup
9 10¾-ounce cans cream of mushroom soup
9 tablespoons chili powder
12 tablespoons Worcestershire sauce
3 tablespoons Beau Monde seasoning
Salt, pepper and Tabasco to taste
4 dozen eggs, hard-boiled
18 cups sharp Cheddar cheese, grated
14 cups Ritz cracker crumbs

In large roasting pan, melt butter and sauté onions, mushrooms, green peppers and celery. Add soups and seasonings. Simmer until well blended. Refrigerate (but don't freeze) for several days before using, if desired. When ready to serve: Cut eggs in half lengthwise and divide equally into 9 greased 13×9-inch Pyrex dishes. Pour sauce over eggs. Top each casserole with cheese and crumbs. Bake at 450° for 15 to 20 minutes or until heated thoroughly. Casserole may be assembled and refrigerated overnight except for cracker crumbs. Sprinkle those over just before baking.

Sausage Grits

12 cups water
4 teaspoons salt
4 cups quick-cooking grits
4 sticks butter
4 rolls garlic cheese
8 eggs
2 cups milk, approximately
8 pounds sausage, browned, drained and set aside

Bring water to boil, add salt, and cook grits as package directs. Melt butter and cheese together in saucepan. Beat eggs and add to milk. Stir into grits with cheese mixture. Crumble sausage into grits. Pour into 2 well greased 3-quart casserole dishes. Bake at 350° for 45 minutes. Make this recipe twice to serve 100 people.

Crisp Bacon

Fry bacon and drain well on paper sacks covered with paper towels. Heat oven to 300°; turn off and place bacon in shallow pan in oven. Will keep warm and remain crisp 45 to 60 minutes.

Hot Biscuits

2 packages yeast
1½ cups warm water
5 cups Bisquick
Melted butter

Dissolve yeast in water; stir into biscuit mix. Mix well. Divide dough into four parts. Knead each part lightly on floured surface. Roll very thin and brush with melted butter. Fold in half and cut with small biscuit cutter (1½-inch). Bake at 450° for 6 to 8 minutes. Make this recipe twice to serve 100 people.

A GRAND OLD-FASHIONED SOUTHERN BREAKFAST

SERVES TWELVE

Whiskey Sour Punch

Stuffed Snow Peas

Pickled Mushrooms

Grillades with Grits

Ratatouille

Sweet and Sour Fruit Salad

Chocolate Shortbread Cookies

Delicious Pecan Bars

Whiskey Sour Punch

1 12-ounce can frozen orange juice
1 6-ounce can frozen pink lemonade
12 ounces bourbon
42 ounces water
2 ounces lime juice
Orange slices and maraschino cherries for garnish

Mix all ingredients except orange slices and cherries. Refrigerate or freeze until ready to serve. Garnish each glass with orange slice and cherries on a toothpick.

Stuffed Snow Peas

2 dozen fresh or frozen snow peas
¾ cup whipped cream cheese, softened
2 tablespoons orange juice
1½ teaspoons prepared horseradish
⅛ teaspoon freshly ground pepper
Grated orange rind

Thaw snow peas, if frozen. Trim ends from snow peas. Place snow peas in a steaming basket. Plunge basket into boiling water, and remove immediately. Place snow peas in a bowl of ice water to cool quickly. Remove from water and then refrigerate. Combine cream cheese, orange juice, horseradish, and pepper; stir until smooth. Chill for at least 1 hour. Using a sharp knife, carefully slit one side of each pea pod. Spoon cream cheese mixture into decorating bag fitted with tip No. 18. Pipe cream cheese mixture into snow peas (about 1½ teaspoons in each). Sprinkle with grated orange rind. Refrigerate until ready to serve.

Yield: 2 dozen.

Pickled Mushrooms

1 12-ounce package fresh mushrooms
¾ cup oil
¼ cup wine vinegar
½ cup Worcestershire sauce
½ teaspoon dry mustard
5 cloves garlic
½ teaspoon salt
1 tablespoon sugar
½ teaspoon paprika
½ teaspoon pepper
Dash cayenne pepper
Dash Tabasco
Dash basil leaves

Clean mushrooms with damp paper towels. Mix all ingredients together in a large ziplock bag and marinate overnight.

The fastest, easiest way to separate eggs is to break the egg into your hand and allow the white to run into a bowl through your fingers. There is less chance of breaking the yolk this way. Both egg yolks and the whites freeze exceptionally well. Place either the yolks or whites in plastic ice trays, freeze, then remove the frozen cubes to plastic bags. Simply remove the number you need, thaw and voilà!

Grillades

- 6 pounds veal round, ¼ inch thick cut into serving pieces
- 1 tablespoon salt
- 1 teaspoon pepper
- ¾ cup bacon drippings
- ½ cup flour
- 2 cups chopped onions
- ¾ cup chopped celery
- 6 green peppers, thinly sliced
- 3 cups green onions, chopped
- 3 cloves garlic, minced
- 3 cups tomatoes, chopped
- 1 teaspoon thyme
- 4 bay leaves
- Tabasco to taste
- Worcestershire to taste
- 1½ cup warm water
- 1 cup parsley

Salt and pepper the veal. In a heavy Dutch oven, brown meat in 4 tablespoons bacon drippings. Remove veal; keep covered and warm. Add remaining drippings and flour to Dutch oven, stirring constantly over low heat to make a dark brown roux. Add celery, peppers, green onions, and garlic. Sauté until limp. Add some of the chopped tomatoes to make the roux slightly pink. Add seasonings and stir in water. Place meat in Dutch oven with the roux, cover and cook slowly for 1 hour. Cool and refrigerate overnight. Reheat by adding a small amount of water and heating slowly. To serve, remove bay leaves and stir in chopped parsley. Serve over Baked Cheese Grits.

Baked Cheese Grits

- 2 cups grits
- 4 cups water
- 1 stick butter
- 2 cups milk
- 4 eggs, beaten
- 1 cup Coon brand cheese
- 1 cup longhorn Cheddar cheese
- 2 teaspoons salt
- 6 drops Tabasco

Cook grits and water as directed on package. Stir in butter, milk, eggs, cheeses, salt and Tabasco. Pour into a baking dish. Bake, uncovered at 350° for 30 to 40 minutes.

Ratatouille

- 4 small eggplants, peeled, halved and sliced fairly thin
- 8 medium tomatoes, peeled and sliced thin
- 4 green peppers, seeded and sliced thin
- 4 zucchini, sliced
- 2 onions, sliced
- Seasoned salt, pepper and garlic powder to taste
- 8 tablespoons olive oil
- 1 cup water

Preheat oven to 350°. Layer vegetables in large shallow pan. Add seasonings to taste. Mix oil and water and sprinkle over top. Cover pan with aluminum foil and bake for 1 hour or till tender. Top with Parmesan cheese.

Sweet and Sour Fruit Salad

1 fresh pineapple
4 bananas, sliced
3 large red apples, unpeeled and coarsely chopped
3 oranges, peeled, seeded, and sectioned
2 cups seedless green grapes
Sweet and Sour Fruit Dressing

Cut pineapple lengthwise into quarters; cut pulp away from skin. Cut pulp into bite-size chunks, discarding core. Combine fruit in a large bowl; add Sweet and Sour Fruit Dressing, and toss gently. Cover and chill.

Sweet and Sour Fruit Dressing

4 egg yolks
1½ cups sugar
½ cup milk
1 teaspoon dry mustard
½ cup vinegar

Combine first 4 ingredients in a medium saucepan; cook over low heat, stirring constantly, until smooth and thickened. Stir in vinegar. Cool.

Makes about 1½ cups.

Delicious Pecan Bars

1 cup flour
1 teaspoon baking powder
¼ cup butter
⅓ cup brown sugar, firmly packed
¼ cup pecans, chopped

Sift together flour and baking powder. In mixing bowl, cream butter and brown sugar. Stir in dry ingredients, mixing until mixture resembles coarse meal. Stir in pecans. Pat mixture into well-greased 12×8 pan. Bake at 350° for 10 minutes. Spread on topping. Return to oven and bake at 350° additional 25-30 minutes. Let cool in pan; cut into bars. Store in tightly covered container.

Makes 2½ dozen bars.

Topping

2 eggs
¾ cup dark corn syrup
¼ cup firmly packed brown sugar
¾ cup chopped pecans
2 tablespoons flour
½ teaspoon salt
1 teaspoon vanilla

Beat eggs until foamy, add corn syrup, brown sugar, flour, salt and vanilla. Mix well and pour over partially baked crust. Sprinkle with chopped pecans.

Chocolate Shortbread Cookies

2 cups all-purpose flour
⅔ cup unsweetened cocoa powder, sifted
1 cup confectioners' sugar, sifted
¼ teaspoon salt
2 sticks (1 cup) cold butter, cut into bits
1 teaspoon vanilla

In a food processor fitted with the steel blade blend the flour, the cocoa powder, the sugar, the salt, the butter, and the vanilla for 1 minute, or until the mixture just forms a dough. Roll the dough out ½-inch thick on a floured surface, cut out rounds with a 2-inch cutter dipped in flour, and arrange them on a buttered baking sheet. Gather the scraps into a ball, reroll the dough, and cut out more rounds in the same manner. Prick each cookie several times with the tines of a fork, going all the way through the cookie, and bake the cookies in a preheated slow oven (300°) for 25 minutes, or until they are firm. Let the cookies cool on a rack.

Makes about 24 cookies.

I find this recipe works much better by turning the dough out into a lightly greased jelly roll pan. Press firmly, working the dough with your fingers to cover the pan. Prick the surface and bake as directed above. When done, remove pan from oven, allow to cool slightly and cut into squares. Sprinkle with granulated sugar and allow to cool completely before removing from pan.

Luncheons

"Elegance at Midday"

Luncheons Large and Small

Elegance At Midday

LUNCHEONS LARGE AND SMALL

Lunch For Two

A Twosome for Lunch
A Simple Saturday Lunch

Lunches For Four

Spanish Flavors
A Summer Afternoon
A Memorable Event
A Birthday Party

Luncheons For Six

Casual Elegance
After the Holidays Luncheon

Luncheons For Eight

The Best Luncheon I
The Best Luncheon II
To Honor the Bride
For Someone Special
The Committee Meets

Luncheons For Twelve

A Lovely Repast
A Quiche for Each
A Little More Than Twelve

Luncheons For Large Groups

Day of the Wedding Luncheon
A Gala Event
A Salad Luncheon
An Appreciation Luncheon

PIE CRUSTS

Single Crust

1 cup flour
1 teaspoon salt
½ teaspoon sugar
⅓ cup shortening
¼ cup ice water
½ teaspoon white vinegar

Mix flour, salt, and sugar in bowl. Cut in shortening until crumbly. Mix ice water and vinegar; sprinkle over flour mixture one tablespoon at a time, stirring with a fork, just until all flour is moistened and will shape into a ball. Don't add too much water or overmix. Gently form into a ball, place on lightly floured surface and flatten with your hand. Roll out to desired size; fold into thirds and place in lightly greased pie pan. Unfold and fit gently and carefully into pan, being careful not to stretch pastry, causing it to be tough and to shrink. Trim the edges, fold, (again making certain that you don't pull too much) and with thumb and forefingers, flute the edges. Cover loosely with plastic wrap and chill *at least* 15 minutes before pricking and baking. Bake at 400° 10 to 12 minutes. If you plan to pour a filling into an unbaked crust, brush the bottom and the sides of the raw crust with slightly beaten egg white. This prevents the crust from becoming soggy. Refrigerate (or freeze up to 4 months, covered with foil).

Double Crust

1½ cups flour
1½ teaspoons salt
1 teaspoon sugar
½ cup shortening
⅓ cup ice water
1 teaspoon white vinegar
1 egg yolk, beaten

Mix as directed for single crust, adding the beaten yolk to water and vinegar before sprinkling over flour. Shape into 2 balls, one slightly larger. Roll and fit the larger one into the lightly greased pie pan, add filling, (usually a fruit filling for a double crust), roll top crust, fit over filling, fold and flute edges and refrigerate until well chilled before baking as pie recipe directs.

Five Crusts

4 cups flour
1 tablespoon sugar
2 teaspoons salt
1¾ cups shortening
½ cup ice water
1 tablespoon white vinegar
1 egg

Mix all ingredients as directed for single crust. Divide into 5 balls. Flatten with hands, wrap in plastic wrap and place in plastic bags in freezer up to 4 months. (Can be kept in refrigerator up to 8 days before using.) When ready to use, let dough come to room temperature before rolling, but chill briefly before baking for a flaky crust.

Meringue for Pies

3 egg whites
1 tablespoon water
¼ teaspoon cream of tartar
Dash of salt
6 tablespoons sugar
1½ teaspoons vanilla

Combine egg whites, water, cream of tartar, and salt. Beat until soft peaks form. Add sugar, one tablespoon at a time, beating until small amount rubbed between thumb and forefinger doesn't feel grainy. Add vanilla and beat until stiff but not dry peaks form. (You may need to beat at a slower speed to allow the sugar to dissolve without the meringue becoming too dry.) Spread meringue over WARM filling and bake at 300° 15 to 20 minutes, or just until LIGHTLY browned. Turn off oven, open oven door and leave pie in to cool slowly. When oven is cold, remove pie and refrigerate until ready to serve.

Meringue for pies seem to create a problem for many people. This recipe will insure a perfect meringue every time and may be easily adjusted to any amount. Just remember that the formula is 1 teaspoon water and 2 tablespoons sugar to each egg white called for in a particular recipe. The difference in this method and most recipes is the water. Don't know why it works—just that it always does! Another important trick is to add the sugar very slowly and be SURE that it has all dissolved. Finally, cooking it at a lower temperature than is usually called for is important, too. Many recipes call for the meringue to be spread over a cooled filling—this DOES NOT mean chilled! The filling should be warm—at least room temperature—to keep it from "weeping". Be sure when you are covering the filling that all edges are well sealed so the meringue won't pull away while baking.

Good pies take a little practice but are certainly worth the effort. A pie crust in the freezer can be a life-saver!

A TWOSOME FOR LUNCH

SERVES TWO

Chicken Imperial

Asparagus and Spaghetti

Red Leaf Lettuce with Creamy Vinaigrette

Jiffy Rolls (see Index)

Strawberry Charlottes

Chicken Imperial

- 2 large chicken breasts, halved and skinned
- 2 tablespoons butter
- ¼ cup onions, chopped
- 1 cup fresh mushrooms, thinly sliced
- 2 tablespoons flour
- ¼ cup white wine
- 1 cup whipping cream
- 1 teaspoon salt
- Dash white pepper

In skillet, cook chicken halves in butter until lightly browned on all sides. Remove chicken and set aside. In same skillet, sauté onions and mushrooms until soft. Blend in flour and slowly add wine, stirring until well blended. Stir in cream, salt and pepper. Cook, stirring, until sauce is thickened. Place chicken pieces in greased baking dish and pour sauce over. Cover and bake at 350° 30 minutes or until chicken is tender.

Microwave Instructions

In 12×8 baking dish, combine butter, onions, and mushrooms. Cover with plastic wrap and microwave at High 3 to 5 minutes, or until vegetables are tender. Add chicken breasts and cover. Microwave on High 5 minutes, rotating dish once.

In 2 cup measure, blend flour and wine. Stir in cream, salt, and pepper. Remove chicken from dish. Stir cream mixture into vegetables. Place chicken into dish, spoon cream mixture over chicken and cover with plastic wrap. Reduce power to Medium. Microwave 9 to 14 minutes or until chicken is tender, rearranging once.

Asparagus and Spaghetti

- 4 tablespoons butter
- 3 tablespoons olive oil
- 2 cloves garlic, smashed
- 8 asparagus spears, (fresh or frozen)
- ½ pound spaghetti
- 2 tablespoons chopped parsley
- 1 teaspoon salt
- ½ teaspoon freshly ground pepper
- ½ cup grated Parmesan cheese

Place butter, oil and garlic in small saucepan over low heat. Cook until garlic is soft. In skillet in boiling, salted water, cook asparagus until tender. Drain well and set aside. While vegetables cook, bring large pot of salted water to boil. Add spaghetti and cook until tender. Toss drained spaghetti with garlic sauce, adding parsley, salt and pepper. Toss until well coated. Arrange half of spaghetti on each plate, and place asparagus spears around in spoke-fashion, tips toward the center. Sprinkle with Parmesan cheese.

To "smash" garlic; place peeled clove of garlic on chopping surface, lay flat side of knife on top of garlic and "smash" with flat of hand. You can then finely mince the garlic and will find much more flavor is released. Follow this method anytime a recipe calls for minced garlic.

Red Leaf Lettuce with Creamy Vinaigrette

- 1 head red leaf lettuce, washed and torn
- 1 tablespoon sour cream
- 2 tablespoons Dijon mustard
- 1 tablespoon red wine vinegar
- ½ teaspoon salt
- Dash pepper
- 2 tablespoons green onion, tops and bottoms, chopped
- ½ cup salad oil

Combine all dressing ingredients except salad oil. Mix well. Slowly beat in oil, continuing to beat until thickened. Pour into tightly covered container and store in refrigerator. This dressing will keep in the refrigerator several weeks.

Never allow garlic to become too brown when cooking it. Overcooking will result in a bitter taste.

Strawberry Charlottes

- 3 egg yolks
- 3 tablespoons sugar
- 3 tablespoons light rum
- ¾ cup whipping cream, divided
- 2 tablespoons sugar
- ½ teaspoon vanilla
- 6 ladyfingers, split
- 1 cup strawberries, sliced (reserve two large ones)

In double boiler over barely simmering water, mix egg yolks and sugar. Slowly whisk in rum, mixing constantly until custard is smooth and thickened, about 7 to 8 minutes. Do not allow to boil. Whisk in 2 tablespoons of the cream, stirring until well blended. Pour into a bowl, cover with plastic wrap and refrigerate until well chilled. Beat remaining cream until thickened. Gradually add sugar, mixing until blended; add vanilla and continue beating until cream holds soft peaks. Refrigerate. When ready to assemble, line two small serving bowls (or use two large balloon wine glasses) with ladyfingers. Spoon ¼ of the custard into each and cover with ¼ of the strawberry slices. Spoon ¼ of whipped cream over the strawberries. Repeat layering of the custard, berries and cream. Place two large, whole strawberries on top to garnish. May be assembled and refrigerated 1 to 2 hours before serving, covered tightly with plastic wrap.

A SIMPLE SATURDAY LUNCH

SERVES TWO

Cream of Lemon Soup

Green Bean and Tuna Salad

Slices of Honeydew and Cantaloupe

Whole Wheat Bread Cut into Fingers, Buttered and Sprinkled with Parmesan Cheese and Toasted

Strawberry Kisses

or

Vanilla Ice Cream with Praline Sauce

French Almond Meringues

Cream of Lemon Soup

⅓ cup fresh lemon juice
2 1½-inch strips of lemon rind
3 cups canned chicken broth (or homemade)
1½ tablespoons cornstarch, dissolved in 2 tablespoons canned chicken broth or water
½ cup well chilled heavy cream
Snipped fresh chives for garnish

In a saucepan combine the lemon juice, the rind, and the broth, bring the liquid to a boil, and boil it for 5 minutes. Discard the rind, stir the cornstarch mixture, and whisk it into the broth mixture. Cook the broth over moderately high heat, stirring, until it is thickened, remove the pan from the heat, and stir in the cream. In a blender blend the soup with ½ cup crushed ice until it is smooth and transfer it to a metal bowl. Skim the froth and chill the soup, covered and set in a bowl of crushed ice and ice water, stirring occasionally, for 30 minutes. Season the soup with salt, ladle it into chilled bowls, and garnish it with the chives.

Makes about 3 cups, serving 2.

Green Bean and Tuna Salad with Herb Dressing

½ pound green beans

Dressing

2½ tablespoons white-wine vinegar
1½ teaspoons minced fresh parsley
1½ teaspoons freshly grated Parmesan
⅛ teaspoon bottled horseradish or to taste
Pinch of dried basil
Pinch of dried thyme
Freshly ground pepper to taste
⅓ cup olive oil

1 hard-boiled large egg, chopped
¼ cup drained julienne strips of pimento
7-ounce can tuna, drained and broken into chunks

In a steamer set over simmering water steam the green beans, covered partially, for 8 to 12 minutes, or until they are just tender but still al dente, refresh them in a colander under cold water, and pat them dry.

Make the dressing: In a food processor or blender blend vinegar, parsley, Parmesan, horseradish, basil, thyme, pepper, and salt to taste; with the motor running add the oil in a stream, and blend the dressing until it is emulsified.

Arrange the beans in the center of a platter, sprinkle the egg over them, and mound the pimento in the center. Scatter the tuna around the edges and drizzle the green bean and tuna salad with the dressing.
Yield: Serves two.

Strawberry Kisses

½ pint strawberry ice cream
1 cup crushed ice
½ cup half-and-half
¼ cup brandy
¼ cup crème de strawberry liqueur
4 fresh strawberries
2 small scoops strawberry ice cream
2 fresh strawberries, sliced

Chill 2 wide-mouthed stemmed glasses. Combine ½ pint ice cream, crushed ice, half-and-half, brandy, liqueur and 4 strawberries in blender and mix well. Pour into chilled glasses. Float 1 scoop of ice cream in each. Garnish with sliced strawberries and mint sprigs. Serve immediately.

Praline Sauce

1 cup light corn syrup
½ cup sugar
⅓ cup butter or margarine
1 egg, beaten
1 tablespoon vanilla extract
1 cup coarsely chopped pecans

Combine first 4 ingredients in a heavy saucepan; mix well. Bring to a boil over medium heat, stirring constantly; boil 2 minutes without stirring. Remove from heat; stir in vanilla and pecans. Serve warm or at room temperature over ice cream.

Yield: 2 cups.

French Almond Meringues

1 6-ounce package semisweet chocolate pieces
3 egg whites
½ teaspoon vanilla extract
1 cup sugar
⅓ cup blanched almonds, finely chopped

Melt chocolate pieces over hot, not boiling, water. Remove from heat, and cool about 5 minutes. Combine egg whites and vanilla and beat until stiff but not dry. Gradually add sugar and beat until very stiff. Fold in finely chopped almonds and cooled melted chocolate. Drop by teaspoonfuls onto greased cookie sheet. Bake at 350° about 10 to 12 minutes.

Yield: 4 dozen.

SPANISH FLAVORS

SERVES FOUR

Mexican Chi Waw-Waw
Corn Chips
Southwestern Quiche
Dilled Tomato Molds   Avocado Mousse
Sausage Bites
Pineapple-Buttermilk Sherbet
with
Cinnamon Sugar Cookies

Mexican Chi Waw-Waw

1 can quartered artichoke hearts
1 8-ounce can chopped ripe olives
1 8-ounce can chopped pimento
1 8-ounce can chopped mushrooms
3 8-ounce cans chopped green chiles
4 large fresh tomatoes, seeded, peeled and chopped
2 medium white onions, chopped
4 tablespoons cider vinegar
2 tablespoons olive oil
3 teaspoons salt
1 clove garlic, minced

Drain all excess juices thoroughly from olives, pimentos, mushrooms and chiles. Best made a day in advance, combined in a large bowl, covered and chilled. Serve with tortillas, Doritos, Fritos, as a dip. Keeps for days in the refrigerator.

Southwestern Quiche

1 9-inch pie shell
¾ cup Cheddar cheese, grated
½ cup Monterey Jack cheese, grated
3 eggs, lightly beaten
1 teaspoon salt
¼ teaspoon white pepper
1½ cups half-and-half
1 4-ounce can diced green chilies (drained)
1 2¼-ounce can sliced ripe olives (drained)
2 tablespoons green onion, tops and bottoms, chopped

Prepare piecrust (see index) as directed in recipe, adding 1½ teaspoons chili powder to dry ingredients. Fit into a 9-inch pie plate, flute edges and set aside.

Mix cheeses together and spread over bottom of prepared shell. In medium bowl, mix eggs, salt, pepper, cream, chilies, olives, and onions. Pour over the cheese. Bake at 350° for 40 to 45 minutes. Serve at once.

Dilled Tomato Molds

1 3-ounce package gelatin, lemon flavored
1 teaspoon salt
1 cup boiling water
2 teaspoons vinegar
½ tray (7 to 10) ice cubes
½ cup peeled, seeded and chopped tomatoes
½ cup chopped celery
2 tablespoons chopped capers
1 tablespoon chopped onion
½ teaspoon dill seed
⅛ teaspoon coarsely ground pepper
Mayonnaise

Dissolve gelatin and salt in boiling water. Add vinegar and ice cubes; stir constantly until thickened—about 3 minutes. Remove any unmelted ice.

Stir remaining ingredients into gelatin. Spoon into a 3-cup mold or individual molds. Chill until firm. Serve with crisp salad greens. Top with mayonnaise.

Serves 4.

Avocado Mousse

2 tablespoons gelatin
1 cup cold water
2 pound can asparagus, drained, liquid reserved
1½ cups hot liquid from asparagus
¾ cup mayonnaise
¾ cup sour cream
2½ teaspoons salt
5 tablespoons strained lemon juice
1½ cups mashed avocado

Soak gelatin in cold water. Add boiling liquid and stir until dissolved. Then add asparagus, mayonnaise, sour cream, salt, avocado and lemon juice. Mix well. Pour into molds that have been greased with mayonnaise and refrigerate.

Pineapple-Buttermilk Sherbet

1 quart buttermilk
1 can (20 ounces) crushed pineapple in heavy syrup
1 cup sugar

Combine the buttermilk, the pineapple with its syrup and the sugar in a large bowl; stir to dissolve the sugar.

Pour the mixture into two standard ice cube trays (without ice cube dividers), filling them to within ¼-inch of the top. Place the trays in the freezer until partially frozen, about 45 minutes, then stir to break up the ice crystals. Return the trays to the freezer, stirring every 30 minutes, until completely frozen. If you are not serving the sherbet the same day, transfer it to a freezer container with a tight-fitting lid.

Makes about 1½ quarts.

Sausage Biscuit Bites

- ¾ pound hot bulk pork sausage
- 2⅔ cups all-purpose flour
- 2 tablespoons sugar
- ½ teaspoon baking soda
- ½ teaspoon salt
- ½ cup shortening
- 1 package dry yeast
- ¼ cup warm water (105-115°)
- 1 cup buttermilk
- Melted butter or margarine

Cook sausage in a skillet until browned, stirring to crumble; drain well, and set aside.

Combine the next 4 ingredients, mixing well; cut in shortening with a pastry blender until mixture resembles coarse meal. Dissolve yeast in warm water; let stand 5 minutes. Add yeast mixture to buttermilk, stirring well. Add buttermilk mixture to dry ingredients, stirring just until the dry ingredients are moistened. Knead in sausage. Turn dough out onto a lightly floured surface; knead lightly 3 to 4 times.

Roll dough to ½-inch thickness; cut with a 1¾-inch round cutter. Place biscuits on an ungreased baking sheet. Brush tops with melted butter. Bake at 425° for 10 minutes or until golden brown.

Yield: 3 dozen biscuits.

Biscuits may be frozen. To freeze, place uncooked biscuits on an ungreased baking sheet; cover and freeze until firm. Transfer frozen biscuits to plastic bags. To bake, place frozen biscuits on an ungreased baking sheet; bake at 425° for 10 minutes.

Cinnamon Sugar Cookies

- ½ cup butter, softened
- 1 cup sugar
- 2 eggs
- 1 teaspoon grated lemon rind
- 2 cups all-purpose flour
- 1 teaspoon baking powder
- ½ teaspoon baking soda
- ½ teaspoon salt
- ¼ cup sugar
- ½ teaspoon ground cinnamon

Cream butter; gradually add 1 cup sugar, beating well. Add eggs and lemon rind, beating well. Combine flour, baking powder, soda, and salt; stir into creamed mixture. Chill dough 2 hours.

Combine ¼ cup sugar and cinnamon, mixing well. Roll dough into 1-inch balls; roll in cinnamon-sugar mixture. Place about 2 inches apart on lightly greased cookie sheets. Bake at 375° for 8 to 10 minutes or until lightly browned. Cool on wire racks.

Yield: about 3 dozen.

A SUMMER AFTERNOON

SERVES FOUR

Cold Peach Soup

Crab - Pecan Salad

Cheddar Pea Salad **Tropical Fruit**

Fresh Mint Dressing

Banana - Jam Bread

Praline Custard Pie

Cold Peach Soup

1½ pounds peaches, peeled, pitted and sliced
2 cups sour cream
1 cup fresh orange juice
1 cup pineapple juice
½ cup dry Sherry
1 tablespoon fresh lemon juice
Sugar (optional)

Purée peaches in food processor until smooth. Add all remaining ingredients except sugar (in batches if necessary) and blend well. Pass soup through fine strainer. Add sugar to taste. Serve chilled.

Fresh ingredients, used whenever possible, are always better. Once you have taken the small amount of time necessary to chop fresh parsley, grate fresh Parmesan cheese, mince garlic, grind pepper—both white and black—and grate fresh nutmeg and compared the quality of the finished dish, you will find it most worthwhile.

Crab-Pecan Salad

- 1 cup mayonnaise, preferably homemade
- 1 tablespoon fresh lemon juice
- 1 teaspoon Dijon-style mustard
- ½ cup minced fresh parsley
- ½ cup minced fresh dill or 2 to 3 teaspoons dried
- 1½ pounds lump crabmeat, preferably Dungeness, broken up
- ⅓ cup thinly sliced celery (1 small rib)
- Tender leaves from 1 large head of Boston lettuce, washed and well dried
- ½ cup (about 2 ounces) pecan halves, slivered and lightly toasted
- Lemon wedges, for garnish

In a small bowl, stir the mayonnaise with the lemon juice and mustard until blended.

Set aside 1 tablespoon each of the parsley and dill and 1 teaspoon of the chives for garnish. Fold the remaining parsley, dill and chives into the mayonnaise.

In a medium bowl, toss the crabmeat with the celery; gently fold about ⅔ cup of the mayonnaise into the crab mixture (enough to moisten and flavor the salad).

Arrange the lettuce leaves on chilled dinner plates or a large platter; loosely mound the crabmeat on the leaves. Sprinkle the reserved parsley, dill and chives and the pecan halves attractively on top. Garnish with the lemon wedges. Serve with the remaining mayonnaise.

This is our favorite crab salad. You may use canned crab if fresh isn't available, or a high quality frozen.

Cheddar Pea Salad

- 1 16-ounce can small English peas, drained
- 1 cup cubed Cheddar cheese
- ½ cup chopped celery
- ¼ to ½ cup sliced pimento-stuffed olives
- 1 hard-cooked egg, chopped
- 1 tablespoon grated onion
- ¼ cup mayonnaise

Combine all ingredients; mix well. Cover salad, and chill at least 1 hour.
Serves 4.

Fresh snow peas are a wonderful addition to this salad. Snap off the stems and string before adding.

Tropical Fruit Salad with Fresh Mint Dressing

1 medium pineapple
1 kiwi, peeled and thinly sliced
1 large banana, peeled and cut into ½-inch chunks
2 medium-size peaches, peeled and sliced
1 cup whole strawberries, halved
3 tablespoons slivered almonds, toasted

Dressing

1 cup sugar
⅓ cup water
½ cup loosely packed fresh mint leaves

For Salad: Cut pineapple in half lengthwise. Scoop out pulp, leaving shells ¼ to ½ inch thick; set aside.

Cut pineapple into bite-size pieces, discarding core. Combine pineapple chunks, kiwi, banana, peaches, and strawberries; toss gently, and spoon into pineapple shells. Sprinkle with toasted almonds. Serve with Fresh Mint Dressing.

For Dressing: Combine sugar and water in a small saucepan; bring to a boil, stirring occasionally. Remove from heat.

Combine sugar mixture and mint leaves in container of electric blender; process until leaves are finely chopped. Chill 2 to 3 hours.
Yield: ⅔ cup.

Banana-Jam Bread

½ cup butter
1 cup sugar
2 eggs
1 cup mashed ripe banana
1 teaspoon lemon juice
2 cups all-purpose flour
1 tablespoon baking powder
½ teaspoon salt
½ cup strawberry jam
1 cup chopped pecans

Cream the butter; gradually add sugar, beating until light and fluffy. Add eggs, one at a time, beating well after each addition.

Combine banana and lemon juice; stir into creamed mixture.

Combine flour, baking powder, and salt; add to creamed mixture, stirring just until moist. Stir in jam and pecans.

Spoon batter into 2 greased and floured 8½×4½×3-inch loafpans. Bake at 350° for 50 minutes or until wooden pick inserted in center comes out clean. Cool in pans 10 minutes; remove from pans, and cool completely on wire racks.
Yield: 2 loaves.

Praline Custard Pie

1 9-inch pie shell, baked
½ cup butter
½ cup brown sugar
½ cup pecans
1 5½-ounce package instant vanilla pudding mix
3 cups milk
1 cup whipped cream, sweetened to taste

Prepare pie shell, (see index) and bake at 400° just until very lightly browned. Remove from oven and set aside. In saucepan, melt the butter; stir in the brown sugar and pecans and cook over medium heat, stirring constantly, until well blended. Do not allow mixture to boil. Pour into the baked pie shell and bake at 400° for 5 minutes. Remove from oven and allow to cool completely. Mix instant pudding with milk. Pour over cooled praline. Spread whipped cream over top and refrigerate until serving time.

A MEMORABLE EVENT

SERVES FOUR

Plum Slush
Chicken-Pasta Salad with Fruit
Sesame Broccoli
Pepper and Cheese Fingers
Rainbow Bombe

Plum Slush

- 1¼ cups light rosé
- 1¼ cups unsweetened white grape juice
- 3 cups peeled, sliced fresh plums
- 1 3-inch stick cinnamon
- ½ teaspoon vanilla extract

Combine first 4 ingredients in a medium saucepan. Bring to a boil; cover, reduce heat, and simmer 15 minutes. Remove from heat; discard cinnamon. Stir in vanilla. Process mixture in container of electric blender until smooth; pour into a plastic container. Then cover and freeze until firm.

Remove container from freezer at least 1 hour before serving; spoon slushy mixture into glasses.
Serves 6.

Chicken-Pasta Salad with Fruit

- 3 whole boneless chicken breasts, cooked and chopped into bite-size pieces
- 2 cups seedless green grapes
- 1 cup snow peas
- 12 spinach leaves, torn into pieces
- 1 large celery heart, chopped
- 7 ounces macaroni, cooked and drained
- 1 6-ounce jar artichoke hearts, with marinade
- 1 kiwi, peeled and sliced
- ½ large cucumber, sliced
- ½ cup raisins
- 1 green onion, chopped
- ⅔ cup mayonnaise
- ½ cup freshly grated Parmesan cheese
- ⅓ cup fresh lemon juice
- Salt and freshly ground white pepper
- Spinach leaves
- Mandarin orange sections (garnish)

Combine first 11 ingredients in large serving bowl and toss gently. Mix mayonnaise, Parmesan cheese, lemon juice, salt and white pepper in small bowl. Pour over salad and toss again. Refrigerate until ready to use. To serve, spoon salad onto spinach-lined plates. Garnish with mandarin orange sections.

Sesame Broccoli

- 1 1½-pound bunch fresh broccoli
- 2 tablespoons vegetable oil
- 2 tablespoons vinegar
- 2 tablespoons soy sauce
- 2 tablespoons sesame seeds, toasted
- 1 tablespoon sugar

Trim off large leaves of broccoli. Remove tough ends of lower stalks, and wash broccoli thoroughly. Remove flowerets from stems; slice stems thinly. Cook, covered, in a small amount of boiling water 10 minutes or until crisp-tender; drain. Arrange broccoli in a serving dish.

Combine remaining ingredients in a small saucepan; bring to a boil. Pour over broccoli.

Serves 6.

Pepper and Cheese Fingers

- ⅔ cup freshly grated Parmesan cheese
- 1 teaspoon cracked pepper
- 2 cups all-purpose flour
- 1 tablespoon baking powder
- ½ teaspoon salt
- ½ teaspoon baking soda
- 3 tablespoons well-chilled butter, cut into ½-inch pieces
- 1 cup buttermilk
- 2 tablespoons (¼ stick) butter

Preheat oven to 450°. Combine cheese and pepper in processor. Sift in flour, baking powder, salt and baking soda and mix to blend. Cut in chilled butter, using on/off turns until mixture resembles coarse meal. With machine running, pour buttermilk through feed tube and blend until dough just begins to gather together; do not let dough form ball.

Flour hands, then gather dough into ball. Knead on lightly floured surface until just smooth, about 10 times. Roll dough out with lightly floured rolling pin into 9×12-inch rectangle. Cut into 1½×3-inch "fingers." Gather scraps, reroll and cut additional biscuits. Arrange on nonstick baking sheet or baking sheet lined with parchment, spacing 1 inch apart. Brush tops with melted butter. Bake until biscuits are golden brown, about 10 minutes.

Note: Can be prepared 1 week ahead. Cool completely on rack. Wrap tightly in foil and freeze. Reheat frozen biscuits in foil in 350° oven until hot, about 30 minutes. Serve biscuit fingers warm.

Rainbow Bombé

2 quarts lemon sherbet
4 tablespoons Curacao
2½ tablespoons lemon rind
1 quart raspberry sherbet
2 tablespoons kirsch
1 pint lime sherbet
2 to 3 tablespoons crème de menthe

Allow the lemon sherbet to soften at room temperature. Beat in the Curacao and lemon rind. Spoon the sherbet into a large chilled mold to within 4 inches of top. Freeze.

When the lemon sherbet is hard, remove from the freezer and spread a 2-inch layer of softened raspberry sherbet beaten with kirsch, over the lemon sherbet, leaving space for the lime sherbet. Freeze the mold again. When the raspberry sherbet is hard, fill the remaining layer with the lime sherbet beaten with the crème de menthe. Smooth the top of the mold and cover with foil. Refreeze.

A BIRTHDAY PARTY

SERVES FOUR

Avocado Bisque
Parmesan Chicken Rolls
Brussels Sprouts Veronique
Bibb Lettuce Chiffonade
Banana Muffins
Amaretto-Peach Cream

Avocado Bisque

- 4 very ripe avocados
- ⅓ cup fresh lime juice
- 1 garlic clove put through a fine garlic press
- 1 tablespoon mayonnaise
- ½ teaspoon curry powder
- 1 cup heavy cream
- 1½ cups canned chicken broth
- 2 tablespoons minced fresh parsley leaves
- 1 tablespoon minced fresh coriander
- ½ teaspoon Tabasco

In a blender blend in batches the avocado, the lime juice, the garlic, the mayonnaise, and the curry powder until the mixture is smooth. Transfer the mixture to a large bowl, stir in the cream, the broth, the parsley, the coriander, the Tabasco, and the white pepper, and chill the soup, covered with foil, for up to 3 days. Stir the soup and ladle it into chilled bowls.

Parmesan Chicken Rolls

- 2 chicken breasts, split, skinned and boned
- ¼ teaspoon salt
- ¼ teaspoon freshly ground pepper
- ½ cup dry white wine
- ¾ teaspoon dried tarragon, crumbled
- 1 large garlic clove, crushed
- ¼ cup freshly grated Parmesan cheese
- Additional freshly grated Parmesan cheese
- Dash of paprika
- Chopped fresh parsley

Cut fillets from chicken breasts and set aside. Pound chicken breasts to thickness of ¼ inch. Season with salt and pepper. Combine wine, tarragon and garlic in shallow dish. Add chicken breasts. Marinate at room temperature 30 minutes.

Preheat oven to 350°. Grease 9×9-inch baking dish. Finely chop reserved fillets in processor. Mix in ¼ cup Parmesan. Remove breasts from marinade. Spread Parmesan mixture over 1 side of each chicken breast. Roll up and secure with toothpicks. Transfer to baking dish. Pour marinade over. Sprinkle with additional Parmesan and paprika. Bake until tender, basting frequently, 25 to 30 minutes. Garnish with chopped parsley and serve.

Brussels Sprouts Veronique

- 1½ pounds fresh brussels sprouts
- 1 tablespoon butter
- 10 ounces seedless red grapes
- 8 grape leaves (optional)

Cook brussels sprouts in large amount of boiling salted water until almost tender, about 7 minutes. Drain and rinse under cold water; drain again. (Can be prepared several hours ahead to this point.) Melt butter in large saucepan over medium heat. Stir in grapes and brussels sprouts and heat through. Arrange grape leaves around bowl. Turn sprouts into bowl and serve.

Bibb Lettuce Chiffonade

- 1 tablespoon white wine vinegar
- 1 tablespoon fresh lemon juice
- ¼ cup olive oil
- 1 hard-cooked egg, finely chopped
- 1 tablespoon snipped fresh chives
- 1 teaspoon chopped parsley
- Pinch of sugar
- ⅛ teaspoon salt
- Pinch of freshly ground pepper
- 3 small heads of Bibb lettuce, torn into bite-size pieces

In a small jar, combine the vinegar, lemon juice, oil, egg, chives, parsley, sugar, salt and pepper; cover and shake well. Just before serving, pour the dressing over the lettuce and toss until well coated.

Banana Muffins

- 1¾ cups all-purpose flour
- ¾ cup sugar
- 1¼ teaspoons cream of tartar
- ¾ teaspoon baking soda
- ½ teaspoon salt
- 2 ripe bananas, mashed
- 2 eggs, beaten
- ½ cup vegetable oil
- ¾ cup chopped pecans

Combine first 5 ingredients in a large bowl; make a well in center of mixture. Combine remaining ingredients; add to dry ingredients; stir just until moistened.

Spoon batter into greased muffin pans, filling three-fourths full. Bake at 400° for 18 minutes or until golden brown.

Yield: 1½ dozen.

Amaretto-Peach Cream

1 cup heavy cream
1 pound frozen peach slices, or any other frozen fruit
2 tablespoons, plus 4 teaspoons amaretto
4 teaspoons superfine sugar
2 ripe peaches, thinly sliced (optional)

Place the cream in the freezer for 1 hour, or until slightly frozen.

Place half the peaches in a food processor or blender and purée for 30 seconds, or until smooth. With the machine on, slowly pour in half of the cream and process for an additional 3 to 5 minutes, using a spatula to scrape down the sides. Add 1 tablespoon of the amaretto and 2 teaspoons of the sugar; blend for 60 seconds. Divide the mixture between 2 individual dessert bowls. Repeat with the remaining peaches, cream and sugar and another tablespoon of the amaretto, and divide the second mixture between 2 more dessert bowls.

Place all 4 bowls in the freezer for 20 to 30 minutes, or until slightly frozen. Before serving, pour 1 teaspoon of amaretto over each serving and decorate with peach slices, if desired.

CASUAL ELEGANCE

SERVES SIX

Hot Spiced Wine

Ham Salad Ring

Gruyère Cheese Soufflé

Avocado Salad or Asparagus Mold

Sour Cream Corn Muffins

Coconut Custard Pie

Hot Spiced Wine

1 cup water
½ cup sugar
1 lemon, sliced
12 whole allspice
12 whole cloves
1 3-inch stick cinnamon
1 25.4-ounce bottle Burgundy or other dry red wine

Combine water, sugar, lemon slices, and orange slices in a Dutch oven. Tie spices in cheesecloth bag; add to sugar mixture, and bring to a boil. Reduce heat, and simmer 5 minutes. Add wine; return to a boil. Reduce heat, and simmer 10 minutes. Discard spice bag. Serve hot.
Yield: 4½ cups.

Ham Salad Ring

1 tablespoon unflavored gelatin
½ cup cold water
2 tablespoons lemon juice
2 tablespoons horseradish
2 teaspoons prepared mustard
1 cup mayonnaise
½ teaspoon salt
2 cups ham, cooked and cubed
1 cup celery, diced
2 tablespoons onion, minced

Soften gelatin in cold water. Dissolve over hot water. Add lemon juice, horseradish, mustard, mayonnaise and salt. Mix thoroughly. Add remaining ingredients and mix well. Pour into oiled 8-inch ring mold and chill until firm. Unmold on crisp lettuce.

Chicken, shrimp, salmon or tuna may be substituted for the ham.

Gruyère Cheese Soufflé

6 slices buttered bread
6 eggs
½ cup white wine
½ cup chicken broth
1½ cups milk
8-ounces grated Gruyère cheese
1 4-ounce can sliced mushrooms
Parsley, onion salt and pepper to taste

Preheat oven to 350°. Place bread, buttered side down, in 9×14-inch shallow casserole dish. Mix eggs and liquids together (blender or egg beater). Sprinkle cheese, mushrooms and seasonings over bread. Add liquid. Bake for 45 minutes.

Get the bread in the casserole and make the liquid ahead of time, so you can easily assemble it before putting in oven. Serves 6 amply as an entree, and will serve 8 hungry eaters at a buffet when there is a meat. Good with ham or ham loaf.

Avocado Salad

2 3-ounce packages lime gelatin (or 1 6-ounce)
2 cups boiling water
1 cup mayonnaise
2 mashed avocados
1 8-ounce package and 1 3-ounce package cream cheese
1 small jar pimentos
2 cups celery
1 small grated onion
Dash Worcestershire
Garlic powder to taste
Salt and cayenne pepper to taste

Mix together the boiling water and lime gelatin. Add remaining ingredients and pour into prepared mold. Chill.

My sister-in-law, Jeanelle Street, has given me many, many wonderful recipes through the years. I have never served this salad that it wasn't well received and I think it is good with any meat.

Asparagus Mold

- 1 can asparagus soup
- 1 3-ounce package lime gelatin
- 1 8-ounce package cream cheese
- ½ cup hot (boiling) water
- ½ cup mayonnaise
- ¾ cup celery - diced
- 1 tablespoon grated onion
- ½ cup chopped green pepper
- ½ cup coarsely chopped pecans

Dissolve the gelatin in hot water. Add cream cheese and work out any lumps. Add other ingredients and jell.

Serves 6.

This is one of the many wonderful recipes that have come from Mary Louise Gee.

Sour Cream Corn Muffins

- 1 cup yellow cornmeal
- 1 cup all-purpose flour
- ¼ cup sugar
- 2 teaspoons baking powder
- 1½ teaspoons salt
- ½ teaspoon baking soda
- 1 cup sour cream
- 2 eggs
- ¼ cup (½ stick) butter, melted

Preheat oven to 425°. Generously butter muffin cups. Mix cornmeal, flour, sugar, baking powder, salt and baking soda in medium bowl. Stir sour cream, eggs and melted butter in small bowl to blend. Add to dry ingredients and stir just until evenly moistened; do not overmix or muffins will be tough. Turn batter into prepared muffin cups, filling almost to top. Bake until muffins are light golden and tester inserted in centers comes out clean, about 10 to 15 minutes for mini, 15 to 20 minutes for regular and 25 to 30 minutes for extra-large muffins. Cool in pans 5 minutes before removing. Serve immediately.

Makes 24 mini, 12 regular, or 6 extra-large muffins.

Very, very good. The cooked muffins freeze well.

Coconut Custard Pie

- 1 9-inch pie shell, unbaked
- 1 cup sugar
- 1 tablespoon flour
- 2 eggs, well beaten
- ⅓ cup very soft butter
- 1 cup milk
- 1 teaspoon vanilla
- 1 cup coconut

Prepare pie shell (see index); set aside. Mix sugar and flour and stir into beaten eggs. Add butter, milk and vanilla and mix well. Stir in coconut. Pour into prepared shell and bake at 350° for 40-45 minutes.

All custard-type pies need to be checked carefully the last several minutes of baking. Shake the pan slightly and when the center seems almost firm but will still move, remove from the oven, set on a solid surface and the middle will continue to set as the pie cools. This is from my husband's aunt, Boots Reaves, and my oldest son, Stephen, has been known to eat a whole one!

AFTER THE HOLIDAYS LUNCHEON

SERVES SIX

Hot Apple Cider Nog

Turkey-Spinach Casserole

Pickled Carrots   Swiss-Apple Salad

Jalapeño-Cheese Loaf

Heavenly Pudding

Hot Apple Cider Nog

2 eggs, beaten
½ cup sugar
1 cup apple cider or apple juice
¼ teaspoon salt
¼ teaspoon ground cinnamon
⅛ teaspoon ground nutmeg
3 cups milk, scalded
½ cup whipping cream, whipped
Ground nutmeg

Combine first 6 ingredients in a medium saucepan, mixing well. Gradually add scalded milk, stirring constantly with a wire whisk. Cook over low heat, stirring constantly, until thoroughly heated (do not boil). Ladle into mugs. Top each serving with a dollop of whipped cream; sprinkle with nutmeg. Serve hot.

Yield: about 4½ cups.

Turkey-Spinach Casserole

6 slices bacon
½ cup chopped onion
1½ cups cooked regular rice
1 10-ounce package frozen chopped spinach, cooked and drained
1 2-ounce jar diced pimento, drained
¼ cup sliced water chestnuts
¼ teaspoon salt
1 10¾-ounce can cream of mushroom soup, undiluted
½ cup commercial sour cream
1 pound sliced cooked turkey
¾ cup soft breadcrumbs
1 tablespoon butter or margarine, melted

Cook bacon in a large skillet until crisp; remove bacon, reserving 2 tablespoons drippings in skillet. Crumble bacon, and set aside.

Sauté onion in bacon drippings until tender; remove from heat. Add rice, spinach, pimento, water chestnuts, half of bacon, and salt; stir well. Combine soup and sour cream; stir half of soup mixture into spinach mixture. Spoon spinach mixture into a lightly greased 12×7×2-inch baking dish; arrange turkey slices on top. Spoon remaining soup mixture over turkey. Combine breadcrumbs and butter; mix well, and sprinkle around edges of casserole. Sprinkle remaining bacon over center of casserole.

Bake, uncovered, at 350° for 30 minutes.

Serves 6.

Toasted almonds may be added and are very good.

Pickled Carrots

2 pounds carrots
1 can tomato soup
½ cup salad oil
¾ cup vinegar
1 medium onion, chopped
1 small green pepper, chopped
1 cup sugar
1 teaspoon dry mustard
Salt and pepper to taste

Peel carrots and cook whole or sliced, until barely tender. Drain. Combine rest of ingredients and pour over hot carrots. Refrigerate 24 hours.

There are many variations of this recipe but it is so good with the turkey casserole we decided to include it.

Jalapeño-Cheese Loaf

1 package dry yeast
1 cup warm water (105-115°)
1 egg, beaten
2 tablespoons butter, melted
4 to 4½ cups all-purpose flour, divided
1 tablespoon sugar
¾ teaspoon salt
¼ teaspoon garlic salt
3 small canned or fresh jalapeño peppers, seeded and chopped
1 cup (4 ounces) shredded sharp Cheddar cheese
1 4-ounce jar diced pimento, well-drained
¼ cup minced onion

Dissolve yeast in warm water in a large bowl; let stand for 5 minutes. Combine yeast, egg, and butter; mix well.

Combine 3 cups flour, sugar, salt, and garlic salt. Gradually add flour mixture to yeast mixture, beating at medium speed of electric mixer until smooth. Beat in peppers, cheese, pimento, onion, and enough of the remaining flour to form a soft dough.

Turn dough out onto a well-floured surface, and knead 5 to 10 minutes or until smooth and elastic. Place dough in a greased bowl, turning to grease top. Cover and let rise in a warm place (85-degrees), free from drafts, 1 hour or until doubled in bulk. Punch dough down.

Turn dough out onto a well-floured surface, and knead 1 minute. Shape dough into a loaf; place in a greased 9×5×3-inch loafpan. Cover and let rise in a warm place (85°), free from drafts, 30 minutes or until doubled in bulk. Bake at 400° for 40 to 45 minutes or until loaf sound hollow when tapped. Remove from pan; let cool on wire racks.
Yield: 1 loaf

You will notice that we usually call for butter instead of margarine in the bread recipes. The flavor of the bread is much improved. Unless a crusty texture is desired, as in French Bread, always brush loaves or rolls with melted butter as soon as they are removed from the oven.

Swiss-Apple Salad

3 large red apples, unpeeled and chopped
2 tablespoons lemon juice
1 cup seedless green grapes, halved
¾ cup diced Swiss cheese
½ cup sliced celery
½ cup coarsely chopped pecans
⅓ cup mayonnaise
Lettuce leaves

Sprinkle apples with lemon juice, and toss lightly. Add the next 5 ingredients and mix well. Serve on lettuce leaves.

Serves 6.

Heavenly Pudding

1 12-ounce box vanilla wafers
1 large bottle maraschino cherries, drained and chopped
1 15¼-ounce can crushed pineapple, well drained
1 cup chopped pecans
2 cups heavy cream, whipped
1 cup butter
2 cups powdered sugar
2 eggs

Cream butter and powdered sugar; add eggs and beat until smooth. Set aside. In separate bowl, place cherries, pineapple, and pecans, mix well and set aside. Spread ⅓ of the vanilla wafer crumbs in a buttered 9×13 inch serving dish. Spread egg mixture over the crumbs. Top with another layer of ⅓ of the vanilla wafer crumbs. Spoon the fruit mixture over the crumbs. Sweeten the whipped cream to taste and spread over the fruit mixture. Top with remaining crumbs. Cover tightly and refrigerate several hours or overnight. This will keep in refrigerator several days and the flavor really improves.

This is the dessert that I served at our very first dinner party 30 years ago! It is from the collection of my mother-in-law, Ruth Thompson, who has cooked some of the finest food I have ever eaten. She no longer entertains on the scale she once did, but the beauty of her table, the excellence of her food, and her graciousness are legendary in Plainview.

THE BEST LUNCHEON I

SERVES EIGHT

Chilled Cherry Soup

A Truly Different Chicken Salad

Snow Peas with Celery

Strawberry Soufflé Salads

Gruyère Shortbread

Fruited Trifle

Chilled Cherry Soup

4 1-pound cans pitted tart red cherries
3 3-inch cinnamon sticks
20 whole cloves
20 whole allspice berries
1 cup sugar
1 lemon slice
2 cups (1 pint) whipping cream
1 tablespoon all-purpose flour
1⅔ cups dry red wine
Unsweetened whipped cream (garnish)

Combine 2 cans cherries with juice in large saucepan. Add juice only from remaining 2 cans (reserve cherries for another use). Tie whole spices in cheesecloth bag. Add to saucepan with sugar, lemon and salt. Bring mixture to boil, stirring occasionally to dissolve sugar completely.

Place cream in medium bowl. Whisk in flour. Stir into cherry mixture with wine. Return soup to boil, then remove from heat and cool. Cover and chill thoroughly. Discard spice bag. Ladle soup into chilled bowls. Top with whipped cream.

NOTE: Soup can be prepared up to 2 weeks ahead, covered and refrigerated. Discard spice bag before refrigerating.

A Truly Different Chicken Salad

8 chicken breast halves, skin removed
1 tablespoon lemon juice
½ teaspoon salt
¾ cup vinaigrette dressing
1 cup mayonnaise
2 teaspoons tarragon, fresh, chopped *or* 1 teaspoon dried
1 lemon rind, grated
1 bunch of lettuce, red-tip, curly leaf, etc.

Put the chicken breasts into a Pyrex dish or pan in a single layer. Mix the lemon juice and salt and pour over the chicken. Cover and bake for 30 minutes at 400°. Cool and cut chicken into small, bite-sized pieces. Marinate it in the vinaigrette dressing for about 3 hours at room temperature. Mix the mayonnaise, tarragon and lemon rind. Combine with the drained chicken pieces. Chill. When ready to serve, put salad on large lettuce leaves.

Serves 8.

Vinaigrette Dressing

½ teaspoon dried parsley
¼ teaspoon basil
¼ teaspoon dried chives
¾ teaspoon salt
½ teaspoon pepper
1 clove garlic, crushed
1 teaspoon dry mustard
¼ cup white wine vinegar
½ cup olive oil
¼ cup salad oil

Mix all of the ingredients by shaking in a jar. Chill. Shake well before serving.

Chicken salad recipes are usually good, but this one is so different from the rest that it is now our favorite.

Snow Peas with Celery

2 tablespoons cornstarch
2 teaspoons sugar
1 teaspoon salt
2 tablespoons soy sauce
1 cup water
2 pounds fresh snow peas
1 cup chopped green onions with tops
1½ cups diagonally sliced celery
4 tablespoons butter

Combine first 5 ingredients, stirring well; set aside.

Wash pea pods; trim ends, and remove any tough strings. Sauté peas, green onions, and celery in butter in a large skillet 2 minutes. Stir in cornstarch mixture; cook, stirring constantly, 2 minutes or until thickened.

Serves 8.

Strawberry Soufflé Salads

1 10-ounce package frozen sliced strawberries, thawed
1 3-ounce package strawberry-flavored gelatin
¼ teaspoon salt
1 cup boiling water
2 tablespoons lemon juice
¼ cup mayonnaise or salad dressing
¼ cup chopped walnuts
Lettuce

Drain berries, reserving syrup. Add enough water to syrup to measure ¾ cup. Dissolve gelatin and salt in boiling water. Add reserved syrup and lemon juice. Beat in mayonnaise or salad dressing. Chill till partially set. Beat with electric mixer till fluffy. Fold in berries and nuts. Pour into individual molds. Chill till set. Unmold on lettuce-lined platter atop pineapple. Serve with additional mayonnaise or salad dressing, if desired.

Serves 4 to 6.

For this menu, double this recipe.

Gruyère Shortbread

3 tablespoons butter, room temperature
½ cup all-purpose flour
¼ teaspoon salt
Pinch of ground red pepper
1 egg yolk
½ cup finely grated Gruyère cheese

Preheat oven to 350°. Cream butter in medium bowl. Blend in flour, salt and red pepper. Add yolk and blend until dough forms ball. Mix in cheese.

Turn dough out onto baking sheet and form into 4-inch squares ½ inch thick. Cut diagonally in both directions to form 4 triangles, separating triangles slightly with knife. Bake until golden, about 25 minutes. If dough spreads during baking, cut triangles apart with knife while hot. Cool on baking sheet 3 minutes, then transfer shortbread to rack. Serve warm.

A poor quality wine will not improve in taste when used in a recipe. Wines for cooking do not have to be expensive but certainly should have a pleasing charm of their own.

Fruited Trifle

2 cups milk
4 egg yolks
½ cup sugar
3 tablespoons cornstarch
¼ teaspoon salt
2 tablespoons (¼ stick) butter
1 teaspoon vanilla
1 16-ounce pound cake, cut into ½-inch slices
¼ to ½ cup cream Sherry or rum
1 pound strawberries, sliced
2 bananas, peeled and sliced (about 2 cups)
1 11-ounce can mandarin orange sections, drained or 1 pint blueberries
2 kiwi, peeled and sliced
1 cup whipping cream
2 tablespoons powdered sugar
Whole strawberries and fresh mint sprigs (garnish)

Combine milk, yolks, sugar, cornstarch and salt in medium saucepan.

Cook on high until thick, about 6 to 7 minutes, stirring. Whisk in butter and vanilla. Cover custard and refrigerate until cool and softly set.

Brush cake slices generously with Sherry or rum. Arrange half of slices in single layer in trifle or other deep bowl. Layer with half of strawberries, bananas, orange sections or blueberries and kiwi. Spoon half of custard over. Repeat layering with remaining ingredients. Whip cream in medium bowl until soft peaks form. Add powdered sugar and continue beating until stiff. Spoon or pipe cream decoratively over top of trifle. Garnish with strawberries and mint sprigs. Chill until ready to serve.

Beautiful to serve buffet!

THE BEST LUNCHEON II

SERVES EIGHT

Cantaloupe Rum Soup

Salmon Mousse with Dill Sauce

Spinach Mornay **Tomatoes Vinaigrette**

Double-Quick Rolls

Easy Ice Cream Balls

Cantaloupe Rum Soup

¼ cup (½ stick) butter
2 medium-size ripe cantaloupes, peeled, seeded and cubed
¼ cup orange marmalade
2 tablespoons unsweetened coconut milk
1 cup (about) fresh orange juice
½ cup whipping cream
¼ cup dark rum
Toasted walnuts (optional)

Melt butter in heavy medium saucepan over medium heat. Add cantaloupe and stir until just soft, about 5 minutes. Blend in marmalade and coconut milk. Add enough orange juice to cover. Simmer until cantaloupe is very soft but not transparent, 10 to 15 minutes (cooking time will vary depending on ripeness of cantaloupe).

Puree cantaloupe mixture in processor or blender. Return to saucepan. Stir in cream and rum. Rewarm over low heat. Ladle soup into bowls. Garnish with walnuts if desired and serve immediately.

Note: May also be served chilled, garnished with fresh mint leaves.

Salmon Mousse

1 envelope unflavored gelatin
¼ cup cold water
½ cup boiling water
½ cup mayonnaise
1 tablespoon lemon juice
1 tablespoon onion, grated
½ teaspoon Tabasco
½ teaspoon paprika
1 teaspoon salt
2 cups red salmon, drained and flaked
1 tablespoon capers, chopped
½ cup heavy cream, whipped
Olives, sliced
Eggs, hard-cooked and sliced
Pimento
Lemon slices or watercress for garnish

Soften gelatin in cold water. Add boiling water and stir until gelatin is dissolved. Cool. Add mayonnaise, lemon juice, onion, Tabasco, paprika and salt; mix well. Chill until consistency of unbeaten egg whites. Add salmon and capers, beat well. Fold in whipped cream.

Garnish bottom and sides of oiled 2-quart fish or other mold with sliced olives, hard-cooked eggs and pimento. Pour mousse carefully into mold and chill. Unmold and garnish with lemon slices or watercress. Serve with dill sauce.

Dill Sauce

1 teaspoon salt
Pinch pepper
Pinch sugar
4 teaspoons lemon juice
1 teaspoon onion, grated
2 tablespoons dill weed, finely cut or tablespoon dry dill weed
1½ cups sour cream
½ cup cucumber, peeled, seeded and grated

Mix all ingredients together. Stir and chill. Serve with Salmon Mousse.

Spinach Mornay

3 10-ounce packages frozen, chopped spinach
4 tablespoons butter
3 tablespoons flour
Salt to taste
Dash cayenne
2 teaspoons Dijon mustard
1 cup milk
3 tablespoons Swiss cheese, grated
½ cup Parmesan cheese, grated
4 tablespoons light cream

Cook spinach without adding any water; drain thoroughly and set aside. Melt butter; remove from heat and add flour, stirring well. Season with salt, cayenne and mustard. Return to heat and add milk, stirring constantly until mixture boils. Add cheeses and light cream. Simmer 5 minutes. Combine with spinach and refrigerate or freeze. To serve, bring to room temperature. Bake at 350° for 15 to 20 minutes. Can also be baked in tomato cases.

Tomatoes Vinaigrette

4 large tomatoes
¼ cup plus 2 tablespoons chopped fresh parsley or 2 tablespoons dried parsley flakes
1 clove garlic, crushed
¼ cup plus 2 tablespoons olive oil
2 tablespoons vinegar
1½ teaspoons minced fresh basil or ½ teaspoon dried whole basil
1 teaspoon salt
⅛ teaspoon pepper
Additional chopped fresh parsley (optional)

Slice tomatoes; place in a serving bowl. Sprinkle with ¼ cup plus 2 tablespoons parsley. Combine next 6 ingredients in a jar; cover tightly, and shake vigorously. Pour over tomatoes. Chill 3 hours. Sprinkle with additional parsley, if desired.
Serves 8

Double-Quick Dinner Rolls

1 package active dry yeast
1 cup warm water (105-115°)
2 tablespoons sugar
1 teaspoon salt
1 egg
2 tablespoons shortening
2¼ cups flour

Dissolve yeast in warm water in large mixer bowl. Add sugar, salt, egg, shortening and 1 cup of the flour. Beat until smooth. Stir in remaining flour; continue stirring until smooth. Scrape batter from side of bowl. Cover; let dough rise in warm place until double, about 30 minutes.

Stir down batter. Spoon into 12 greased large muffin cups, filling each about ½ full. Let rise until batter reaches tops of cups, 20 to 30 minutes. Heat oven to 400°. Bake 15 minutes.
Yield: 1 dozen rolls.

These rolls are really quick, really good - even better if you add some grated cheese to the batter.

Easy Ice Cream Balls

½ gallon peppermint or vanilla ice cream
14 chocolate wafers, crushed
2 (1-ounce) squares semisweet chocolate
½ cup butter
1 5.33-ounce can evaporated milk
2 cups sifted powdered sugar
Whipped cream (optional)
Maraschino cherries (optional)

Scoop ice cream into 2½-inch balls. Lightly roll in cookie crumbs. Cover and freeze until firm.

Combine chocolate and butter in top of a double boiler; bring water to a boil. Reduce heat to low; cook until chocolate melts. Stir in milk and sugar. Cook, stirring constantly, until sauce is thickened and smooth.

Arrange ice cream balls in individual serving dishes. Garnish with whipped cream and cherries, if desired. Spoon warm sauce over ice cream balls just before serving.

Yield: 18 2½-inch ice cream balls.

The sauce needs to be warm when served for this to be at its very best. If you have trouble finding the chocolate wafers, use the cream-filled cookies.

TO HONOR THE BRIDE

SERVES EIGHT

Cheese Soup
Avocado Crab Mornay
Honey-Glazed Carrots
Herbed Rice and Pea Salad
Cheese Herb Bread
Walnut Jumbles
Cherry-Nut Ice Cream

Cheese Soup

- 1/3 cup carrots, finely chopped
- 1/3 cup celery, finely chopped
- 1 cup green onions, finely chopped
- 2 cups water
- 1 medium white onion, chopped
- 1/2 cup butter
- 1 cup flour
- 4 cups milk
- 4 cups chicken broth
- 1 jar (15-ounce) Kraft Cheese Whiz
- Salt to taste
- Pepper to taste
- 1/4 teaspoon cayenne pepper
- 1 tablespoon prepared mustard

Boil carrots, celery and green onions in 2 cups of water for 5 minutes. Sauté white onion in butter. Add flour and blend well. Boil milk and chicken broth. Stir briskly into white onion mixture with a wire whisk. Add cheese, salt, pepper and cayenne. Stir in mustard and the boiled vegetables including the water in which they were cooked. Bring to a boil and serve immediately.

Don't tie your pleasure in creating an unusual dish or special meal to anyone else's appreciation. Learn to receive the compliments as a bonus but enjoy the creation as your own special expression of your unique talent.

Avocado Crab Mornay

¼ cup butter
¼ cup flour
1 cup light cream
½ cup chicken broth
½ cup sherry
¼ cup grated Parmesan cheese
2 tablespoons shredded Swiss or Gruyere cheese
Dash of nutmeg
Dash of cayenne pepper
Dash of salt
6 scallions, minced
¼ cup butter
3 avocados, peeled, pitted and diced
1½ pounds crab meat
Freshly grated Parmesan cheese

In a saucepan, melt ¼ cup butter and stir in flour with a whisk. Add the cream and chicken broth and stir until smooth. Blend in sherry, ¼ cup Parmesan cheese, Swiss cheese, nutmeg, cayenne pepper, and salt. Remove from heat. At this point, the sauce may be refrigerated, then reheated in a double boiler.

In a large skillet, gently sauté the scallions in ¼ cup butter until barely limp. Add the sauce and heat, gently stirring, but do not boil. Fold in avocados and crab meat.

Mound the crab meat mixture in scallop shells or individual ramekins, sprinkle with cheese. Bake 5 minutes at 500°. Serve immediately.

NOTE: Served in smaller shells or individual au gratin dishes, it becomes a special first course.

Honey-Glazed Carrots

12 medium (about 1½ pounds) carrots, scraped and cut into 2 to 2½ inch pieces
¼ cup honey
3 tablespoons orange juice
1½ teaspoons salt
1 teaspoon grated orange rind
¼ teaspoon ground ginger

Position slicing blade in processor bowl. Arrange carrots horizontally in the food chute; slice, applying firm pressure with food pusher. Stack carrot slices, keeping ends even. Position slicing blade in processor; place slices in bottom of the food chute with cut sides parallel to chute sides. Reattach processor lid, and slice again to make julienne strips.

Sauté carrots in butter 5 minutes. Combine remaining ingredients. Pour over carrots, and cook over medium high heat 15 minutes or until the liquid evaporates.

Serves 8.

Herbed Rice and Pea Salad

- 1 cup long-grain rice
- 2 tablespoons fresh lemon juice
- ½ teaspoon Dijon-style mustard
- ⅓ cup olive oil
- 3 tablespoons plain yogurt
- ⅓ cup minced fresh parsley leaves
- ¼ cup minced scallions
- 1 cup cooked fresh or thawed frozen peas
- White pepper to taste

Into a saucepan of boiling salted water sprinkle the rice, stirring until the water returns to a boil, and simmer, covered, for 12 minutes or until done and all water is absorbed. Drain the rice. Transfer the rice to a bowl and let it cool for 10 minutes.

In a small bowl whisk together the lemon juice, the mustard, and salt to taste, add the oil in a stream, whisking, and whisk the dressing until it is emulsified. Whisk in the yogurt, add the dressing to the rice with the parsley, the scallions, the peas, and the white pepper, and toss the salad with 2 forks.

Serves 6 to 8.

Cheese-Herb Bread

- ½ cup water
- ¼ cup shortening
- 2 tablespoons sugar
- ¾ teaspoon salt
- 1 package dry yeast
- 1 5-ounce jar process cheese spread, coarsely chopped
- 2 cups all-purpose flour, divided
- 1 egg, beaten
- 1 tablespoon butter or margarine
- 2 tablespoons grated Parmesan cheese
- 1 teaspoon poppy seeds
- ½ teaspoon dried whole basil

Combine water, shortening, sugar and salt in a large glass bowl; microwave at HIGH for 2½ minutes or until shortening melts. Cool to lukewarm (105 to 115°). Add yeast, cheese spread, 1 cup flour, and egg to liquid mixture; beat 30 seconds on low speed of an electric mixer, scraping sides of bowl. Beat 3 minutes on high speed. Stir in remaining 1 cup flour.

Turn dough out onto a lightly floured surface, and knead 1 to 2 minutes. Roll dough into a 9-inch circle. Place dough in a well-greased 9-inch pie plate, and set in a larger, shallow dish; pour about 1 inch hot water in bottom dish. Cover dough loosely with waxed paper. Microwave at MEDIUM-LOW (30% power) for 2 minutes; let stand in oven 5 minutes. Repeat microwaving and standing 3 times or until dough is doubled in bulk. Remove from oven, and remove waxed paper.

Place butter in a custard cup; microwave at HIGH for 35 seconds or until melted. Brush over loaf. Combine remaining ingredients; sprinkle over loaf.

Place pieplate with loaf in microwave oven on an inverted custard cup or saucer. Microwave at MEDIUM (50% power) for 6 to 8 minutes or until surface springs back when touched lightly with finger, giving dish a quarter turn at 2-minute intervals. Remove from microwave, and place pie plate on foil. Let stand 5 minutes. Remove from pan, and cool on wire rack.

Yield: one 9-inch loaf.

Walnut Jumbles

1¾ cups flour
¾ teaspoon soda
Dash salt
1 stick butter
1 teaspoon vanilla
1 cup brown suggar
1 egg
½ cup sour cream
1 cup chopped walnuts

Cream butter and sugar. Add vanilla and egg. Mix in sour cream alternately with flour mixture. Stir in nuts. Drop by teaspoonsful onto greased cookie sheet. Bake at 375° for 12 minutes.

Sharon Larson gave me this recipe after a delightful weekend at their lake house.

Cherry-Nut Ice Cream

6 eggs
2 cups sugar
1 can Eagle Brand
1 pint coffee cream
¼ teaspoon red food color
6 tablespoons cherry juice
2 #2 cans Bing cherries
1½ cups pecans, chopped
1 tablespoon vanilla

Beat eggs until lemon colored. Add sugar and beat until blended. Add remaining ingredients and enough milk to fill gallon freezer.

This is an unusual, as well as delicious, ice cream from Toni Jenkins.

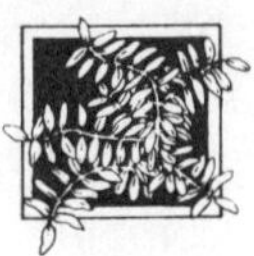

FOR SOMEONE SPECIAL

SERVES EIGHT

Cold Asparagus Soup

Crab and Rice

Creole Beans Orange Salad

Jiffy Rolls (see index)

Lime-Sour Cream Pie

or

Lemon Chess Pie

Cold Asparagus Soup

14 ounces chicken broth
10 ounces canned asparagus, drained
2 cups sour cream
Dash cayenne pepper
Salt, lemon juice, curry powder, to taste
1 cucumber, peeled (optional)

Purèe all ingredients in blender. Strain to remove strings. Chill and serve.

Crab and Rice

1 cup rice, cooked
1 pound crab meat
5 eggs, hard-cooked and chopped
1½ cups mayonnaise
½ teaspoon salt
¼ teaspoon cayenne pepper
Dash black pepper
⅛ teaspoon crushed tarragon
1 tablespoon minced parsley
2 teaspoons onion, finely chopped
5 ounces canned evaporated milk
8½ ounces canned water chestnuts, drained and sliced
½ cup Cheddar cheese, grated

Combine first 3 ingredients. Blend together remaining ingredients except cheese. Combine with first mixture until well blended. Fill 8 buttered sea shells or ramekins. Sprinkle with cheese. Bake at 350° for 20 minutes or until hot and cheese is melted.

Creole Beans

- 1½ cups thinly sliced onion
- 1 cup chopped green pepper
- 1 cup diced celery
- 3 tablespoons butter
- 2 teaspoons salt
- ¼ teaspoon pepper
- 3 cups diced fresh or drained canned tomatoes
- 3 cups cooked or canned green beans

Cook onion, green pepper, and celery in butter until tender. Mix in remaining ingredients and cook until beans are heated thoroughly.

Serves 8.

Orange Mandarin Salad

- 3 3-ounce packages orange-flavored gelatin
- 2 cups boiling water
- 1 pint orange sherbet
- 1 large can mandarin oranges or 3 small cans, undrained

Dissolve the gelatin in boiling water. Stir well, add orange sherbet. Stir until melted. Add oranges and juice. Pour in mold and refrigerate. Serve with Topping.

Yield: 10 servings.

Topping

- 1 pint whipping cream
- 1 3-ounce package cream cheese
- ½ cup marshmallow whip

Whip cream. Add softened cream cheese and marshmallow whip.

You can make one cup of powdered sugar by blending ½ cup of granulated sugar in a blender.

Lime Sour Cream Pie

¾ cup sugar
3 tablespoons cornstarch
Freshly grated peel of 2 large limes (2½ teaspoons)
⅓ cup fresh lime juice
¼ cup (½ stick) butter, room temperature
1 cup sour cream
1 baked 9-inch pie shell
1 cup whipping cream
1 to 2 tablespoons sugar

Combine ¾ cup sugar with cornstarch and lime peel in medium saucepan and mix well. Add lime juice and stir until smooth. Blend in sour cream and butter. Place over medium heat and stir until mixture thickens and starts to boil, about 10 to 12 minutes. Remove from heat and let cool, stirring occasionally. Fold in sour cream. Turn mixture into baked pie shell. (See Index for Recipe.)

Combine whipping cream and 1 to 2 tablespoons sugar in medium bowl and whip to soft peaks. Spread atop pie and serve.

You will need two pies for this menu.

Lemon Chess Pie

1 9-inch pie shell
½ cup butter, softened
2 cups sugar
5 eggs
3 tablespoons flour
½ cup fresh lemon juice
4 tablespoons grated lemon rind

Prepare pie shell (see index); set aside. Cream butter and sugar; add eggs, beating well after each addition. Add flour and continue beating until well blended and mixture is thickened. Add lemon juice slowly, beating as you pour. Stir in rind. Pour into pie shell. Bake at 300° for 30 to 45 minutes. Cool completely before serving.

There are many recipes for Lemon Chess Pie but this one of my mother's is the best I've ever used. There is a "just right" time to take it out of the oven so that it will have a velvety texture after it has cooled and set. The secret is to not overbake. Set your timer for the 30 minute period and check it often after that. When the top is puffed and browned and the middle will still move when you carefully shake the pan, remove it from the oven. Set it on a solid surface and the middle will continue to set.

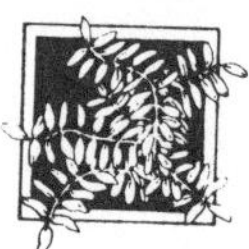

THE COMMITTEE MEETS

SERVES EIGHT

Sparkle Punch
Shrimp Alexander
Zucchini Casserole
Cucumber-Pineapple Salad
Orange Muffins
Fresh Peach Pie

Sparkle Punch

1 10-ounce package frozen raspberries, thawed
1 6-ounce can frozen lemonade concentrate, thawed and undiluted
2 cups water
1 32-ounce bottle lemon-lime carbonated beverage, chilled
Fresh mint sprigs (optional)

Process raspberries in food mill or container of electric blender; strain, discarding seeds.

Combine raspberry pulp, lemonade concentrate, and water; chill.

To serve, combine raspberry mixture and lemon-lime beverage; stir well. Serve over ice. Garnish with mint sprigs, if desired.
Yield: 7 cups.

Shrimp Alexander

1 pound cooked shrimp
¾ cup raw rice
2 tablespoons butter
¼ cup minced onion
¼ cup minced green pepper
⅛ teaspoon pepper
⅛ teaspoon mace
Cayenne pepper
1 can tomato soup
1 cup heavy cream (or half-and-half)
½ cup sherry
½ cup slivered almonds
paprika

Preheat oven to 350°. Cook rice. Melt butter in skillet. Sauté green pepper and onion in butter 5 minutes. Combine all ingredients except ⅛ cup of almonds. Put in 9×13-inch baking dish. Top with reserved almonds, sprinkle with paprika and bake 55 minutes.
Serves 8.

Zucchini Casserole

- 4 eggs
- ½ cup half-and-half
- 3 tablespoons all purpose flour
- 2 teaspoons baking powder
- Salt
- ¾ pound Monterey Jack cheese, grated
- ½ cup cottage cheese
- 1 medium onion, chopped
- 1 4-ounce can diced green chilies, drained
- 1 tablespoon dried basil, crumbled
- 1 garlic clove, minced
- 4 medium zucchini, sliced ¼ inch thick
- 1 2¼-ounce can sliced black olives, drained

Preheat oven to 350°. Butter 9×9-inch baking dish. Mix eggs with half-and-half in large bowl. Beat in flour and baking powder. Season with salt. Stir in cheeses, onion, chilies, basil and garlic. Arrange zucchini slices in bottom of prepared dish. Pour egg mixture over. Top with olives. Bake until golden and set, 35 to 40 minutes. Let casserole stand 10 minutes before serving.

Cucumber-Pineapple Salad

- 1 6-ounce package lemon-flavored gelatin
- 1½ cups boiling water
- 1 8-ounce package cream cheese, softened
- 1 8-ounce carton sour cream
- ½ cup mayonnaise
- 1 teaspoon lemon juice
- 1 teaspoon Worcestershire sauce
- 1 15½-ounce can crushed pineapple, drained
- 1 cup grated, seeded cucumber
- ¾ cup chopped celery
- 1 4-ounce jar diced pimento, drained
- 1 tablespoon prepared horseradish
- 1 tablespoon grated onion
- Cucumber slices (optional)

Dissolve gelatin in boiling water; cool slightly. Beat cream cheese until smooth. Gradually add gelatin mixture; beat well. Add sour cream, mayonnaise, lemon juice, and Worcestershire sauce. Chill until consistency of unbeaten egg white. Stir in next 6 ingredients. Pour into a lightly oiled 7-cup mold. Chill until firm. Unmold on a bed of cucumber slices, if desired.

Serves 12.

Orange Muffins

- 1 orange
- ⅓ cup fresh orange juice
- ½ stick (¼ cup) butter, softened
- 1 large egg
- ½ cup raisins
- 1½ cups all-purpose flour
- ¾ cup sugar
- 1 teaspoon double-acting baking powder
- 1 teaspoon baking soda
- 1 teaspoon salt

Grate the rind from the orange, reserving it, discard the pith, and quarter and seed the orange. In a blender blend the reserved orange rind, the orange quarters, the orange juice, the butter, and the egg. Add the raisins, blend the mixture for 5 seconds, and transfer it to a bowl. Into another bowl sift together the flour, the sugar, the baking powder, the baking soda, and the salt, stir the mixture into the orange mixture, and stir the batter until it is just combined. Divide the batter among 16 buttered and floured ⅓-cup muffin tins, bake the muffins in a preheated 400° oven for 15 to 20 minutes, or until they are golden, and turn them out onto a rack.

Makes 16 muffins.

Fresh Peach Pie

- 1 9-inch pie shell, unbaked
- 1 cup heavy cream, whipped
- 4 tablespoons flour
- 1 cup sugar
- 1 teaspoon almond extract
- 1 teaspoon cinnamon
- ½ teaspoon nutmeg
- ¼ teaspoon cloves
- ¼ teaspoon allspice
- 4-5 peaches, peeled and sliced

Prepare pie shell (see index). Set aside. Whip cream. Mix in flour, sugar, almond extract, and spices. Arrange peach slices in pie shell and pour cream mixture over. Bake at 350° for 30 to 40 minutes. Cool completely before serving.

Serves 8.

Bealah Reaves, better known as "Aunt Boots", is my husband's aunt who has shared her marvelous cooking skills with all of Plainview. The trick is to be sick enough for her to come but not too sick to eat what she brings!

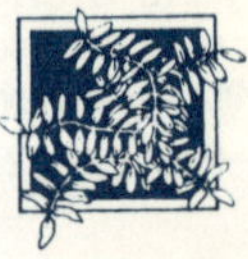

A LOVELY REPAST

SERVES TWELVE

Honeydew and Lime Bisque
Congealed Cranberry-Chicken Salad
Florentine Crepe Cups
Fruit Bread
Cream Cheese Tarts

Honeydew and Lime Bisque

1 large honeydew melon (5½ to 6 pounds), peeled, seeded, and diced, about 5 cups
2 cups (1 pint) lime sherbet
Juice of 1 large lime or to taste
Crushed ice
Fresh mint sprigs (garnish)

Combine melon, sherbet, and lime juice in processor (in batches if necessary) and purée until smooth. Divide among bowls set into ice. Garnish with mint and serve.

Congealed Cranberry-Chicken Salad

1 envelope unflavored gelatin
½ cup cold water
½ cup hot water, boiling
2 cups cooked, diced chicken breast
1 cup celery, chopped
1 cup mayonnaise
1 can jellied cranberry sauce
1 3-ounce package lemon gelatin
¾ cup boiling water
½ cup orange juice

Soften unflavored gelatin in cold water. Add boiling water and stir until gelatin is dissolved. Cool, then chill until slightly thickened. When thickened to consistency of egg whites, add chicken, celery, and mayonnaise. Grease a 9×13 inch Pyrex dish with mayonnaise. Pour in chicken mixture and chill until firm. With a fork, whip cranberry sauce. Dissolve lemon gelatin in boiling water, stirring until completely dissolved. Add orange juice and stir to mix well. Stir in cranberry sauce, and continue stirring until mixture is smooth. Set aside to cool. When chicken layer is firm, pour cranberry layer over. Cover and chill overnight.

Serves 12.

Florentine Crepe Cups

3 eggs, slightly beaten
⅔ cup flour
½ teaspoon salt
1 cup milk

1½ cups shredded sharp Cheddar cheese
3 tablespoons flour
3 eggs, slightly beaten
⅔ cup mayonnaise
1 10-ounce package frozen chopped spinach, thawed and drained
1 4-ounce can mushrooms, drained
6 crisply cooked bacon slices, crumbled
½ teaspoon salt
Dash pepper

Combine eggs, flour, salt and milk; beat until smooth. Let stand 30 minutes. For twelve crepes, pour 2 tablespoons batter into hot lightly greased 8-inch skillet. Cook on one side only, until underside is lightly browned.

Toss cheese with flour, add remaining ingredients; mix well. Fit crepes into greased muffin pan; fill with cheese mixture. Bake at 350° for 40 minutes or until set. Garnish with bacon curls, if desired.

Note: This recipe serves 6. For 12, double recipe. This is the crepe recipe that I use for any filling. The cooked crepes freeze well stacked, with waxed paper between each, in a plastic bag. Take out and thaw as many as needed.

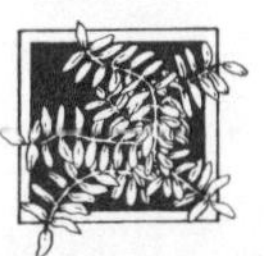

Anytime you boil chicken to be used in a recipe and don't need the liquid, pour it into a container and freeze it. Sour cream and cottage cheese cartons are good for this, stack easily in the freezer and you have a pre-measured amount.

Fruit Bread

- 1 cup sugar
- ¾ cup (1½ sticks) butter, melted and cooled
- 2 eggs
- 2 tablespoons apricot brandy
- 2 tablespoons almond liqueur
- 2 teaspoons vanilla
- 1 cup mashed ripe banana (about 2 medium-large)
- 2 teaspoons pumpkin pie spice
- 2 teaspoons cinnamon
- 1 teaspoon baking soda
- 1 teaspoon baking powder
- ½ teaspoon salt
- 2 cups flour
- 1 6-ounce package dried apricots, finely chopped
- 1 cup chopped walnuts

Preheat oven to 350°. Grease and lightly flour a 9×5-inch loaf pan. Combine sugar, melted butter, eggs, apricot brandy, almond liqueur and vanilla in large bowl and whisk until well blended, about 2 to 3 minutes. Stir in mashed banana. Combine pumpkin pie spice, cinnamon, baking soda, baking powder and salt in small bowl and mix well, making sure no lumps remain.

Whisk into banana mixture, blending well. Fold in flour using spatula; batter will be thick. Stir in chopped apricots and walnuts. Spoon batter into prepared pan. Bake until tester inserted in center comes out clean, about 50 to 55 minutes (top will split).

Let bread cool in pan 15 minutes. Remove from pan and cool completely on rack, about 2 to 3 hours. Wrap tightly in aluminum foil and store at room temperature for at least 2 days before serving. To serve 12, make 2 loaves.

Cream Cheese Tarts

- 2 8-ounce packages cream cheese, softened
- 1 cup sugar
- 2 eggs
- 1 teaspoon vanilla extract
- 12 vanilla wafers
- Blueberry pie filling or whipped cream

Beat cream cheese in a medium mixing bowl until soft and creamy. Gradually add sugar, beating until light and fluffy. Add eggs, one at a time, beating well after each addition. Stir in vanilla. Place a vanilla wafer in each paper-lined muffin cup; spoon cream cheese mixture over wafer, filling cups full. Bake at 350° for 20 minutes. Leave in muffin pans, and refrigerate overnight.

To serve, remove paper liners, if desired and top with a small amount of blueberry pie filling or whipped cream. (Reserve leftover pie filling for other uses.)
Serves 12.

A QUICHE FOR EACH

SERVES TWELVE

Cream of Cucumber Soup

Individual Quiches

Deluxe English Peas **Sunshine Salad**

Lemon-Cream Loaf

White Chocolate Cheesecake

Cream of Cucumber Soup

6 cucumbers, peeled and seeded
2 cups chilled buttermilk
2 cups chilled sour cream
2 tablespoons distilled white vinegar
3 teaspoons olive oil
5 teaspoons snipped fresh dill or 1½ teaspoons dried

In a food processor purée coarse the cucumbers. In a metal bowl whisk the cucumbers with the buttermilk, the sour cream, the vinegar, the oil, the dill, and salt to taste and chill the soup, covered and set in a bowl of crushed ice and ice water, stirring occasionally, for 30 minutes.

12 small servings - Double if you wish to use something larger than a punch cup to serve in.

Individual Quiches

Pastry for 2-crust pie
¾ cup chopped cooked shrimp
¼ cup sliced green onion, tops and bottoms
4 ounces Swiss cheese (1 cup)
½ cup mayonnaise
2 eggs
⅓ cup milk
¼ teaspoon salt
¼ teaspoon dill weed

On floured surface roll half of pastry into 12-inch circle (see Index for recipe). Cut six 4-inch circles. Repeat with remaining pastry. Fit into twelve 2½-inch muffin pan cups. Fill each with some shrimp, onion and cheese. Beat remaining ingredients. Pour over cheese. Bake in 400° oven 15 to 20 minutes or until browned.

Makes 12.

Deluxe English Peas

- 4 pounds fresh English peas, or frozen peas cooked and drained
- 2 tablespoons butter
- 2 cups sliced celery
- 4 tablespoons finely chopped onion
- 8 ounces fresh mushrooms, sliced
- 2 2-ounce jars diced pimento, drained
- ½ teaspoon salt
- ½ teaspoon ground savory
- Freshly ground pepper

Shell and wash peas; add water to cover. Bring peas to a boil; cover, reduce heat, and simmer 8 to 12 minutes or until tender. Drain and set aside.

Place skillet over medium heat until butter is melted. Add celery and onion; sauté 3 minutes. Add next 5 ingredients, and cook until thoroughly heated, stirring occasionally.

Sunshine Salad

- 1 6-ounce package lemon-flavored gelatin
- 2 cups boiling water
- 1 5-ounce jar process pimento cheese spread
- 1⅓ cups mayonnaise
- 1 15¼-ounce can crushed pineapple, undrained
- 1 cup chopped celery
- ½ cup shredded carrot

Dissolve gelatin in boiling water. Add pimento cheese spread, beating with a wire whisk until smooth. Let cool.

Add mayonnaise, beating with a wire whisk until smooth. Stir in pineapple, celery, and carrot; mix well. Pour into a lightly oiled 8-cup mold; chill until firm.
Serves 12.

Often a recipe will call for a small amount of tomato paste, leaving the remainder of the can unused. Line a cookie sheet with waxed paper and spoon the paste out in Tablespoon portions. Freeze. When frozen, remove from paper and place in a plastic bag, fasten tightly and store in freezer. Remove Tablespoon amounts as needed.

Lemon-Cream Loaf

1 8-ounce package cream cheese, softened
½ cup butter or margarine, softened
1¼ cups sugar
2 eggs
2¼ cups all-purpose flour
1 tablespoon baking power
½ teaspoon salt
¾ cup milk
⅔ cup chopped pecans
1 teaspoon grated lemon rind
2 to 3 tablespoons lemon juice
⅓ cup sifted powdered sugar

Combine cream cheese and butter, creaming well. Gradually add sugar, beating until light and fluffy. Add eggs, one at a time, beating mixture well after each addition.

Combine flour, baking powder, and salt; add to creamed mixture alternately with milk, beginning and ending with flour mixture. Mix well after each addition. Stir in pecans.

Pour batter into 2 greased and floured 8½×4½×3-inch loafpans. Bake at 350° for 45 minutes or until a wooden pick inserted in center comes out clean. Combine lemon rind, lemon juice, and powdered sugar, mixing until smooth; pour over hot loaves. Cool in pans 10 minutes; remove to wire rack, and cool completely.

Yield: 2 loaves

This bread is good toasted, too.

White Chocolate Cheesecake

1½ cups graham cracker crumbs
5 tablespoons melted butter
1 to 2 tablespoons sugar
2 pounds cream cheese, room temperature
½ cup (1 stick) butter, room temperature
4 eggs, room temperature
10 ounces white chocolate, melted
4½ teaspoons vanilla
Pinch of salt

Mix graham cracker crumbs, melted butter and sugar in large bowl. Press into bottom and sides of 9-inch springform pan. Refrigerate.

Preheat oven to 300°. Combine cream cheese and butter in large bowl of electric mixer and beat until smooth. Add eggs one at a time, blending well after each addition. Add white chocolate, vanilla and salt and beat 1 to 2 minutes at medium speed. Turn mixture into prepared graham cracker crust. Bake 1 hour. Let stand 2 hours at room temperature, then refrigerate for about 12 hours before serving.

Serves 12 to 16.

All of the cheesecake recipes in this book are exceptionally good but this one is most unusual. A square of dark chocolate, melted and drizzled over the top doesn't hurt a bit!

A LITTLE MORE THAN TWELVE

SERVES TWELVE TO FOURTEEN

Cold Raspberry Soup
Sensational Salad
Melon Ball Salad
Pecan Muffins
Lemon Cheesecake

Cold Raspberry Soup

- 2 10-ounce packages frozen Raspberries, thawed
- 2½ cups water
- 2 cups dry red wine
- 1 stick cinnamon
- ⅓ cup sugar
- 2 tablespoons cornstarch
- Sour cream

Combine raspberries, water, wine, cinnamon stick, and sugar in large saucepan. Bring to boil, reduce heat and simmer 30 minutes. Press mixture through a fine sieve to remove seeds. Return mixture to pan. Mix small amount of hot raspberry liquid with cornstarch and stir until smooth. Bring raspberry mixture back to boil, reduce heat and stir in cornstarch. Cook, stirring constantly, until slightly thickened. Chill at least 8 hours or overnight. (May be made several days ahead of serving.) Serve cold with small dollop of sour cream on top of each serving.
Yield: 6 to 8 cups.

Double recipe for this menu.

NEVER FORGET!! You feed the eye before you ever taste a dish. Give as much thought to the appearance of your various dishes as you plan a meal as you do to the recipe. To create an attractive combination of color, shape, and texture is as important to an excellent menu as the ingredients in the recipes.

Sensational Salad

6 to 8 potatoes, cooked and chopped
2 green onions, tops and bottoms, chopped
½ cup celery, chopped
2 hard-boiled eggs, chopped
salt and pepper
1 tablespoon Dijon mustard
½ to ¾ cup mayonnaise

Mix all of the ingredients in a bowl with a rounded bottom. Pack down firmly and refrigerate.

1 head lettuce, shredded (set aside largest outer leaves)
6 tomatoes, cut into wedges
4 small cucumbers, unpeeled and cut into sticks
4 avocados, peeled and sliced
12 to 14 thin slices ham
12 to 14 thin slices turkey
½ pound thinly sliced cheese (Cheddar, Monterey Jack or Swiss)
2 bell peppers, cut into rings
1 large can ripe olives, pitted, well-drained

To assemble salad:

Line a large round platter with outer leaves of lettuce. Unmold potato salad in center of platter. Chop remaining lettuce and place it around the base of the salad covering the salad halfway up. Make tight rolls of ham and turkey. Arrange meats and cheeses around the platter alternating. Garnish salad with the vegetables creating an attractive pattern. Cover and refrigerate. May be made 1 day ahead of serving.

Before serving, drizzle with vinaigrette dressing. To serve, cut into wedges.

Vinaigrette

3 tablespoons white wine vinegar
1¼ teaspoons Dijon-style mustard
½ teaspoon salt
½ teaspoon white pepper
8 tablespoons salad oil
2 tablespoons parsley
½ teaspoon basil

Mix vinegar and mustard in small jar with tight lid. Shake well to mix. Add remaining ingredients and shake again. Keep stored in refrigerator in tightly closed jar until ready to use.

This is a very pretty salad—be prepared for compliments when you serve this!

Melon Ball Salad

- 1 envelope plus 1 teaspoon unflavored gelatin
- ¼ cup cold water
- ¾ cup hot water
- 3 tablespoons sugar
- ½ cup orange juice
- 1 tablespoon grated lemon rind
- ¼ cup lemon juice
- 1 cup watermelon balls
- 1 cup cantaloupe balls or honeydew balls
- ½ cup seedless green grapes
- 3 peaches, peeled and sliced

Soften gelatin in cold water; let stand 5 minutes. Add hot water and sugar; stir until gelatin dissolves. Add next 3 ingredients; mix well. Chill mixture until consistency of unbeaten egg white. Fold in fruit; pour into a lightly oiled 8-cup mold. Chill until set.

Cottage Cheese Layer

- 1 envelope unflavored gelatin
- ¼ cup cold water
- ¾ cup hot water
- ⅓ cup lemon juice
- ¼ cup plus 1 tablespoon sugar
- 2 cups cream-style cottage cheese
- Lettuce leaves

Soften gelatin in cold water; let stand 5 minutes. Add hot water, lemon juice, and sugar; mix well. Place cottage cheese in container of electric blender; process until smooth. Gradually stir cottage cheese into lemon juice mixture; pour over melon ball layer. Chill until firm. Unmold salad on lettuce leaves.

Pecan Muffins

- 1 cup brown sugar
- ⅓ cup flour
- Dash salt
- 1 cup pecans
- 2 eggs
- ½ teaspoon vanilla

Mix all ingredients well. Bake in at 350° oven for 20 minutes. These freeze well. For 16, triple recipe.

Lemon Cheesecake

Crust

¾ cup butter, softened
1 egg
1¼ cups flour
⅓ cup plus 1 teaspoon sugar
Peel of 1 small lemon, grated
4 drops lemon extract

In a small bowl and at low speed of mixer, mix butter, egg, flour, ⅓ cup sugar, lemon peel and lemon extract. Shape the dough into a ball. Wrap in waxed paper and chill 1 hour. Preheat oven to 400°. Press one-third of the dough into the bottom of a spring form pan. Sprinkle with remaining 1 teaspoon sugar. Bake for 8 minutes. Cool. Reset oven temperature to 475°.

Filling

5 8-ounce packages cream cheese, room temperature
¼ cup milk
1¾ cups sugar
3 tablespoons flour
4 eggs
Peel of 1 small lemon, grated

In a large bowl and at medium speed of mixer, beat cream cheese with milk until smooth and fluffy. Slowly beat in sugar. With mixer on low speed, beat in flour and remaining ingredients. Beat at medium speed for 5 minutes.

Press remaining dough around sides of pan to within 1 inch of the top. Do not bake. Pour cream cheese mixture into pan. Bake for 12 minutes. Turn oven to 300° and bake 35 additional minutes. Turn off oven. Leave cheese cake in oven at least 30 minutes to cool, then cool on a wire rack. Chill overnight if possible, remove from spring form pan and serve.

If cake appears to be too soft in the center after the 35 minutes at 300°, extend the time 10 to 20 minutes.

DAY OF THE WEDDING LUNCHEON

SERVES TWENTY

Cold Dill Soup

Shrimp Mousse

Herbed Spinach

Fresh Tomato Tart (Make Two)

Mandarin Salad

Lemon Poppy-Seed Bread (Make Three Loaves)

Daiquiri Pie (Make Three)

Cold Dill Soup

- 2 pints half-and-half
- 4 8-ounce cartons plain yogurt
- 4 cucumbers, peeled, seeded and diced
- 4 tablespoons minced fresh dillweed or 2 tablespoons dried whole dillweed
- 2 tablespoons chopped green onions
- 1 teaspoon salt
- ½ teaspoon white pepper
- Sliced cucumber (optional)
- Sprigs of fresh dillweed (optional)

Combine first 8 ingredients, sitrring well; chill thoroughly. Stir well; garnish with sliced cucumber and dill sprigs, if desired.

Shrimp Mousse

- 3 pounds peeled, deveined, cooked shrimp, chopped
- 1 cup mayonnaise
- 2 cups sour cream
- 2 8-ounce packages cream cheese
- ½ cup bell pepper, finely chopped
- ½ cup green onion, finely chopped
- ½ cup celery, finely chopped
- ¼ cup pimento, finely chopped
- 1 tablespoon Worcestershire sauce
- ½ to 1 teaspoon salt
- ½ cup chili sauce
- 2 tablespoons unflavored gelatin
- ¼ cup cold water
- 6 tablespoons lemon juice
- Dash Tabasco

Measure shrimp to equal at least 6 cups. Cream mayonnaise, sour cream and cream cheese. Add chopped vegetables and seasonings. Soften gelatin in cold water. Add lemon juice. Stir over low heat until gelatin is dissolved. Fold into the cheese mixture. Add shrimp and mix well. Pour into a 2-quart fish mold or Pyrex dish. Chill until firm. May be made two days ahead of serving.

Serves 12 generously. Make two for twenty.

Herbed Spinach

2 10-ounce packages frozen chopped spinach, cooked and drained
4 cups cooked rice
1½ cups shredded sharp American cheese
4 eggs, slightly beaten
4 tablespoons soft butter
1 teaspoon Worcestershire
⅔ cup milk
4 tablespoons chopped onions
2 teaspoons salt
½ teaspoon rosemary
Stuffed eggs for garnish

Mix all together in order given. Pour into a 8×13×1½-inch baking dish. Refrigerate overnight. Preheat oven to 350°. Bake 20 to 25 minutes. Cut in squares to serve. Garnish with stuffed eggs.

Serves 20.

Fresh Tomato Tart

Buttermilk Pastry

4 cups all purpose flour
3 tablespoons baking powder
1 tablespoon sugar
1 teaspoon salt
¾ cup (1½ sticks) margarine
1¼ cups buttermilk

Tomato-Basil Filling

12 medium tomatoes (about 3¾ pounds), diced
2 cups chopped fresh basil leaves (6 tablespoons dried basil may be used.)
1 teaspoon salt
4 cups grated Cheddar cheese
4 cups grated Swiss cheese
1½ cups mayonnaise, preferably homemade

For Pastry: Preheat oven to 400°. Combine flour, baking powder, sugar and salt in large bowl. Cut in margarine with pastry blender or 2 knives until mixture resembles coarse meal. Gradually mix in buttermilk until dough just comes together.

Roll dough out between 2 sheets of waxed paper to fit shallow 3-quart baking dish. Peel off 1 sheet of paper; invert dough into dish. Press dough into bottom and up sides; flute edges. Bake until puffed and golden, about 15 minutes (if center rises, gently press down). Set crust aside. Reduce oven temperature to 375°. (Crust may be frozen or refrigerated at this point. Fill and bake when ready to serve.

For filling: Mix tomatoes, basil and salt. Spoon into crust, spreading evenly. Blend cheeses and mayonnaise. Pat evenly over tomato mixture. Bake until filling is heated through and cheese melts, 20 to 25 minutes. Serve tomato tart immediately.

Make 2 to serve 20.

Mandarin Salad

- 1 cup chopped walnuts
- 6 tablespoons sugar
- 2 medium heads romaine lettuce, torn into bitesize pieces
- 2 cups chopped celery
- 4 medium size green onions, thinly sliced
- 2 11-ounce cans mandarin oranges, drained

Dressing

- ¼ cup vegetable oil
- 2 tablespoons cider vinegar
- 2 tablespoons sugar
- 1 tablespoon chopped fresh parsley
- ½ teaspoon salt
- Dash of freshly ground pepper
- Dash of hot pepper sauce

For Dressing: Combine all ingredients in jar with tight-fitting lid and shake well. Refrigerate until ready to use. (Can be prepared up to 3 days ahead.)

Sauté walnuts and sugar in heavy small skillet over low heat until sugar dissolves and walnuts are glazed, about 5 minutes, watching carefully to prevent burning. Cool completely. (Can be prepared 1 week ahead. Store in airtight container.) Toss lettuce, celery and green onions in large bowl. Add walnuts and oranges. Shake dressing, pour over salad and toss well. Serve immediately.

Lemon Poppy Seed Bread

- ¾ cup sugar
- 2 eggs
- ½ cup milk
- ½ cup (1 stick) butter, melted and cooled
- 1 tablespoon lemon extract
- 1½ cups all-purpose flour
- 1 teaspoon baking powder
- 1 teaspoon baking soda
- ½ teaspoon salt
- 3 tablespoons poppy seed

Preheat oven to 325°. Grease and flour a 4×7½-inch loaf pan. Combine sugar and eggs in large bowl and beat until very light and fluffy. Slowly beat in milk. Add butter and lemon extract and blend well.

Sift together flour, baking powder, baking soda and salt. Add to sugar mixture with poppy seed and stir to blend. Turn batter into prepared pan. Bake until bread is golden and tester inserted in center comes out clean, about 50 to 60 minutes.

Make 3 loaves to serve 20.

Daiquiri Pie

1 envelope unflavored gelatin
1½ cups sugar
½ teaspoon salt
4 egg yolks
½ cup lemon juice
2 tablespoons lime juice
1 teaspoon grated lemon peel
6 drops green food color
½ cup light rum
4 egg whites
½ cup heavy cream, whipped
1 (9-inch) baked pie shell

Make pie shell. (See Index.) Bake until lightly browned. Set aside. In the top of a double boiler, combine gelatin with 1 cup sugar and the salt. In a small bowl, beat egg yolks with lemon and lime juices just until combined. Stir into gelatin mixture. Cook over boiling water, stirring constantly, until gelatin is dissolved and mixture is thickened, 10 to 12 minutes. Remove from water; stir in lemon peel, food coloring, and rum. Set in a bowl filled with ice cubes and water. Cool, stirring occasionally until mixture is thick and mounds when it is dropped from a spoon, about 30 minutes. In a large bowl, beat egg whites until soft peaks form. Gradually add remaining sugar, 2 tablespoons at a time, beating well until stiff peaks form. Fold gelatin mixture and whipped cream into egg whites just until combined. Turn half of mixture into baked pie shell. Refrigerate along with the rest of the mixture, 20 minutes. Spoon rest of chilled mixture in center of pie, mounding high. Refrigerate until firm, 4 hours or overnight. If desired, decorate with whipped cream and grated chocolate before serving.

Makes 8 servings.

A GALA EVENT

SERVES FORTY

Nearly Champagne
Pineapple Lemonade
Turkey with Mushroom Sauce
Broccoli-Corn Bake Beet Salad
Lemon-Herb Buttered French Bread
Apricot Brandy Cake (Make Three)

Nearly Champagne

1 gallon sauterne, chilled
2 ounces lemon juice, chilled
4 ounces vodka, chilled
3 quarts gingerale, chilled

Mix all ingredients in large punch bowl. Serve immediately.
Double to serve forty.

Pineapple Lemonade

12 cups sugar
12 cups water
6 cups fresh lemon juice
12 cups unsweetened pineapple juice
12 cups club soda

In large saucepan combine the sugar and water, bring the mixture to boil over medium heat, stirring until sugar is dissolved. Let simmer without stirring for 10 minutes. Let syrup cool. Stir in pineapple juice, club soda, and lemon juice. Serve over ice and garnish with lemon slices and mint sprigs.

Turkey with Mushroom Sauce

1 cup chopped green onions
½ cup chopped green pepper
2 cups chopped celery
1 cup margarine or bacon drippings
2 10½-ounce cans undiluted cream of mushroom soup
2 10½-ounce cans golden mushroom soup
4 soup cans water
8 cups cooked, chopped turkey
2 tablespoons Worcestershire sauce
Salt and pepper to taste
4 tablespoons chopped pimento
2 tablespoons minced parsley
1 cup Sauterne wine
40 individual tart shells, baked

Make tart shells (see Index for pastry recipe). Bake as directed and set aside.

Sauté green onions, pepper, and celery in margarine or bacon drippings until tender. Add soups and water. Add turkey and all other ingredients except wine. Cook slowly for 30 minutes. Stir in wine and pour in chafing dish. Serve hot in tart shells.

Serves 40.

Beet Salad

6 tablespoons unflavored gelatin
2 cups cold water
8 16-ounce cans beets, drained (Reserve liquid.)
6 teaspoons salt
2 cups sugar
2 cups white wine vinegar
6 cups chopped celery
½ cup chopped green onion, tops and bottoms
1 cup prepared horseradish

Dissolve gelatin in water. Heat and stir in 6 cups of beet liquid. Combine beets with remaining ingredients and gelatin mixture. Pour into 4 9×13-inch Pyrex dishes. Cut into squares to serve.

Kneaded Butter is handy to keep in your freezer for thickening soups or pan juices — without lumps! Process 1 cup butter in food processor until soft. Add 1¼ cups flour and process briefly to blend. Turn out onto foil and shape into long roll. Refrigerate until firm. Cut into ¼ inch slices and place in plastic bag. Freeze. When needed, two ¼ inch slices will thicken 1 cup liquid to medium consistency. Simmer several minutes, stirring.

Broccoli-Corn Bake

4 16-ounce cans cream style corn
4 10-ounce packages broccoli
4 beaten eggs
2 cups cracker crumbs
4 tablespoons onion
8 tablespoons melted butter
2 teaspoons salt

Mix together and spoon into greased Pyrex dishes. Double this recipe to serve 40, using 4 9×13 casseroles.

Sprinkle over top:

1 cup cracker crumbs
4 tablespoons melted butter

Bake at 350° for 35 to 40 minutes.

Ernestine Bain gave me a real treasure with this recipe.

Lemon-Herb Bread

1 teaspoon dried rosemary
1 teasoon dried oregano
1 teaspoon dried basil
1 tablespoon minced fresh dill or 1 teaspoon dried dill weed
1 tablespoon lemon juice
4 tablespoons butter, softened
1 loaf crusty, French or Italian bread, about 13 inches long

In a small bowl, mix the herbs, dill, lemon juice and butter until well blended.

Cut the bread into 1-inch slices, leaving the bottom crust intact. Reserving 1½ teaspoons, spread the herbed butter evenly on one side of each slice. Spread the reserved butter over the top of the loaf. Wrap the loaf tightly in aluminum foil and bake at 350° for 10 to 12 minutes, or until the bread is hot and the butter is melted. Use 4 loaves of bread for this menu.

Apricot Brandy Cake

1 cup butter
3 cups sugar
6 eggs
3 cups flour
½ teaspoon salt
¼ teaspoon baking soda
1 cup sour cream
½ cup apricot brandy
1 teaspoon vanilla
½ teaspoon rum extract
½ teaspoon lemon extract
¼ teaspoon almond extract

Cream together butter and sugar. Add eggs one at a time. Sift flour, salt and baking soda together. Mix sour cream, apricot brandy and all extracts together. Now alternately add sour cream mixture and flour mixture into creamed butter and sugar. Pour into a greased and floured angel food cake pan. Bake at 325° for 70 minutes or until done.

Use this recipe for Christmas gift-giving, too. It freezes well or keeps several days, tightly wrapped.

SALAD LUNCHEON

SERVES FIFTY TO SIXTY

Tropical Cooler
Bourbon Slush
Layered Ham and Egg Salad
Dilled Green Beans
Watermelon Boat with Poppy-Seed Dressing
Chicken Finger Sandwiches
Cheese Finger Sandwiches
Chocolate Frumps
Blueberry-Cream Cheese Squares

Tropical Cooler

- 9 tablespoons sugar
- 3 tablespoons instant tea
- 4½ cups water
- 3 12-ounce cans apricot nectar, chilled
- 3 6-ounce cans frozen lemonade concentrate, thawed
- 6 12-ounce cans lemon-lime carbonated beverage, chilled

Combine first 3 ingredients; stir until sugar dissolves. Add remaining ingredients; mix well. Serve over ice.

Yield: about 2 gallons. Double to serve 50-60.

Bourbon Slush

- 9 cups water
- 2 to 3 cups bourbon
- 1 12-ounce can frozen orange juice concentrate, thawed and undiluted
- 1 12-ounce can frozen lemonade concentrate, thawed and undiluted
- 1¾ cups sugar
- 1 tablespoon instant tea
- 3 16-ounce bottles lemon-lime carbonated beverage

Combine first 6 ingredients; stir well. Freeze mixture overnight or until firm. Remove from freezer 30 minutes before serving (mixture should be slushy); combine with lemon-lime beverage, stirring well.

Yield: about 1½ gallons. Double to serve fifty to sixty.

Layered Ham and Egg Salad

½ cup cold water
2 tablespoons unflavored gelatin

Egg Salad

2 dozen hard-cooked eggs, chopped
2 cups celery, chopped
1 cup pimento-stuffed olives, chopped
3 teaspoons salt
1 teaspoon pepper
1 cup mayonnaise
5 tablespoons above prepared gelatin mixture

Ham Salad

3 cups ground, cooked ham
⅔ cup mayonnaise
½ cup sweet pickle relish
2 tablespoons green onion, tops and bottoms, chopped
1 tablespoon chopped parsley
2 teaspoons Dijon mustard
3 tablespoons prepared gelatin mixture

In a small saucepan, sprinkle gelatin over water. Stir over low heat until gelatin is dissolved; cool. In very large bowl, combine all Egg Salad ingredients except gelatin mixture; blend well. Stir in gelatin. Spoon ⅓of mixture into 12-cup bundt pan. Set aside. In another large bowl, mix all Ham Salad ingredients, except gelatin mixture; blend well. Stir in gelatin. Carefully spoon Ham Salad over Egg Salad in pan, spreading evenly. Spoon remaining Egg Salad over ham, making sure all ham is evenly covered. Cover tightly with plastic wrap, chill until firm. Unmold on serving platter and garnish with softened cream cheese whipped with a small amount of mayonnaise and decorate with parsley and pimento-stuffed olives.

Make 3 of these to serve 50 to 60.

Dilled Green Beans

1 quart salad oil
1 quart white wine vinegar
1 cup water
2 cloves garlic, minced
¼ cup sugar
2 tablespoons dry mustard
1 tablespoon celery seed
1 tablespoon dill weed
1 teaspoon salt
1 teaspoon pepper
3 6-pound, 9-ounce cans green beans, drained
5 white or red onions, thinly sliced

Mix all ingredients except beans and onions, heat to boiling in very large pan. Add beans and return to boil; remove from heat and let beans cool in pan. With slotted spoon, remove beans and layer with onions in 9×13-inch Pyrex dishes (use 2 or 3 dishes). Pour marinade over beans. Cover with plastic wrap and refrigerate at least 24 hours. Serve cold.

May be made up to 1 week ahead. Stir occasionally.

Watermelon Boat

- 1 large watermelon, cut in half and all meat removed and cut into bite-size chunks
- 2 cantaloupe, peeled and cut into chunks
- 2 honeydew, peeled and cut into chunks
- 1 pineapple, peeled, cored and cut into chunks
- 2 quarts strawberries, left whole with stems
- 4 pounds peaches, peeled, sliced and sprinkled with lemon juice
- 2 pounds seedless green grapes, left whole
- ½ cup sugar
- Poppy-Seed Dressing (see recipe below)

Mix all fruit and sugar, chill. Pile into reserved watermelon halves. Serve with poppy-seed dressing served in a separate bowl.

Poppy-Seed Dressing

- 1½ cups sugar
- 2 teaspoons salt
- 2 teaspoons mustard
- 5 tablespoons grated onion
- ⅔ cup vinegar
- 2 cups salad oil
- 4 tablespoons poppy seeds

Combine all ingredients except oil and poppy seeds in blender or food processor. Mix well. With machine running, slowly add oil. Stir in poppy seeds by hand. Refrigerate.

Yield: 1 quart.

Chicken Salad Spread

- 4 cups cooked, chopped chicken
- 1 cup minced celery
- 1 cup toasted almonds, finely chopped
- 4-5 tablespoons mayonnaise, or enough to moisten for proper spreading consistency

Combine all ingredients, mixing well to completely blend.

Spread on bread of choice, trim and cut into fingers. Wrap tightly in plastic wrap, store in refrigerator in tightly closed container. May be made 3 to 4 days in advance or up to 1 month in advance, then frozen.

Cheese Spread

Grate 4 pounds sharp Cheddar cheese, mix with 1 cup green onion, tops and bottoms, chopped, 2 (4-ounce) cans chopped green chilies, drained, 1 (4-ounce) can chopped ripe olives, drained, 1 cup chopped pecans, enough mayonnaise to moisten. Make sandwiches as directed for chicken spread.

Chocolate Frumps

- 1 cup butter
- 2 cups sifted powdered sugar
- 4 ounces unsweetened chocolate, melted
- 1½ teaspoons peppermint flavoring
- 4 eggs
- 2 teaspoons vanilla
- 1 cup crushed vanilla wafers
- Whipped cream
- Maraschino cherries

Cream butter and sugar. Add chocolate, eggs and extracts, beating after each addition. Sprinkle half of crumbs in bottom of 18 cupcake tins lined with paper baking cups. Spoon chocolate mixture on top, then top with remaining crumbs. Freeze till firm. Remove frumps from tins. Store in freezer in plastic bags. Before serving, thaw about 15 minutes and top each with a swirl of whipped cream and a cherry.

Serves 18. Make this recipe four times to serve this party.

Blueberry-Cream Cheese Squares

- 1½ cups graham cracker crumbs
- ½ cup powdered sugar
- ½ cup (1 stick) butter melted
- 1 cup sugar
- 1 8-ounce package cream cheese, room temperature
- 2 eggs, beaten to blend
- 2½ tablespoons fresh lemon juice
- 1 21-ounce can blueberry pie filling

Preheat oven to 350°. Butter a 9×13-inch baking dish. Mix crumbs, powdered sugar and butter in medium bowl. Press into bottom of prepared dish using fork. Mix sugar, cream cheese and eggs in medium bowl until smooth. Spread over crust. Bake 20 minutes. Cool.

Stir lemon juice into pie filling. Spread over cheese mixture. Cover tightly and refrigerate. Cut into squares to serve. Make four times to serve this party.

AN APPRECIATION LUNCHEON

FOR SIXTEEN

Chilled Tomato Cheese Soup
Ham Rolls with Orange Rice
Williamsburg Salad
Peach stuffed with Mincemeat
Hot Rolls (see Index) or
Sweet Potato Muffins
Strawberry Satin Pie

Chilled Tomato Cheese Soup

1 can condensed tomato soup
2 cups light cream
2 tablespoons lemon juice
1 tablespoon horseradish
5 drops Tabasco sauce
½ cup small curd cottage cheese
1 teaspoon salt
¼ teaspoon pepper
¼ cup green pepper, chopped fine

Combine first 5 ingredients. Beat with rotary beater. Add remaining ingredients. Mix well. Chill at least 8 hours.

Serves 4 to 6 — triple to serve 16.

Ham Rolls With Orange Rice

1⅓ cups orange juice
⅔ cup raw rice
2 (11 ounce) cans mandarin oranges, drained and chopped
⅔ cup mayonnaise
¼ cup chopped pecans
4 tablespoons chopped parsley
2 tablespoons green onion, tops and bottoms, chopped
16 thin slices ham
½ cup orange marmalade
2 tablespoons lemon juice
½ teaspoon ginger

Bring orange juice to a boil, stir in rice. Lower heat, cook covered 20 to 30 minutes, or until rice is tender. Combine chopped oranges with rice and mix in mayonnaise, pecans, parsley and onion. Spoon mixture onto ham slices and roll as tightly as possible. Place in greased baking dishes, seam side down.

Combine marmalade, lemon juice and ginger. Brush tops of ham rolls. Bake at 350° for 25 to 30 minutes. Continue to baste with remaining marmalade sauce every few minutes. Allow 1 ham roll per serving.

NOTE: May be made a day ahead before baking.

Williamsburg Salad

2 envelopes unflavored gelatin
½ cup cold water
1 cup boiling water
½ cup cold water
½ cup vinegar
½ teaspoon salt
2 cups sugar
Few drops green food coloring
1 cup diced, blanched almonds
1 cup sliced sweet pickles
1 cup crushed pineapple, drained
1 cup sliced stuffed olives

Soften gelatin in ½ cup cold water. Add to boiling water and stir until dissolved. Add ½ cup cold water, vinegar, salt, sugar and a few drops of green food coloring.

Chill until mixture thickens. Fold in other ingredients. Chill until ready to serve. Serves 8 — double for this menu.

Peach Stuffed With Mincemeat

Drain 2 large cans peach halves, making sure there are 16.

Melt ½ stick butter in saucepan, add 1 jar prepared mincemeat (either with brandy and rum or without). Stir to mix well. Place peach halves, cut side up, in a shallow pan. Fill cavities with mincemeat. Place under broiler until bubbly. Serve immediately.

Sweet Potato Muffins

1¼ cups sugar
1¼ cups cooked, mashed sweet potatoes or yams (fresh or canned)
½ cup (1 stick) butter, room temperature
2 eggs
1½ cups flour
2 teaspoons baking powder
1 teaspoon cinnamon
¼ teaspoon nutmeg
¼ teaspoon salt
1 cup milk
½ cup chopped raisins
¼ cup chopped walnuts or pecans
2 tablespoons sugar mixed with ¼ teaspoon cinnamon

Thoroughly grease 24 muffin cups (paper liners may be used instead). Preheat oven to 400°.

Beat sugar, sweet potatoes and butter until smooth. Add eggs and blend well.

Sift together flour, baking powder, spices and salt. Add alternately with milk to sweet potato mixture, stirring just to blend. Do not overmix.

Fold in raisins and nuts. Spoon into muffin cups and sprinkle each with sugar/cinnamon mixture. Bake 25 to 30 minutes or until muffins test done. Serve warm.

NOTE: Muffins may be frozen and reheated.

Strawberry Satin Pie

- 1 pie shell baked
- ½ cup almonds
- ½ cup sugar
- 3 tablespoons cornstarch
- 3 tablespoons flour
- ½ teaspoon salt
- 2 cups milk
- 1 egg
- ½ cup whipping cream
- 1 teaspoon vanilla
- 1½ cups fresh strawberries, sliced

Prepare pie shell (see index). Bake as directed. Cool.

Cover bottom of pie shell with almonds. Combine sugar, cornstarch, flour, and salt. Add the milk. Cook until thick. Add beaten egg slowly. Cook just till bubbling. Chill thoroughly.

Whip cream and fold into cool custard. Add vanilla. Pour into shell. Slice 1½ cups strawberries over filling. Spoon Glaze over all.

Glaze

- ½ cup water
- ¼ cup sugar
- 1 tablespoon cornstarch
- ½ cup strawberries, crushed

To the crushed strawberries add the water and sugar. Mix together the sugar and cornstarch. Add to the strawberries and cook until thick and clear. Chill.

Dinners

"Elegance at Eight"

Elegance At Eight

DINNERS TO TEMPT EVERY PALATE

HIS BIRTHDAY DINNER

FOR TWO

Hot Beef and Tomato Drinks
Chutney-Cheese Paté
Assorted Crackers
Filet Mignons in Cognac Cream
Potatoes Venetian
Bibb Lettuce with Chiffon Dressing
Cheese-Olive Bread
Chilled Custard with Fresh Fruit
Cabernet-Sauvignon
or
Bordeaux

Hot Beef and Tomato Drinks

2 cups tomato juice
½ cup canned beef broth
2 tablespoons fresh lime juice
Celery salt to taste

In a small stainless steel or enameled saucepan combine the tomato juice, the broth, and the lime juice, bring the liquid just to a boil, and divide it between mugs. Sprinkle the drinks with the celery salt.

Makes 2 drinks.

Chutney-Cheese Paté

1 3-ounce package cream cheese, softened
½ cup (2 ounces) shredded sharp Cheddar cheese
2 teaspoons dry sherry
¼ teaspoon curry powder
⅛ teaspoon salt
½ cup chutney
Finely chopped green onions with tops

Combine first 5 ingredients; beat until smooth. Shape mixture into a ½-inch thick circle; chill until firm. Spread chutney over top, and sprinkle with green onions. Serve paté with crackers.

Yield: 1 cup.

Filet Mignons in Cognac Cream Sauce

2 filet mignons, cut 1½-inches thick
Freshly ground pepper
½ cup Cognac
1 teaspoon salt
4 tablespoons unsalted butter
1 tablespoon vegetable oil
2 shallots, minced
½ cup heavy cream
½ teaspoon fresh lemon juice

Season the steaks liberally with pepper. Marinate in ¼ cup of the Cognac at room temperature, turning occasionally, for 30 minutes. Remove the steaks and reserve the marinade. Pat the steaks dry and season with the salt. In a large heavy skillet, melt 2 tablespoons of the butter in the oil over moderately high heat. Sear the steaks, turning once, until well browned, about 2 minutes on each side. Lower the heat to moderate and cook, turning occasionally, until rare, about 6 minutes, or medium-rare, about 8 minutes. Remove the steaks to a platter and cover loosely with foil to keep warm. Pour off the fat in the skillet. Melt the remaining 2 tablespoons butter and add the shallots. Cook over low heat until softened, about 1 minute. Pour in the reserved marinade and the remaining ¼ cup Cognac. Increase the heat to moderately high and bring to a boil, scraping up the browned bits clinging to the bottom of the skillet. Cook until reduced by half. Add the cream and boil until reduced by half again. Season with the lemon juice and salt and pepper to taste. Spoon the sauce over the steaks.

Absolutely elegant.

Potatoes Venetian

4 cups hot mashed potatoes
1 8-ounce package cream cheese (room temperature)
1 egg, well beaten
⅓ cup finely chopped onion
¼ cup finely chopped pimento
1 teaspoon salt
1 dash pepper

Mix in order. Bake in 350° oven for 45 minutes.

Bibb Lettuce with Chiffon Dressing

1½ teaspoons white wine vinegar
1½ teaspoons fresh lemon juice
2 tablespoons olive oil
1 hard-cooked egg, finely chopped
1½ teaspoons chives, fresh or dried
½ teaspoon parsley
Pinch each salt and sugar
Freshly ground pepper to taste
1 small head Bibb lettuce, torn into bite-size pieces and well chilled

In small jar, combine vinegar, lemon juice, oil, egg, chives, parsley, sugar, salt and pepper; cover and shake well. Just before serving, pour dressing over lettuce and toss until well coated.

Cheese-Olive Bread

1 16-ounce loaf unsliced French bread
½ cup butter or margarine, softened
¼ cup mayonnaise
2 cups (8 ounces) shredded mozzarella cheese
½ cup finely chopped ripe olives
1 teaspoon garlic powder
1 teaspoon onion powder

Cut French bread in half lengthwise. Combine butter and mayonnaise; stir in remaining ingredients. Spread mixture on cut side of bread. Bake at 350° for 10 to 15 minutes or until cheese melts.

Yield: 1 loaf.

Chilled Custard with Fresh Fruit

5 tablespoons sugar
¼ cup cornstarch
Pinch of freshly grated nutmeg
1 cup milk
½ cup half-and-half
2 egg yolks, room temperature, beaten to blend
½ teaspoon vanilla
Fresh fruit

Combine sugar, cornstarch and nutmeg in top of double boiler. Gradually whisk in milk, half-and-half, yolks and vanilla until smooth. Set over simmering water. Stir until thick, about 10 minutes. Spoon custard into two 1-cup molds, smoothing evenly. Refrigerate until firm, at least 4 hours. Invert custards onto plates. Top each with fresh fruit and serve.

BECAUSE YOU'RE SPECIAL

FOR TWO

Lemon-Carrot Bisque

Herb-Glazed Pork Chops

Zucchini Sauté Celebrity Rice

Fresh Apple Salad

Quick Buttermilk Rolls

Cheesecake Flowers

Chardonnay

or

Fumé Blanc

Lemon-Carrot Bisque

2 tablespoons (¼ stick) butter
2 medium carrots, grated
¼ cup minced onion
¾ cup chicken broth
1 tablespoon fresh lemon juice
1 tablespoon grated lemon peel
¾ cup half-and-half
Salt and freshly ground pepper
Dash of hot pepper sauce
2 lemon slices (garnish)
Minced fresh mint or parsley (garnish)

Melt butter in heavy medium saucepan over low heat. Add carrots and onion. Cover and cook, stirring occasionally, 5 minutes. Blend in chicken broth, lemon juice and peel. Cover and cook, stirring occasionally, 15 minutes. Add half-and-half and cook 10 minutes. Transfer to blender and puree until smooth. (Strain soup if finer texture is desired.) Season with salt, pepper and hot pepper sauce. Ladle soup into bowls. Garnish with lemon slices and minced mint or parsley and serve immediately.

The flavors of this soup are delightfully light.

Herb-Glazed Pork Chops

2 1-inch thick pork chops
Coarse salt
Cracked black pepper
½ teaspoon dried thyme, crumbled
½ teaspoon paprika
¼ teaspoon dried marjoram, crumbled
1 tablespoon butter
1 tablespoon olive oil
1 large garlic clove
½ cup chopped onion
½ cup beef broth
¼ cup dry white wine
⅓ cup whipping cream
¼ cup diced pimento
½ teaspoon crushed green peppercorns, rinsed and drained
Salt and freshly ground pepper

Sprinkle pork chops on both sides with coarse salt and cracked black pepper. Mix thyme, paprika and marjoram in small bowl. Press herb mixture onto both sides of pork chops. Melt butter with oil in heavy small skillet over medium-low heat. Add garlic and stir until golden; discard. Add pork and brown on both sides. Remove from skillet and set aside. Add onion and stir until lightly browned, 2 to 3 minutes. Blend in broth and wine and bring to boil. Return pork to skillet. Cover and simmer gently, about 25 minutes until tender. Remove pork chops from skillet. Increase heat to high. Whisk in cream, scraping up any browned bits, and boil until sauce thickens, about 2 minutes. Stir in pimento and peppercorns. Season with salt and pepper. Spoon sauce over chops and serve immediately.

Zucchini Sauté

2 medium zucchini
1 tablespoon chopped onion
1 tablespoon chopped green pepper
2 tablespoons olive oil
¼ teaspoon salt
¼ teaspoon pepper
Pinch of sugar

Cut washed and trimmed zucchini into ½ inch slices. Sauté onion and pepper in oil until tender. Reduce heat, add zucchini; cook until tender-crisp, stirring often. Stir in salt, pepper, and sugar. Mix well.

Celebrity Rice

½ cup raw rice
1 cup chicken broth
Dash salt
¼ cup chopped green onion, tops and bottoms
2 tablespoons chopped parsley
2 tablespoons butter

Combine rice, broth and salt in saucepan; cover and cook over medium heat 20 minutes or until rice is done and all liquid absorbed. Set aside. Sauté green onion in butter until soft. Add parsley. Stir into rice.

Fresh Apple Salad

¾ cup chopped apple
½ cup chopped celery
¼ cup raisins
1 tablespoon mayonnaise
2 teaspoons sugar
Dash salt

Combine apple, celery and raisins. Mix mayonnaise, sugar and salt. Pour over apple mixture, toss gently. Serve on lettuce leaves.

Quick Buttermilk Rolls

4 to 4½ cups flour, divided
2 packages dry yeast
3 tablespoons sugar
1 teaspoon salt
½ teaspoon baking powder
1¼ cups buttermilk
½ cup water
½ cup shortening

Combine 1½ cups flour, yeast, sugar, salt and soda in large mixing bowl. Combine buttermilk, water and shortening in saucepan; place over low heat until very warm. Gradually stir milk mixture into dry ingredients, mixing well to form soft dough. Stir in remaining flour. Turn dough onto lightly floured surface and knead about 5 minutes until smooth. Place dough in greased bowl, cover and let rise about 45 minutes. Punch down and shape into 1½-inch balls; place balls in greased pans. Let rise 30 minutes. Bake at 400° for 15 to 18 minutes. Will freeze.

Cheesecake Flowers

2 3-ounce packages cream cheese, room temperature
⅓ cup sugar
2 eggs
1 teaspoon vanilla
1 teaspoon fresh lemon juice
Sour cream
Shaved chocolate (optional)

Preheat oven to 350°. Butter two 8-ounce custard cups. Combine cream cheese, sugar, eggs, vanilla and lemon juice in processor or blender and blend until smooth (or use electric mixer). Divide mixture between prepared custard cups. Bake until tops of cheesecakes are golden brown and tester inserted in centers comes out clean, about 35 to 40 minutes. Let cheesecakes cool, then chill. To serve, remove cheesecakes from cups and transfer to dessert plates. Spoon dollop of sour cream into centers. Top with chocolate if desired.

IMPRESSIVELY ELEGANT

SERVES FOUR

Tuna Ball Cheese Spread

Assorted Crackers

Almond Chicken

Hot Rice

Salad Romanoff

Spoon Rolls

Mendy's Favorite Apple Pie

Fumé Blanc

Tuna Ball

3 ounces cream cheese
1 tablespoon mayonnaise
1 7-ounce can tuna, drained
1 teaspoon prepared horseradish
¼ teaspoon garlic salt
¼ teaspoon onion salt
¼ teaspoon MSG
½ teaspoon soy sauce
1 tablespoon capers, chopped
⅓ cup chopped pecans

Soften cheese, blend in mayonnaise and tuna. Mix well. Add other ingredients except nuts and beat until fluffy. Chill thoroughly. Form into ball and roll in pecans. Better if removed from refrigerator an hour or so before serving. Serve with assorted crackers.

Cheese Spread

1 pound sharp Cheddar cheese
1 medium onion
6 hard-cooked eggs
1 7-ounce can chopped green chilies
1 4.2-ounce can chopped black olives
1 8-ounce can tomato sauce
½ cup (1 stick) butter, melted
½ teaspoon Worcestershire sauce
¼ teaspoon garlic salt

Grate cheese, onion and eggs in processor or blender. Transfer to large bowl. Add remaining ingredients and mix thoroughly. Refrigerate until ready to serve. Serve with assorted crackers.

Makes about 6 cups.

Almond Chicken

- 2 whole chicken breasts, halved and boned
- Salt and pepper, to taste
- 3 tablespoons butter
- ½ teaspoon salt
- ¼ teaspoon pepper
- 6 ounces canned frozen orange juice concentrate, thawed
- ½ cup salted almonds, toasted and chopped
- 2 tablespoons bourbon

Season chicken with salt and pepper, to taste; brown in butter over medium heat. Reduce heat to low. Add orange juice, ½ teaspoon salt and ¼ teaspoon pepper. Cover and cook until chicken is done, 20 to 30 minutes; spoon sauce over chicken while cooking. Remove chicken from pan and sprinkle with almonds. Keep warm. Reduce liquid over high heat and stir until slightly brown. Add bourbon and stir. Pour over chicken and serve over rice.

Salad Romanoff

- ½ cup cooked asparagus
- ½ cup cooked string beans
- ½ cup cooked green peas
- 4 radishes, sliced
- 2 hearts of artichoke, chopped
- 2 hard-cooked eggs, chopped
- 1 teaspoon mixed herbs
- ⅓ cup French dressing
- ¼ cup mayonnaise

Toss lightly all ingredients except mayonnaise, and marinate for at least 30 minutes. Before serving, blend in mayonnaise.

Alcohol evaporates when heated and you have the flavor left. Remember that "more" is not better as it tends to result in a bitter taste if too much is used.

Mendy's Favorite Apple Pie

1 cup sugar
2 tablespoons flour
1 teaspoon cinnamon
Dash of salt
6 apples, peeled, cored and thinly sliced
½ cup flour
¼ cup sugar
½ cup Cheddar cheese, grated (packed)
¼ cup butter, melted
1 9-inch pie crust, unbaked

Mix the sugar, 2 tablespoons flour, cinnamon and salt. Sprinkle the apple slices with the mixture and place in a 9-inch pie crust. (See index for pie crust recipe.) Mix the ½ cup flour, the ¼ cup sugar, the cheese and butter. Crumble the mixture over the apples. Bake at 400° for 30 to 35 minutes. Serve warm with sour cream spread over top, if desired.

I have a standing order to have this pie ready when our daughter, Melinda Hampton, comes home.

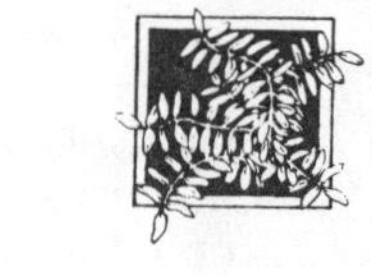

Spoon Rolls

1 package dry yeast
2 cups very warm water
1½ sticks margarine, melted
¼ cup sugar
1 egg
4 cups self-rising flour

Place yeast in 2 cups warm water. Melt butter; cream with sugar in a large bowl; then add beaten egg. Add dissolved yeast to creamed mixture. Then add the flour and stir until well mixed. Place in airtight bowl and keep in refrigerator. To cook, drop by spoonfuls into well-greased 2½-inch muffin tins and bake at 350° about 20 minutes or until browned. This dough keeps for several days.

Yield: 2 dozen.

SHRIMPLY DELICIOUS

FOR FOUR

Stuffed Mushrooms
Shrimp Scampi
Parsley Peas Hot Rice
Tossed Salad Greens
with Cheddar Cheese Dressing
Italian Dinner Rolls
An Adult Banana Split
Chardonnay
Finish with European Coffee

Stuffed Mushrooms

18 large mushrooms
3 ounces cream cheese
2 tablespoons milk
1 teaspoon Worcestershire sauce
¼ cup chopped water chestnuts
1 teaspoon minced green pepper
2 tablespoons minced onion
2 tablespoons cooked, crumbled bacon
Salt to taste

Wipe mushrooms and remove stems. Chop stems finely. Mix cheese, milk, and Worcestershire sauce until well blended. Add chopped water chestnuts, stems, green pepper, onion, bacon and salt. Blend. Fill mushroom caps with mixture and place on ungreased baking sheet. Bake at 350° for 12 to 15 minutes.

Excellent!

Shrimp Scampi

½ cup butter, melted
3 cloves garlic, crushed
2 tablespoons olive oil
24 large or jumbo shrimp, peeled and deveined
2 tablespoons parsley, chopped
2 tablespoons dry white wine
1 tablespoon lemon juice
Salt and pepper to taste

Heat butter, garlic and olive oil in a large skillet. Add shrimp and sauté on both sides until done (about 5 minutes). Pour off pan drippings into a small saucepan. Add the remaining ingredients. Cook over high heat 1 minute. Pour sauce over shrimp and serve with rice to absorb the juices.

Parsley Peas

3 tablespoons butter
¼ cup chopped onion
1 10-ounce package frozen peas, unthawed
1 tablespoon chopped fresh parsley
½ teaspoon salt
1 to 1½ cups chopped lettuce
3 tablespoons chicken stock

Melt butter in small saucepan over low heat. Increase heat to medium-high. Add onion and sauté until tender, about 10 minutes. Add peas, parsley and salt. Cover and steam, stirring frequently, about 5 minutes. Stir in lettuce and chicken stock. Reduce heat and simmer until heated through, 2 minutes.

Cheddar Cheese Salad Dressing

1½ cups mayonnaise
½ cup buttermilk
½ cup finely shredded Cheddar cheese
Dash of Worcestershire sauce
Dash of red wine vinegar or to taste
Pinch each of salt, freshly ground pepper and ground red pepper

Combine all ingredients in medium bowl and blend thoroughly. Store in tightly covered container in refrigerator. Makes about 2½ cups.

Fresh mushrooms have become so popular that they are available throughout the year in most places. They are far better than canned in any cooked dish and always add eye appeal as well as taste to salads. Do not wash them before storing in your refrigerator. They will keep longer in a paper sack or with a paper towel in a plastic bag, stored in the vegetable keeper in your refrigerator.

Italian Dinner Rolls

1 cup milk
3 tablespoons butter
2 tablespoons sugar
1½ teaspoons dried Italian herbs
1 teaspoon salt
2 packages dry yeast
½ cup warm water
2 eggs, beaten
4½ cups flour
½ cup grated Parmesan cheese
2 tablespoons melted butter
Additional Parmesan cheese

Combine milk, butter, sugar, Italian seasonings, and salt in saucepan. Heat, stirring, until butter melts. Dissolve yeast in warm water. Let stand 5 minutes. Combine milk, eggs, and 1½ cups flour. Mix well. Stir in Parmesan cheese and enough remaining flour to make stiff dough. Turn onto floured surface and knead 5 to 7 minutes until smooth. Place in well greased bowl. Cover and let rise 45 minutes. Punch down; let rest 10 minutes. Shape into 16 2-inch balls. Dip into melted butter then tops into Parmesan cheese. Arrange rolls in greased pans. Cover. Let rise 15 minutes. Bake at 375° for 20 to 25 minutes.

An Adult Banana Split

½ cup (1 stick) butter
½ cup plus 2 tablespoons firmly packed brown sugar
2 medium bananas, peeled and sliced into rounds
Juice of ½ medium orange, strained (2 generous tablespoons)
Juice of ½ medium lemon, strained (2 generous tablespoons)
½ tablespoon Grand Marnier
½ tablespoon orange liqueur
½ tablespoon banana liqueur

½ quart vanilla ice cream
Unsweetened whipped cream
2 to 3 tablespoons coarsely chopped toasted macadamia nuts

Melt butter in medium saucepan over medium heat. Add brown sugar and stir until smooth. Add banana slices and stir until coated. Blend in juices and liqueurs and bring to simmer. Let simmer 2 minutes. Divide ice cream among individual dishes. Spoon hot sauce over. Top with whipped cream, sprinkle with nuts and serve.

HAUTE CUISINE

SERVES FOUR

Shrimp Puffs and Assorted Cheeses with Crackers
Veal Aix-en Provence or Veal Suzanne
Hot Asparagus Vinaigrette
Spinach Rice Salad
Sherry Sautéd Mushrooms
Easy Cheese Bread or Onion Cheese Bread
Frangelico Cream over Pears
Orange Butter Cookies
Rosé

Shrimp Puffs

1 8¼-ounce can crushed pineapple (juice pack), well drained
⅔ cup shredded carrot
½ cup small-curd cottage cheese, drained
½ cup plain yogurt
1 teaspoon lemon juice
2 4½-ounce cans small shrimp, drained
2 hard-cooked eggs, chopped
Appetizer Cream Puffs

Combine pineapple, carrot, cottage cheese, yogurt and lemon juice. Fold in shrimp and eggs. Cover and chill. Just before serving, spoon a rounded tablespoon of filling into each puff.

Makes 36 to 40 cream puffs.

Appetizer Cream Puffs

In a saucepan melt ½ cup butter or margarine in 1 cup boiling water. Add 1 cup all-purpose flour and ¼ teaspoon salt all at once; stir vigorously. Cook and stir till mixture forms a ball. Cool slightly. Add 4 eggs, one at a time, beating till smooth after each. Drop level tablespoons of dough 3 inches apart on greased baking sheet. Bake in 400° oven for 25 minutes. Cool on rack. Cut off the top third of each puff. Remove any soft dough from inside.

Veal Aix-en Provence

2 tablespoons butter
1 tablespoon vegetable oil
½ teaspoon each: garlic salt, marjoram, thyme
4 veal chops, ¾ inch thick
¼ cup dry white wine
1 cup mushrooms, drained
1 tablespoon flour
¾ cup half-and-half cream
½ cup grated Gruyere cheese

In large skillet, heat butter and oil. Combine seasonings and sprinkle over chops. Brown chops on both sides. Add wine and cover and cook 10 minutes over low heat. Place chops in 12-inch casserole. Cover with mushrooms. Loosen meat sediment from bottom of skillet and stir in flour. Add cream and cheese. Stirl till it starts to thicken. Pour over veal and mushrooms. Bake at 350° for 20 to 25 minutes.

Veal Suzanne

12 round veal scallops, cut ⅛ inch thick
Flour
½ cup butter
Juice of 2 lemons
3 tablespoons chopped fresh parsley
Salt
Pepper, freshly ground

Place the veal scallops between sheets of wax paper and pound them with the flat side of a meat cleaver to make them thin without breaking through them. Season them with salt, pepper and dust them with flour. Heat 5 tablespoons of the butter in a large frying pan over fairly high heat until golden and quickly brown the veal slices. This takes only about 2 minutes on a side. Transfer them to a platter and keep warm. Add the lemon juice and parsley to the pan, remove from the heat and swirl in the remaining butter, bit by bit and pour over the scallops.

Hot Asparagus Vinaigrette

¼ cup salad oil
2 teaspoons white wine vinegar
1 small sweet pickle, finely chopped
¼ teaspoon dry mustard
Dash salt
¼ teaspoon pepper
1 teaspoon minced parsley
½ teaspoon minced chives
1 10-ounce package frozen asparagus, cooked and drained-keep warm

Heat oil, vinegar, pickle, mustard, salt and pepper to boiling. Remove from heat; stir in parsley and chives. Pour over hot asparagus.

Spinach Rice Salad

1 cup Uncle Ben's Converted Brand Rice
½ cup bottled Italian salad dressing
1 tablespoon soy sauce
½ teaspoon sugar
2 cups fresh spinach, cut into thin strips
½ cup sliced celery
½ cup sliced green onions, including tops
⅓ cup crumbled crisp bacon

Cook rice according to package directions. Transfer to bowl. Cool slightly. Combine dressing, soy sauce and sugar. Stir into warm rice. Cover and chill. Fold in remaining ingredients before serving.

Makes 6 to 8 servings.

Sherry-Sautéd Mushrooms

2 tablespoons (¼ stick) butter
2 tablespoons olive oil
¾ pound fresh mushrooms, thickly sliced (5 cups)
½ cup chopped onion
1 cup dry sherry
Salt and freshly ground pepper
1 tablespoon minced fresh parsley

Melt butter with 1 tablespoon olive oil in large skillet over medium-high heat. Add mushrooms and sauté 2 minutes. Remove mushrooms from skillet and set aside. Reduce heat to medium-low and add remaining 1 tablespoon olive oil to skillet. Add onion and cook until soft and golden but not brown, about 5 minutes. Stir in sherry, increase heat to high and boil until reduced by half, about 6 minutes. Reduce heat to medium-low. Return mushrooms to skillet. Season with salt and pepper. Simmer gently 5 minutes. (Can be prepared ahead and reheated just before serving.) Stir in minced parsley and serve immediately.

Makes about 2 cups.

Easy Cheese Bread

2½ cups Bisquick
1 cup sharp Cheddar cheese, grated
2 teaspoons poppy seed
1 egg, beaten
1 cup milk

In mixing bowl, combine Bisquick, cheese and poppy seed. Blend beaten egg into milk. Add to dry mixture, stirring to mix well. Pour into greased 8-inch square glass dish. Smooth top and microwave on high 7 to 8 minutes.

This is one of the best "quick breads" I've ever used.

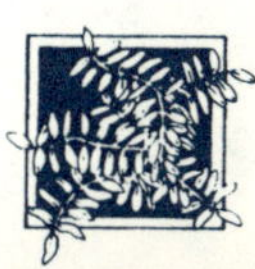

Onion-Cheese Bread

½ cup chopped onions
1 tablespoon butter
1 beaten egg
½ cup milk
1½ cup Bisquick
1 cup grated cheese
1 tablespoon poppy seed
1 tablespoon melted butter

Sauté onions in butter until tender. Combine egg and milk. Add to Bisquick and stir only until dry ingredients are just moist. Add onion and half of cheese. Spread dough in greased 8 × ½-inch round pie pan. Sprinkle top with remaining cheese and poppy seed. Drizzle melted butter over all. Bake in hot oven at 400° for 20 to 25 minutes. Serve hot.

This is almost the same recipe but for the conventional oven and too good to leave out.

Frangelico Cream Over Drained, Canned Pears

4 egg yolks, room temperature
¼ cup sugar
Pinch of salt
1 cup half-and-half cream
¼ cup Frangelico liqueur

Combine yolks, sugar and salt in large saucepan and whisk until light colored and creamy, about 3 minutes. Add milk in steady stream, place over medium heat and cook, stirring constantly, until mixture is thickened and coats back of wooden spoon. Blend in liqueur. Strain. Serve warm.

Makes about 1½ cups.

This sauce is a favorite.

Fresh Orange Butter Cookies

1 tablespoon grated orange rind
1 teaspoon grated lemon rind
1 cup (2 sticks) butter
¼ teaspoon salt
1 cup sugar
1 large egg
¼ cup fresh orange juice
2 cups sifted all-purpose flour

Blend orange and lemon rinds with softened butter. Mix in salt and sugar. Beat in egg and orange juice. Stir in flour. Mix well. Chill dough until stiff enough to handle; then shape into 1-inch balls. Place 2 inches apart on ungreased cookie sheets. Bake in a preheated moderate oven, 375°. for 10 to 12 minutes or until done. Cool on wire racks. Store in airtight container.

Yield: about 4 dozen.

AN EARLY SPRING EVENT

SERVES FOUR

Crab Soup with Sherry and Gruyère Toast
Veal Scallops with Mustard Cream over Rice
Fresh Asparagus with Pecan Sauce
Honey-Kissed Carrots
Red Green Salad
Toasted Herb Loaf
Brandy Alexander Pie
White Burgundy
Finish with Madiera

An elegant menu that will impress any guest.

Crab Soup with Sherry

1 pound crab meat
2 tablespoons butter
3 cups half-and-half
1 teaspoon salt
½ tablespoon Worcestershire sauce
1 tablespoon flour
2 tablespoons onion, grated
3 to 4 tablespoons sherry

Heat all ingredients except crab and flour in double boiler. Do not boil. Mix flour with a little milk and add with crab to milk mixture. Reduce heat and simmer ½ hour, stirring frequently.

Gruyère Garlic Toast

1 10-ounce loaf Italian or French bread, cut into ½-inch slices
1 to 2 large garlic cloves, halved
3 tablespoons olive oil
½ pound sliced Gruyère cheese

Preheat oven to 425°. Arrange bread in single layer on baking sheets. Bake, turning once, until crisp and golden, about 5 minutes per side. (Can be prepared up to 1 day ahead to this point. Cool completely. Store in airtight container.) About 15 minutes before soup is ready, preheat oven to 425°. Line baking sheets with foil. Arrange toast on prepared baking sheets. Rub surfaces of toast with cut side of garlic clove. Drizzle with olive oil. Top with Gruyère. Bake until cheese is lightly browned, 5 to 7 minutes. Serve immediately. For stronger flavor, use ⅓ cup freshly grated Parmesan cheese instead of Gruyère. Sprinkle cheese evenly over each slice of toast before second baking.

Makes about 15 slices.

Veal Scallops with Mustard Cream

- 8 veal scallops dredged in seasoned flour
- 6 tablespoons butter
- ¼ cup dry white wine
- 1 teaspoon minced onion
- ⅓ cup heavy cream
- 2 tablespoons Dijon mustard
- White pepper to taste

Sauté veal in butter until browned on each side. Transfer to platter; keep warm. Add to the skillet the wine, onion, and deglaze skillet. Add cream and cook until thickened. Stir in mustard and white pepper. Pour over veal. Allow 2 scallops per serving.

Fresh Asparagus with Pecan Sauce

- ½ cup dry white wine
- 5 tablespoons white wine vinegar
- 2 teaspoons minced fresh shallot
- 2 tablespoons crème fraiche
- 1 cup (2 sticks) butter, cut into tablespoon-size pieces
- 4 ounces toasted pecans, coarsely chopped (1 cup)
- 3 tablespoons fresh lemon juice
- Salt and freshly ground white pepper
- 2 pounds asparagus, stalks trimmed and peeled

Combine wine, vinegar and shallot in heavy medium saucepan over medium-high heat and boil until reduced to 2 tablespoons, watching carefully to prevent burning. Reduce heat to very low and whisk in crème fraiche. Remove from heat and whisk in 2 pieces butter, then return to very low heat and whisk in remaining butter 2 pieces at a time. (If at any time sauce begins to separate, remove from heat and quickly whisk in 2 pieces chilled butter. Return to heat and proceed as directed.) Stir in pecans, lemon juice, salt and ground white pepper. Transfer sauce to vacuum bottle to keep warm. Bring large pot of salted water to boil over high heat. Add asparagus and cook until crisp-tender. Drain well. Arrange asparagus on 1 side of heated plates. Spoon sauce onto other side of plate. Serve immediately.

Sour cream may be used instead of crème fraiche, if desired.

Honey-Kissed Carrots

- 1 pound carrots, scraped and cut into ½-inch slices
- 1¼ cups water
- ⅓ cup golden raisins
- ⅓ cup honey
- 2 tablespoons butter

Combine carrots and water in a medium saucepan; cover and simmer 15 minutes or until tender. Add remaining ingredients; cook, uncovered, over medium heat an additional 10 minutes or until carrots are glazed, stirring occasionally.

Serves 4.

Red Green Salad

1 bunch red-leaf lettuce, washed and well drained

Add

1 can Mandarin oranges, drained
1 small red onion, thinly sliced and separated into rings
1 avocado, sliced
1 cup red grapes, seeded and halved

Combine all salad ingredients and toss gently with dressing.

Mix together:

1 cup salad oil
⅓ cup vinegar
2 tablespoons sugar
2 teaspoons ketchup
2 teaspoons chili sauce
2 teaspoons prepared mustard
1 teaspoon salt

Toasted Herb Loaf

1 16-ounce loaf unsliced French bread
¼ cup butter, softened
1 small clove garlic, crushed
⅛ teaspoon salt
⅛ teaspoon dry mustard
⅛ teaspoon dried whole thyme
⅛ teaspoon paprika
⅛ teaspoon ground savory

Slice French bread into ½-inch slices. Combine remaining ingredients, mixing well; spread butter mixture between bread slices. Wrap loaf in foil; bake at 400° for 15 minutes or until thoroughly heated.

Yield: 1 loaf.

Brandy Alexander Pie

1 tablespoon unflavored gelatin
½ cup cold water
⅔ cup sugar
Dash salt
3 eggs, separated
¼ cup brandy
¼ cup crème de cocao
2 cups heavy cream, whipped
10-inch chocolate wafer crust, baked and cooled
Chocolate curls for garnish

Sprinkle gelatin over cold water in saucepan. Add ⅓ cup sugar, salt and egg yolks. Stir to blend. Cook over very low heat. Stir until gelatin dissolves and mixture thickens. Do not boil. Remove from heat. Stir in brandy and crème de cocao. Chill, stirring occasionally. When mixture will mound on a spoon, beat egg whites until stiff. Gradually beat remaining ⅓ cup sugar into whites, forming a glossy meringue. Fold into gelatin mixture with 1 cup of whipped cream. Turn into cooled crust. Chill. Top with remaining cup of whipped cream and chocolate curls.

A HEARTY WINTER EVENING

FOR SIX

Quick Mushroom Consommé
Pork Chops in Wine Sauce
Squash Bake
Green Beans
Grapefruit and Avocado Salad with Celery Seed Dressing
Winter Waldorf Salad
Monkey Bread
Fruit Crumble
Rich Burgundy

Quick Mushroom Consommé

2 10½-ounce cans beef consommé
1 cup thinly sliced mushrooms
1 cup water
½ cup sherry

Simmer consommé, mushrooms and water for 10 minutes. Add sherry; bring to boil. Remove from heat. Serve at once.

Pork Chops in Wine Sauce

6 1-inch thick pork chops
1 tablespoon olive oil
1 tablespoon minced garlic
1½ cups dry red wine
½ cup Marsala
¼ cup blanched almonds, ground fine and combined with 2 teaspoons flour
Grated rind of 1 lemon
2 tablespoons minced fresh parsley leaves

In a large stainless steel or enameled skillet brown the pork chops, patted dry, in batches in the oil over moderately high heat, transferring them as they are browned, to a plate. Pour off all but 1 tablespoon of the fat from the skillet and reduce the heat to moderate. Add the pork chops in one layer, sprinkle them with the garlic and salt and pepper, and turn them. Add the red wine and the Marsala, bring the liquid to a boil, and braise the chops, covered, over low heat for 45 minutes to 1 hour, or until they are very tender. Transfer the chops to a platter and keep them warm, covered. Skim the fat from the sauce, whisk in the almond mixture, and simmer the sauce for 5 minutes, or until it is thickened slightly. Nap the chops with the sauce and sprinkle them with the lemon rind and the parsley.

Serves 6.

Squash Bake

6 tablespoons butter
1 cup chopped onion
1 cup chopped celery
6 cups squash cut in chunks, any kind
2 cups cooked rice
1 can cream of mushroom soup
1 8-ounce package herb-seasoned stuffing mix

Preheat oven to 350°. Melt half of butter in large skillet. Sauté onion and celery until partially cooked. Add squash, cover and cook until tender. Add rice, soup and half the stuffing mix. Pour into greased 2-quart casserole. Melt remaining butter in pan and add remainder of stuffing mix. Stir until well mixed. Spread on top of casserole. Bake 30 minutes.

Serves 6-8.

This, too, is from Faye Ashby and is especially good.

Fresh Green Beans

- 1½ pounds fresh green beans, trimmed, washed and cut
- 3 quarts boiling water in a large kettle
- 1 tablespoon salt
- 6 tablespoons softened butter, cut in pieces
- Salt and freshly ground pepper to taste
- 2 teaspoons lemon juice
- 2 tablespoons minced parsley

To blanch beans, drop a handful at a time into the boiling, salted water. Bring water back to a boil as quickly as possible, reduce heat and boil beans slowly, uncovered. After 7 minutes, test the beans frequently by biting into one each time.

When they are tender but still slightly crunchy, drain immediately. Run cold water over beans 3 to 4 minutes, then drain. (Beans may be refrigerated at this point until ready to finish.)

Toss the beans in a large, heavy skillet over moderately high heat. Toss briefly with a piece of butter and salt and pepper to taste. Add rest of butter gradually, alternating with drops of lemon juice while still tossing.

Taste for seasoning. Turn into a hot vegetable dish. Sprinkle with parsley and serve immediately.

Serves 6.

These are quite different in taste but almost addictive, they are so good.

Grapefruit and Avocado Salad

Toss together ½ head torn iceberg lettuce, 3 sliced avocados, 3 sectioned grapefruits, 1 red onion, thinly sliced. Toss with celery seed dressing.

Celery Seed Dressing

- ½ cup sugar
- ⅓ cup wine vinegar
- ½ teaspoon salt
- 1 teaspoon dry mustard
- ½ teaspoon onion salt
- 1 cup salad oil
- 1 tablespoon celery seed

Combine sugar, mustard, salt, onion and ½ of vinegar. Beat well with rotary beater. Gradually add rest of vinegar. Gradually add oil. Stir in celery seed. Chill.

Winter Waldorf Salad

- 4 apples, cored and sliced into bite-size pieces
- 2 rib celery, thinly sliced
- 1 cup seedless green grapes, halved
- ¾ cup walnut pieces
- ½ cup mayonnaise
- ¼ cup dry white wine

In large bowl, combine apples, celery, grapes and walnuts. In small bowl, combine mayonnaise and wine; blend thoroughly. Toss lightly with dressing just before serving.

Serves 8.

Monkey Bread

- 1 cup milk, scalded and cooled to lukewarm
- 2 packages dry yeast
- ¼ cup sugar
- 1 teaspoon salt
- 1 cup melted butter, divided
- 2¼ cups flour

Add yeast to cooled milk; stir until dissolved. Add sugar, salt and ½ cup of the melted butter. Mix well. Stir in flour and beat well. Cover and let rise until doubled, about 1 hour. Turn out onto floured surface, knead several times and roll out to ¼-inch thickness. Cut into squares about 2½". Dip each piece in remaining butter. Arrange in well greased bundt (or tube) pan. Cover and let rise 30 to 40 minutes or until doubled. Bake at 400° 20 to 25 minutes. Remove from pan; brush top with additional melted butter.

Fruit Crumble

1 stick butter
1 cup brown sugar
1 cup flour
4 apples, peeled and thinly sliced
½ cup brown sugar
½ cup white sugar
1 teaspoon cinnamon

In bowl or food processor, mix butter, 1 cup brown sugar and flour until crumbly. Layer apple slices in a greased 9×13 Pyrex dish. Mix remaining ingredients and sprinkle over apple slices. Spread crumb mixture evenly over top. Bake at 300° for 1 hour.

You may vary this dessert by using canned fruits such as peaches, cherries, blueberries, etc. Mix crumbs as directed adding ½ cup white sugar and 1 teaspoon cinnamon to mixture. Drain 2 cans fruit, pour into greased dish and top with crumb mixture. Bake as directed.

Serve topped with whipped cream, ice cream or Custard Sauce (see index).

This is the easiest, best dessert ever. Becky McLeary shared this with me.

Keep a file of your entertaining. List the obvious things like menu and guests, but also make a note of reactions to table, any changes that you think would improve the same menu served to different guests, and especially comments that are more than the expected. This is certainly a handy reference to have as you plan the next party, but it is an absolute wonder to pull out and read over on those days when you're wondering if you have EVER done anything right!

A CRISP FALL NIGHT

SERVES SIX

Hot Spinach Dip

Becky's Spread

Elegant Ham Casserole

Molded Berry Salad **Green Pepper Casserole**

Cheesy Garlic Bread

Key Lime Pie

Beaujolais

Hot Spinach Dip

3 boxes frozen chopped spinach
4 tablespoons butter
2 tablespoons flour
½ cup heavy cream
1 8-ounce jar Jalapeño Cheez Whiz
2 tablespoons chopped onions
Worcestershire sauce
Cayenne
Celery salt
Garlic salt

Cook spinach in least amount of salted water necessary. Drain and reserve ½ cup cooking water. In large saucepan, melt butter and stir in flour. When blended, add spinach water, cook until thick and smooth, stirring constantly. Add remaining ingredients. Taste and correct seasoning. Transfer to chafing dish and serve hot with tortilla chips.

Becky's Spread

1 can artichoke hearts, drained
Juice of 2 small lemons
2 green onions, chopped
Mayonnaise
Bacon Bits

Tear the artichoke hearts apart. Mix with the lemon juice and onions. Mix in enough mayonnaise to hold it together. Add Bacon Bits as desired. Garnish with fresh parsley and serve with crackers.

Becky McLeary, a "fabulous friend" and very talented cook from Palm Beach, Florida gave us many good recipes. This spread is one of my favorites!

Elegant Ham Casserole

1 pound cooked ham
4 medium sweet potatoes
2 apples
1 tablespoon brown sugar
½ pound butter
Dash ground cloves, cinnamon and allspice
1 cup seedless green grapes
¼ cup brandy (apple juice)

Dice ham; cook peeled, sliced sweet potatoes, drain and set aside; peel and slice apples. Mix ham, potatoes, apples and grapes. Place in greased casserole. Mix brown sugar and spices; dot generously with butter; pour brandy over all. Bake at 350° for 45 to 60 minutes.

Green Pepper Casserole

6 large green bell peppers
1½ cups buttered cracker crumbs, divided
½ pound sharp Cheddar cheese, grated
1 cup half-and-half
Additional milk

Cut the seeded bell peppers in strips and boil slowly in salted water until tender (about 15 minutes). Drain well. Butter a shallow casserole dish and spread half of the buttered cracker crumbs in bottom. Arrange the drained peppers over the crumbs and top with the cheese. Correct seasoning with additional salt, if necessary. Pour half-and-half over, adding enough additional milk to bring the liquid almost to the top of the casserole. Cover with remaining cracker crumbs. Sprinkle with paprika and bake, uncovered, at 375° for 45 minutes.

This may be prepared several hours in advance except for final topping of cracker crumbs.

A most delightful friend in Miami, Florida, Martha Ann Haas, shared this different and delicious casserole. It is especially good with ham.

Candlelight is the very best spice to add to any dinner. It can cover the most ordinary meal with such a sparkle that nobody will remember that it was tuna fish!!

Molded Berry Salad

- 1 3-ounce package strawberry gelatin
- 1 3-ounce package raspberry gelatin
- 2 cups boiling water
- 1 10-ounce package frozen strawberries
- 1 10-ounce package frozen blueberries
- 1 10-ounce package frozen raspberries
- 1 large banana, sliced
- ½ pint sour cream
- ⅓ cup chopped walnuts

Dissolve each package of gelatin in a separate bowl, pouring 1 cup boiling water over each. Stir to dissolve well. To the strawberry gelatin, add the strawberries and blueberries. To the raspberry gelatin, add raspberries, banana and walnuts. Pour one mixture into lightly greased 1½-quart mold. Chill until firm. Leave other bowl at room temperature. Spread sour cream evenly on set fruited gelatin. Pour on remaining fruit mixture. Chill until serving time for at least 3 hours.

Cheesy Garlic Bread

- 1 16-ounce loaf unsliced French bread
- 1 cup (4 ounces) shredded Swiss cheese
- ½ cup butter or margarine, softened
- ¼ teaspoon garlic powder
- ¼ teaspoon celery seeds
- ¼ teaspoon parsley flakes

Slice French bread into 1-inch slices. Combine remaining ingredients, mixing well; spread butter mixture between bread slices and on top and sides of loaf. Wrap loaf in foil; bake at 350° for 15 minutes or until thoroughly heated.

Key Lime Pie

- 1 tablespoon gelatin
- ¼ cup water
- 1 cup sugar
- Dash salt
- 4 egg yolks and whites
- ½ cup lime juice
- Grated rind of 1 lime
- 1 cup whipped cream
- Few drops green food coloring
- 1 baked pie crust or Graham cracker crust, baked; or chocolate cookie crust

If using pie crust, see Index for recipe. Bake as directed and set aside.

Soften gelatin in ¼ cup water. In saucepan, combine ½ cup sugar and salt. Beat egg yolks; gradually adding lime juice. Stir into sugar and mix well. Cook over medium heat until thickened. Remove from heat; stir in softened gelatin and lime peel. Stir until gelatin is completely dissolved. Add food color and cool. Beat egg whites to soft peaks, adding ½ cup sugar. Beat to stiff peaks. Fold into chilled gelatin mixture. Fold in whipped cream. Pour into prepared crust and chill until firm.

A DINNER WITH FRIENDS

SERVES SIX

Lemon-Pepper Cheese Patty

Chicken and Avocado over Green Noodles

Tomato Aspic Ring filled with Cold Pea Salad

Fruit Bouquet Salad

French Fantan Rolls

Chocolate Mousse in Grand Marnier Sauce

Chenin Blanc

Lemon-Pepper Cheese Patty

2 8-ounce packages cream cheese, softened
2 cloves garlic, crushed
2 teaspoons caraway seeds
2 teaspoons dried whole basil
2 teaspoons dried whole dillweed
2 teaspoons chopped chives
2 to 3 tablespoons lemon-pepper marinade

Combine first 6 ingredients; mix well. Shape into a 5×1-inch round patty; coat top and sides with lemon-pepper marinade. Cover and chill 10 to 12 hours; serve cheese patty with assorted crackers.

Makes one 5-inch round.

Chicken and Avocado over Green Noodles

½ stick butter
4 tablespoons flour
¼ teaspoon garlic powder
¼ teaspoon onion powder
¼ teaspoon basil
¼ teaspoon marjoram
¼ teaspoon thyme
1½ cups milk
1 cup half-and-half
3 tablespoons sherry
3 cups cooked chicken, diced (use breasts)
3 avocados, peeled and sliced
2 cups grated Cheddar cheese
1 package green noodles, cooked as package directs

(You may want to cook the noodles in the broth after you have removed the chicken breasts. Drain the noodles well after cooking.) In heavy skillet melt the butter. Whisk in flour and cook until thick. Slowly stir in milk and half-and-half, stirring to prevent lumping. Stir in seasonings and cook until thickened. Remove from heat, stir in sherry. In a well-greased 13×9 inch casserole, layer ½ noodles, ½ avocados, ½ chicken, ½ sauce, ½ cheese. Repeat layers, ending with cheese. Bake at 350° for 30 minutes. This dish doesn't freeze well but everything can be cooked separately ahead, layered and refrigerated 1 to 2 hours before baking.

Tomato Aspic

- 3 cups V-8 juice
- 4 tablespoons unflavored gelatin softened in ¾ cup cold water
- 2 tablespoons Worcestershire sauce
- 2 teaspoons lemon juice
- 1 teaspoon salt
- 2 teaspoons white pepper
- 3 dashes Tabasco sauce

Heat V-8 juice; stir in softened gelatin until completely dissolved. Cool slightly and add remaining ingredients. Mix well. Grease a ring mold with mayonnaise and pour in aspic. Chill until firm. Unmold on platter lined with lettuce leaves. Fill ring with cold English pea salad.

Cold English Pea Salad

- 1 large can tiny English peas, drained
- ½ cup celery, chopped
- 2 green onions, tops and bottoms, chopped
- 2 hard-boiled eggs, chopped
- 1 small jar pimento, drained
- Salt and pepper to taste
- ½ cup mayonnaise
- ½ cup sour cream

Combine all ingredients; mix well. Refrigerate until ready to serve.

Fruit Bouquet Salad

- 2 apples, thinly sliced
- 2 bananas, sliced
- 1 orange, sliced
- 1 can pineapple chunks, drained
- 1 cup whipped cream
- 1 can lemon pie filling

Combine fruits, mix well. Combine whipped cream and pie filling. Toss with fruit. Refrigerate until served.

Always use ½ cup of white wine (dry Vermouth is an excellent choice for this), an onion, a couple of stalks of celery-leaves, too, salt and a dash or two of cayenne pepper added to the water when boiling chicken. The broth is wonderful for any further use and is even very tasty served in small cups as an appetizer.

French Fantan Rolls

1 cup milk, scalded
½ cup shortening
½ cup sugar
1 teaspoon salt
2 packages dry yeast
¼ cup warm water
4 eggs, beaten
6 cups all-purpose flour
¼ cup melted butter, divided

Combine milk, shortening, sugar and salt; stir until shortening melts. Cool. Dissolve yeast in warm water in a large mixing bowl. Stir in milk mixture and eggs. Gradually stir in flour to make a soft dough. Turn dough out onto a floured surface, and knead until smooth and elastic (about 5 minutes). Place in a well-greased bowl, turning to grease top. Cover and let rise in a warm place, free from drafts, 1 hour or until doubled in bulk. Punch dough down, and divide in half. Turn dough out onto a lightly floured surface. Roll each half into a 12×6 inch rectangle. Brush 2 tablespoons butter over top of each. Cut each rectangle into 6 (1-inch) strips. Stack 6 strips of dough, butter side up, on top of one another. Cut each stack of dough, butter side up, on top of one another. Cut each stack of dough into 12 pices about 1-inch wide. Place in greased muffin cups sideways (cut side down). Cover and let rise in a warm place free from drafts, for 30 minutes. Bake at 425° for 10 to 12 minutes or until golden brown.
Yield: 2 dozen.

Chocolate Mousse in Grand Marnier Sauce

1 cup water
1 cup sugar
¼ cup chopped walnuts
¼ pound semisweet chocolate, coarsely chopped
½ cup (1 stick) unsalted butter
¾ cup unsweetened cocoa powder
2 egg yolks, room temperature, beaten
2 egg whites, room temperature
Grand Marnier sauce

Bring water and sugar to boil in heavy small saucepan over low heat, swirling pan occasionally; do not stir. Let boil 1 minute. Cool sugar syrup completely. Butter and sugar 2-cup loaf pan. Sprinkle walnuts in bottom. Melt chocolate and butter in top of double boiler set over gently simmering water. Stir in cocoa powder and ¼ cup sugar syrup (reserve remainder for another use). Remove from over water. Blend in yolks. Beat whites in medium bowl until stiff but not dry. Gently fold into chocolate mixture. Pour into prepared pan. Cover and refrigerate at least 2 hours. To unmold, run very sharp knife along edges of mousse and invert onto platter. To serve, cut into slices. Ladle some of sauce onto plate. Top with slice of mousse.

The mousse isn't as heavy as some and the sauce makes it heavenly.

Grand Marnier Sauce

2 egg yolks
1 tablespoon sugar
1 cup milk, scalded
3 ounces vanilla ice cream
2 tablespoons Grand Marnier

Blend yolks and sugar in top of double boiler until creamy. Set over gently simmering water and whisk in milk in slow steady stream. Continue whisking until mixture is thick, about 12 minutes. Remove from over water. Stir in ice cream and Grand Marnier. Transfer to small bowl. Refrigerate sauce until ready to use.

Makes about 1½ cups.

A SPECIAL FISH DINNER

SERVES SIX

Texas Turnovers
Baked Pecan Catfish
Caraway Coleslaw
Layered Vegetable Casserole
Baked Potato Chips
Cheddar Cornbread
Raspberry Dream
Vouvray Pétillant

Texas Turnovers

1 5-ounce jar Old English cheese
½ cup butter
1 cup flour
2 tablespoons water
1 4-ounce jar hot pepper jelly

Cut cheese into flour with pastry knife. Stir in water, mixing with fork. Shape dough into a ball. Chill. Roll out dough on floured surface and cut into 2 inch circles. Place ½ teaspoon jelly in center of each circle; fold over and crimp edges with a fork. Bake at 375° for 10 to 12 minutes. May be frozen before or after baking. If frozen before they don't need to thaw before baking. Makes 2 to 3 dozen. These are very good filled with apricot jam or orange marmalade for breakfast or brunch.

Caraway Coleslaw

2½ pounds cabbage, cored and finely chopped
1 medium carrot, grated
1 tablespoon plus 1 teaspoon caraway seed
½ cup plain yogurt
½ cup mayonnaise, preferably homemade
½ teaspoon freshly ground pepper
¾ teaspoon salt

In a large bowl combine the cabbage, carrot and caraway seed. Stir in the yogurt, mayonnaise, pepper and salt, tossing until thoroughly combined. Serve at once or refrigerate, covered, overnight. Stir again before serving.

Baked Pecan Catfish

2 pounds catfish
1 cup buttermilk
1 egg, beaten
1 cup flour
1 tablespoon salt
1 tablespoon paprika
1/8 teaspoon pepper
1 cup ground pecans
1/4 cup sesame seed
1/2 cup margarine, melted
1/4 cup pecan halves
Lemon wedges
Parsley sprigs

Combine egg with milk. Sift together flour, salt, pepper and paprika. Add to ground pecans and sesame seed. Add dry ingredients to milk; blend well. Place margarine in baking dish, 13×9×2. Coat the fish with the batter. Place in baking dish. Put pecan halves on top of fish. Bake at 350° for 30 minutes, or until fish is golden brown and flakes easily. Garnish with lemon wedges and parsley. Fish can be made ahead and baked when needed.

We can only encourage you to try this recipe once. It will become a favorite — we promise!

Layered Vegetable Casserole

2 egg plants, sliced
2 onions, sliced
3 green peppers, sliced
3 tomatoes, sliced
Cavender's seasoned salt
Parmesan cheese
1 8-ounce package shredded mozzarella cheese
1 stick butter

Oil a 9×13 baking dish with olive oil. Layer vegetables in order listed. Sprinkle Cavender's salt over vegetables. Dot with butter. Bake at 350° for 30 minutes. Sprinkle Parmesan and mozzarella cheeses over casserole (cover completely) and bake 10 minutes more.

Baked Potato Chips

3½ pounds red or white boiling potatoes, cut crosswise into ⅛- inch-thick slices
6 tablespoons (¾ stick) butter, melted
Salt and freshly ground pepper

Position racks in upper and lower third of oven and preheat to 500°. Lightly grease 2 baking sheets. Arrange potato slices in single layer on prepared baking sheets. Brush generously with butter. Bake 7 minutes. Switch pan positions and continue baking until potatoes are crisp and browned around edges, about 7 to 9 minutes. Transfer to heated platter. Sprinkle with salt and pepper. Serve immediately.

Cheddar Cornbread

1 cup yellow cornmeal
1 cup all-purpose flour
2 tablespoons sugar
1 tablespoon baking powder
1 teaspoon salt
1 cup milk
2 eggs, beaten
2 cups (8 ounce) shredded Cheddar cheese

Combine first 5 ingredients in a large mixing bowl; set aside. Combine milk, eggs and cheese; add to dry ingredients, mixing well. Pour batter into a hot, greased 10½-inch cast-iron skillet. Bake at 425° for 15 minutes or until cornbread is golden.

Serves 10 to 12.

Raspberry Dream

1 envelope (1 tablespoon) unflavored gelatin
¼ cup cold water
1 8-ounce package cream cheese, softened
½ cup sugar
½ teaspoon almond extract
Dash salt
1 cup milk
½ pint whipping cream, whipped
Raspberry Sauce

Soften gelatin in water and heat until dissolved; set aside.

Combine cream cheese, sugar, almond extract and salt; blend until smooth. Gradually add milk and gelatin; fold in whipped cream.

Pour into 8 small molds or a 1-quart mold. Refrigerate until set. (This can be frozen and thawed when ready to use.) Serve topped with Raspberry Sauce.

Raspberry Sauce

1 10-ounce package frozen raspberries
1 tablespoon cornstarch
2 tablespoons sherry

Thaw and drain raspberries. Combine raspberry syrup, cornstarch and sherry; cook over low heat until thick. Add raspberries; blend well. Refrigerate and serve over molds.
Yield: 1 cup.

TO GREET NEW NEIGHBORS

SERVES SIX

Special Cheese Ring **Avocado-Oyster Dip**
Brandied Chicken Breasts
Lima Bean Casserole
Cherry Salad
No-Knead Refrigerator Bread
Double Chocolate Pie
White Burgundy

Special Cheese Ring

1 pound sharp Cheddar cheese, grated
1 cup pecans, chopped
1 cup (scant) mayonnaise
1 small onion, grated
Black pepper, to taste
Dash cayenne
Strawberry preserves

Mix all ingredients except preserves. Mold into desired shape (a ring mold is good). Place in refrigerator until chilled. When ready to serve, unmold and fill center with strawberry preserves.

Avocado-Oyster Dip

1 ripe avocado
1 cup sour cream
1 4-ounce can smoked oysters, drained and chopped
½ cup ripe olives, chopped
2 tablespoons chopped onions
1 teaspoon vinegar
¼ teaspoon salt
⅛ teaspoon Tabasco

Mash avocado, add sour cream and blend well. Add oysters and remaining ingredients. Chill well before serving.

Brandied Chicken Breasts

6 whole chicken breasts, halved, skinned and boned
Brandy
1 teaspoon salt
1 teaspoon pepper
1 teaspoon marjoram
8 tablespoons butter
¾ cup dry sherry
6 egg yolks
2½ cups half-and-half
Salt, pepper and nutmeg, to taste
1 cup Swiss cheese, grated
1 cup buttered bread crumbs

Rub breasts with brandy and let stand a few minutes. Season with salt, pepper and marjoram. Heat butter and sauté chicken 6 to 8 minutes on each side. Remove to an ovenproof platter and keep warm. Add sherry to remaining butter in pan and simmer over low heat until liquid is reduced by half. Beat egg yolks into cream and add to liquid in pan, stirring constantly. Season with salt, pepper and nutmeg. Stir and cook until slightly thickened. Pour sauce over chicken breasts and sprinkle with Swiss cheese and crumbs. Run under broiler for a few minutes to brown topping.

Lima Bean Casserole

2 tablespoons butter
¼ cup chopped onion
1 small jar chopped pimento
1 cup sour cream
2 cans lima beans, drained or 2 packages frozen lima beans cooked and drained
Salt and pepper to taste

Sauté onion in melted butter until soft. Add remaining ingredients and simmer just until heated through. Don't allow mixture to boil after sour cream has been added. Sprinkle top with paprika before serving.

Cherry Salad

1 6-ounce package cherry gelatin
1 small can crushed pineapple and juice
2½ cups hot water
1 can cherry pie filling

Dissolve gelatin in hot water, add pie filling and pineapple. Mold in 8½×13-inch Pyrex pan. Serve with dabs of sour cream mixed with sugar and lemon juice.

Cherry Salad is the easiest salad ever, but it is treasured because it came from my dear friend Marty Gee.

No-Knead Refrigerator Bread

1 package dry yeast
1½ cups warm water
⅔ cup sugar
⅔ cup shortening
2 eggs
1 cup warm mashed potatoes
1½ teaspoons salt
6 to 7½ cups flour

Dissolve yeast in warm water in large mixing bowl. Add sugar, shortening, eggs, potatoes, salt and 4 cups flour. Beat on low speed of mixer 1 minute; beat at medium speed 2 minutes. By hand, stir in enough remaining flour to make stiff dough. Place in well-greased bowl, turning to grease top. Cover tightly and refrigerate 8 hours or up to 3 days. To shape: Divide dough in half; shape each half into a loaf. Place in 2 greased 9×5 loafpans. Cover and let rise 3 hours or until doubled in bulk. Bake at 400° for 20 to 25 minutes.

Double Chocolate Pie

1 package (8½ ounces) chocolate wafers
⅓ cup pecans
¼ cup butter, chilled and cut into bits
1 package (12 ounces) chocolate chips
4 eggs, separated
¼ cup coffee liqueur
½ cup whipping cream, whipped until stiff
1 ounce white chocolate, grated

Place wafers, pecans and butter into workbowl of food processor. Process until mixture is coarsely crumbled. Press onto bottom and sides of a well buttered 10-inch pie plate. Set aside. Melt chocolate chips. In separate bowl, beat egg yolks until thick. Blend in melted chocolate and slowly stir in coffee liqueur. In separate bowl, beat egg whites until stiff but not dry. Fold into chocolate mixture. Fold grated white chocolate into stiffly whipped cream. Pour half of the dark chocolate mixture into the reserved pie shell. Spoon all of the whipped cream mixture over and top with remainder of dark chocolate, spreading evenly. Cover with plastic wrap and freeze for at least 30 minutes before serving.

You may want to reserve ½ cup of the crust mixture and sprinkle it over the top of the pie before freezing.

DINNER BEFORE THE CONCERT

SERVES SIX TO EIGHT

Marinated Mushrooms

Eggs La Russe

Shrimp and Wild Rice Casserole

Avocado Spinach Salad **Herbed Carrots**

Cheese-and-Pepper Muffins

Orange Cheesecake

Amaretto Coffee

Chardonnay

or

Sauvignon Blanc

Eggs La Russe

6 eggs, hard boiled
¼ cup mayonnaise
¼ cup caviar
6 toasted bread rounds
6 lettuce leaves
6 slices tomato
6 tablespoons mayonnaise
Red Sauce
Fresh parsley sprigs

Cut each egg in half; remove yolk. Mash the yolks with the ¼ cup mayonnaise and the caviar. Stuff this mixture into half of each egg and press egg halves back together. Cut rounds from 6 slices of bread and toast. On each plate place a lettuce leaf, a toasted bread round, slice of tomato, an egg, topped with 1 tablespoon of mayonnaise, 2 tablespoons Red Sauce, and garnish with a sprig of parsley. The eggs may be stuffed and kept refrigerated several hours before serving.

Red Sauce

½ cup chili sauce
2 tablespoons olive oil
2 tablespoons lemon juice
Dash Worcestershire sauce

Mix all ingredients together until well blended. Refrigerate until ready to assemble eggs. Will keep several days, covered, in refrigerator.

This is a very elegant, different first course. Becky McLeary shared this with us. It comes from Memphis, Tennessee.

Mayonnaise is called for in all of our recipes and you should always use a high quality brand. Many people are disappointed in the results when salad dressing is substituted. Homemade mayonnaise is even better than commercial and there is an excellent recipe included. (See the Index.)

Marinated Mushrooms

- ¾ cup salad oil
- 3 tablespoons soy sauce
- ⅛ cup Worcestershire sauce
- 1 teaspoon salt
- 3 tablespoons lemon juice
- ¼ teaspoon garlic powder
- 1 teaspoon pepper
- ½ cup red wine
- 3 cans button mushrooms

Mix all of the ingredients except the mushrooms in a saucepan. Simmer 5 minutes. Add mushrooms and simmer 15 minutes. Cool. Refrigerate one day. To serve, reheat and serve warm with toothpicks. May be made several days ahead.

We like to keep these in the refrigerator at all times. They are great with steaks. Sue Terney in Indianola, Ms. gave me this recipe.

Shrimp and Wild Rice Casserole

- 2 pounds shrimp, cooked and deveined
- ½ stick butter
- 4 green onions, tops and bottoms, chopped
- 4 ribs celery, chopped
- 1 small green pepper, chopped
- 1 package Uncle Bens Long Grain and Wild Rice, cooked as package directs
- 2 cans cream of chicken soup
- 1 cup mayonnaise
- Small jar chopped pimentos
- 1 16-ounce can green beans, well drained
- 1 5-ounce can water chestnuts, sliced and drained
- 1 cup Monterey Jack cheese, grated
- ½ cup Parmesan cheese, grated
- 1 cup Cheddar cheese, grated
- 1 cup buttered bread crumbs
- Dash each Tabasco and Worcestershire
- Salt and pepper to taste

In saucepan, sauté the onions, celery and green pepper until soft. Combine remaining ingredients, except bread crumbs, mix until well blended. Pour into greased 13×9 Pyrex dish. Top with buttered bread crumbs and bake at 350° for 30 minutes. Will freeze.

We like this just as well with chicken instead of the shrimp. However you do it, you will be delighted with the results.

Avocado Spinach Salad

- 10 ounces fresh spinach, stemmed and torn into pieces
- 1 cup seasoned croutons
- ¼ pound Swiss cheese, cut into ¼-inch strips
- 4 hard-cooked eggs, quartered
- 2 avocados, peeled, halved, pitted and sliced crosswise
- ½ Bermuda onion, thinly sliced
- Lemon-Mustard Vinaigrette

Combine spinach, croutons, cheese, eggs, avocado and onion in large salad bowl and toss gently. Just before serving, shake dressing thoroughly, pour over salad and toss again.

Lemon-Mustard Vinaigrette

- ½ cup oil
- 1½ tablespoons vinegar
- 1½ tablespoons fresh lemon juice
- ¼ to ½ teaspoon salt
- ¼ teaspoon Dijon mustard
- Freshly ground pepper

Combine all ingredients in jar with tight-fitting lid and shake well. Refrigerate until ready to use.

Makes about ¾ cup.

One of the best salads.

Herbed Carrots

- 8 to 10 carrots
- 6 tablespoons butter
- 1½ teaspoons sugar
- ½ teaspoon salt
- ½ teaspoon tarragon
- Chives and parsley
- 4 tablespoons Madeira wine

Peel carrots and slice. Melt butter in saucepan. Add carrots, sugar, salt, and Madeira. Cover and cook over medium heat for 6 to 8 minutes. Lower heat and cook additional 10 minutes. Remove lid, sprinkle with tarragon, chives and parsley.

Cheese-and-Pepper Muffins

3 tablespoons finely chopped green pepper
¼ cup finely chopped onion
1 2-ounce jar diced pimento, drained
¾ cup (3 ounces) shredded Cheddar cheese
2½ cups all-purpose flour
¼ cup yellow cornmeal
2 tablespoons baking powder
1 teaspoon salt
¼ teaspoon red pepper
¼ cup sugar
2 eggs, beaten
1½ cups milk
¼ cup shortening, melted

Combine first 10 ingredients in a medium mixing bowl; make a well in center of mixture. Combine eggs, milk, and shortening; add to dry ingredients, stirring just until moistened. Spoon into greased muffin pans, filling two-thirds full. Bake at 400° for 20 to 25 minutes.

Yield: 1½ dozen.

Orange Cheesecake

1 cup flour, sifted
¼ cup sugar
1 tablespoon orange rind, grated
½ cup butter
1 egg yolk
½ teaspoon vanilla
Orange sections, for garnish
Mint sprigs, for garnish

Combine flour, sugar and rind. Cut in butter until mixture resembles coarse meal. Add egg yolk and vanilla and blend well. Pat ⅓ of the dough onto the bottom of a 9-inch springform pan. Bake in a hot oven at 400° for 5 minutes or until golden brown. Remove and cool. Pat remaining dough evenly around sides of pan to ½ inch from top. Pour orange cheese filling (below) into pan. Place aluminum foil under pan on oven rack and bake in hot oven at 400° for 8 to 10 minutes until the crust browns slightly. Reduce heat to 225° and bake 1 hour and 20 minutes longer. Remove and cool slowly, then refrigerate. Serve garnished with orange segments and mint sprigs.

Orange Cheese Filling

5 8-ounce packages cream cheese, room temperature
1¾ cups sugar
3 tablespoons flour
1 tablespoon orange rind, grated
¼ teaspoon salt
¼ teaspoon vanilla
5 eggs
2 egg yolks
¼ cup frozen orange juice concentrate, thawed and undiluted

Combine cheese, sugar, flour, orange rind, salt and vanilla in a large bowl. Beat at low speed until smooth. Add eggs and egg yolks, one at a time, beating well after each addition. Stir in orange juice. Pour mixture into prepared pan.

BACKPORCH SUPPER

SERVES SIX TO EIGHT

Bacon and Gruyère Squares

Curried Olives

Cheesy Fish Fillets

Rice Salad   Cran-Raspberry Ring

Zesty Garlic Bread

Peppermint Ice Cream Pie

with Hot Fudge Sauce

Soft Red Italian

Bacon and Gruyère Squares

1 pound bacon, chopped fine
1 cup grated Gruyère
1 cup mayonnaise
1 4-ounce tin mushroom stems and pieces, drained and chopped
8 slices of square rye bread or pumpernickel bread, crusts removed

In a skillet cook the bacon over moderately high heat, stirring, until it is crisp and transfer it with a slotted spoon to paper towels to drain. In a bowl combine the bacon, the Gruyère, the mayonnaise and the mushrooms, spread the mixture on the bread squares, and quarter the squares. Arrange the squares on a baking sheet and put them under a preheated broiler about 6 inches from the heat for 2 minutes, or until the topping is golden and bubbly.

Makes 32 hors d'oeuvres.

Curried Olives

3 tablespoons lemon juice
½ cup salad oil
1 tablespoon finely grated white onion
1 tablespoon curry powder
1 9-ounce jar (1½ cups) stuffed green olives

Put lemon juice in bowl and add oil as for mayonnaise. Add other ingredients and beat. Pour over drained olives. Keep in jar in refrigerator for at least 3 days before serving. Keeps indefinitely in refrigerator. Turn jar upside down from time to time to move liquid. Drain on paper towel before serving. Some martini drinkers like these in martinis.

Cheesy Fish Fillets

6 to 8 fish fillets
½ cup freshly grated Parmesan cheese
¼ cup flour
Salt to taste
Freshly ground pepper to taste
1 teaspoon paprika
1 egg, lightly beaten
1 tablespoon milk
¼ cup melted butter
¼ cup sliced almonds

Preheat oven to 350°. Pat fish dry. Blend together the cheese, flour, salt, pepper, and paprika. Combine egg and milk in a flat dish. Dip fish fillets in the egg mixture and coat with the cheese mixture. Arrange the fillets in a well greased baking dish and pour the butter over all. Sprinkle almonds over. Bake, uncovered, 40 minutes.

A Delta delight—good anytime! Sybil Arant developed the recipe.

Rice Salad

⅓ cup Ranch style dressing
½ cup Italian dressing
½ cup mayonnaise dressing
vegetables
2 tablespoons chopped fresh parsley, basil or dill
2 tablespoons finely chopped onion
3 cups cooked rice

In large bowl, blend dressings with mayonnaise. Stir in vegetables, parsley and onion. Add rice and toss well; pack into 5½-cup ring mold or bowl; chill. Garnish center if desired with vegetables tossed with Italian dressing.
Serves 6 to 8.

Vegetables: Use combination equal to 1½ cups carrots, green pepper, mushrooms, olives, radishes and green onions.

Cran-Raspberry Ring

1 3-ounce package raspberry gelatin
1 3-ounce package lemon gelatin
2 cups boiling water
1 10-ounce package frozen raspberries
1 14-ounce jar cranberry-orange relish
1 7-ounce bottle lemon-lime carbonated beverage

Dissolve gelatins in 2 cups boiling water. Sitr in frozen raspberries, breaking up pieces with fork. Add relish. Chill until cold but not set. Carefully pour in carbonated beverage. Stir gently. Chill until partially set. Turn into a 6-or 6½-cup ring mold. Chill until firm. Unmold on crisp greens.

Zesty Garlic Bread

1 cup butter, softened
1 cup grated Parmesan cheese
½ cup mayonnaise
5 cloves garlic minced
3 tablespoons chopped parsley
½ teaspoon oregano
1 large loaf French Bread

Combine all ingredients. Mix well and spread on bread. Wrap in foil and bake at 375° for 20 minutes.

Faye Ashby gave us this recipe. The bread, buttered and wrapped in foil can be frozen. It only needs to thaw slightly before baking.

Keep a few simple things handy for garnishing—the real secret to beautiful food! Paprika added to the cheese or breadcrumbs to be used for a topping on a casserole will add just the right amount of color to brighten a plate. A jar of long-stemmed cherries will keep a long time in the refrigerator and will make any dessert look company-perfect.

Peppermint Ice Cream Pie with Hot Fudge Sauce

20 Oreo cookies
¼ stick butter (melted)
1½ quarts peppermint ice cream

Crush Oreo cookies and moisten with melted butter. Press into 9-inch pie pan. This crust is delicious; for a thicker crust use more Oreos. Fill crust with peppermint ice cream. See index for ice cream recipe, or use commercial ice cream.

Hot Fudge Sauce

1 tablespoon butter
1 ounce semi-sweet chocolate
⅓ cup boiling water
1 cup sugar
2 tablespoons Karo
½ teaspoon vanilla
½ teaspoon salt

Melt one tablespoon butter and one ounce chocolate and add ⅓ cup boiling water, 1 cup sugar and 2 tablespoons Karo. Boil 5 minutes. Add ½ teaspoon salt. Spoon 2 teaspoons of hot fudge sauce over each piece of pie as it is served.

Everyone, especially the children love this dessert. Sue Terney shared this with us.

AN ANNIVERSARY PARTY

SERVES EIGHT

Brie in Puff Pastry

Squash Bisque with Parmesan Rounds

Crab and Artichoke Extravaganza

Baked Tomatoes

Fresh Spinach Salad with Vinaigrette Dressing (See Index)

Refrigerator Rolls (See Index)

Strawberry Mousse

Best Butter Cookies

Chardonnay

Brie in Puff Pastry

1½ cups flour
½ teaspoon salt
1½ sticks butter, cut into pieces
¾ cup sour cream
1 round of Brie
1 egg

Place flour, salt and pieces of butter in bowl of food processor. Process briefly until butter is coarsely cut into flour. Remove cover and add sour cream. Process until mixture forms a ball. Remove from bowl, flatten and wrap in plastic. Refrigerate one hour. Roll chilled pastry into a rectangle about 16×12 and ⅜ inch thick. Fold into thirds, creating a smaller rectangle. Turn 90° and repeat the rolling and folding as above. You will need to make 6 "turns", chilling dough about 30 minutes between each turn. After final rolling, fold again into small rectangle, wrap and chill in refrigerator (up to five days) or place in freezer until ready to shape. Remove packet of pastry from refrigerator. (If frozen, allow to soften enough to roll.) Roll pastry into a rectangle about 16×12 and ⅛ inch thick. Trim edges to form a square large enough to encase Brie. Place Brie on pastry and bring each corner of pastry to center. Pinch corners and seams together. Beat egg until well blended. Brush over pastry. (Cut the pastry scraps into desired shapes to decorate top and cover seams.) Cut 2 to 4 small slits in top to allow steam to escape. Bake in upper third of oven at 450° for 15 to 20 minutes, until pastry is nicely browned. Serve either hot or at room temperature. Pastry may be shaped over Brie and either refrigerated or frozen for several days. (Refrigerate 4 to 5 days or freeze up to 1 month.) Bake as directed above but dough need not come to room temperature before baking.

You certainly won't regret the time spent in making the dough for this excellent appetizer.

Squash Bisque

1 medium onion, chopped

Sauté in 1 stick butter

Add

2 potatoes, cubed
2 carrots, sliced
2 boxes frozen squash
3 cans chicken broth
1 teaspoon white pepper
¼ teaspoon thyme
½ clove garlic
1 cup heavy cream

Simmer until mushy. Put in blender and purée in batches. Return to boiler and add 1 cup heavy cream. Heat and serve in mugs.

Yield: 11 cups

Kathy Lovelace shared this recipe with me after we were served this delicious soup in Baton Rouge, LA. I have never served it to anyone who didn't love it. It freezes beautifully.

Parmesan Rounds

2 loaves sliced white bread
Butter
2 8-ounce packages cream cheese, room temperature
½ cup (1 stick) butter, melted
¼ cup plus 2 tablespoons mayonnaise
6 green onions, chopped
Freshly grated Parmesan cheese

Preheat broiler. Using 1-inch round cutter, cut 3 to 4 circles from each bread slice. Butter one side of each circle. Arrange in single layer on baking sheet. Broil until lightly toasted. Turn and broil unbuttered side until lightly toasted. Transfer to rack and cool. Combine cream cheese, ½ cup butter, mayonnaise and green onion in large bowl. Spread about 1 teaspoon mixture over buttered side of bread. Dip into Parmesan cheese. (Can be prepared ahead to this point and frozen.) Preheat broiler. Arrange rounds on baking sheet. Broil until bubbly and golden, about 5 minutes. Serve immediately.

Makes about 10 dozen.

Butter is essential to good baking. There are many places that it is simply tastier, but it is an important part of really high quality cakes, pies, or cookies, and most especially for excellent breads.

Crab and Artichoke Extravaganza

- ½ stick butter
- ½ pound fresh mushrooms, thinly sliced
- 2 tablespoons flour
- 1¾ cup half-and-half
- ½ teaspoon chicken soup base
- ½ cup dry sherry
- 2 cups grated Gruyère cheese
- ¼ teaspoon thyme
- ¼ teaspoon Worcestershire sauce
- Dash Tabasco
- 2 pounds King crabmeat, cut into bite-size pieces
- 1 14-ounce can artichoke hearts, drained and sliced
- ½ cup grated Parmesan cheese

Preheat oven to 350°. In a large skillet sauté the mushrooms in the butter until soft. Add the flour and cook, stirring, until the roux is lightly brown. Add the next 7 ingredients and cook, stirring, until the sauce is smooth and thick. Remove from the heat and fold in the crabmeat. Line a shallow baking dish with the artichoke hearts. Pour the crabmeat mixture on top and sprinkle with the cheese. Bake for 30 minutes or until bubbly.

Baked Tomatoes

- 8 tomatoes
- ½ cup sour cream
- ½ cup mayonnaise
- 1 teaspoon curry powder
- 1 tablespoon fresh parsley
- salt and pepper to taste

Cut off top of tomatoes and remove about half of the pulp. Mix the next 5 ingredients and add the tomato pulp to it. Stuff the tomatoes with the mixture. Top with dry bread crumbs. Bake at 350° for 20 to 30 minutes.

Fresh Spinach Salad

- 1 bunch fresh spinach, washed and dried and torn
- 1 can mandarin oranges, drained
- 1 red onion, separated into rings
- 2 avocados, peeled and sliced
- 8 slices bacon, cooked crisp and crumbled

Toss all together. Serve with Vinaigrette Dressing. (See Index for recipe.)

Strawberry Mousse

2 egg whites, room temperature
¼ teaspoon cream of tartar
Pinch of salt
2 cups whipping cream
1¼ cups powdered sugar, sifted
2 cups strawberries, puréed and chilled
Whipped cream (garnish)

Beat egg whites, cream of tartar and salt in small bowl until stiff and glossy. Whip 2 cups cream with sugar in medium bowl until stiff. Whisk strawberry purée into cream until mixture is very thick. Gently fold in egg whites, blending well. Spoon mousse into champagne glasses. Refrigerate at least 1 hour. Garnish each with whipped cream just before serving. Can be prepared 1 day ahead.

Serves eight.

Best Butter Cookies

1 cup flour
½ cup sugar
½ cup butter
1 egg yolk
1 teaspoon vanilla or
1 tablespoon rum or brandy

Mix flour and sugar together in bowl. Cut in butter until fine. Mix egg yolk and flavoring in small dish with fork. Slowly add to flour mixture, mixing well with fork. Gather in ball. Turn dough out onto waxed paper and firmly form into a log. Roll in paper and chill until firm. When ready to bake, slice and bake at 350° for 8 minutes. This recipe is ideal for the food processor.

THE VERY BEST EVER FISH DINNER

FOR EIGHT

Tipsy Cheese with Crackers
Dill Crisps and Herb Dip
Elegant Baked Fish
Special Vegetable Casserole
Avocado Salad with Lime Dressing
French Bread (See Index)
Amaretto Cheesecake
Montrachet

Tipsy Cheese Spread

12 ounces sharp Cheddar cheese
6 ounces Swiss cheese
6 ounces cream cheese
1 large onion, chopped
⅓ cup chopped parsley
2 to 4 dashes Tabasco
¼ teaspoon salt
¼ cup gin
⅛ teaspoon dried tarragon

Grate all cheese; mix all ingredients together well. Chill. Bring to room temperature before serving. Keep in refrigerator.

Dill Crisps

1 egg
1 teaspoon salt
4 ounces cream cheese, room temperature
1½ teaspoons dried dillweed
6 tablespoons (¾ stick) butter, cut into 6 pieces and well chilled
1 tablespoon cold water
1 cup unbleached all purpose flour
½ teaspoon baking powder

In food processor bowl with steel knife: Blend egg and ½ teaspoon salt 2 seconds. Set aside for glaze. Blend cream cheese and dill until smooth. Add butter and 1 tablespoon water and mix using 5 on/off turns, then process continuously 5 seconds. Mix flour, baking powder and remaining ½ teaspoon salt in small bowl. Add to work bowl and blend just until dough begins to come together (do not form ball). Gather dough into ball and wrap in plastic. Chill at least 1 hour. Position rack in center of oven and preheat to 350°. Grease 2 baking sheets and sprinkle with water. Divide dough into quarters. Roll out 1 portion on lightly floured surface to thickness of ⅛ inch. Cut out 3-inch rounds with cookie cutter; firm remaining scraps in refrigerator. Arrange rounds on prepared sheets ½ inch apart. Repeat with remaining dough. Brush rounds with glaze. Bake until light brown, about 15 minutes. Cool on racks. Repeat rolling, cutting and baking with dough scraps. Store crackers in airtight container.

Makes about 40.

Herb Dip

1 cup mayonnaise
½ tablespoon lemon juice
½ teaspoon salt
¼ teaspoon paprika
¼ cup chopped parsley (or dried)
1 tablespoon grated onion
1 tablespoon chopped chives (or dried)
¼ teaspoon curry powder
½ teaspoon Worcestershire sauce
Garlic salt to taste
1 tablespoon capers
½ cup sour cream

Mix all ingredients in given order. May be made up to 3 days ahead of serving. Keep in refrigerator until ready to serve.

Yield: 1½ cups.

Elegant Baked Fish

1½ cup Hellmann's mayonnaise
1 tablespoon creole mustard
1 tablespoon lemon juice
1 tablespoon Tabasco
1 tablespoon Worcestershire sauce
2 teaspoons garlic powder
¾ teaspoon curry powder
Ritz crackers

Mix well and spread over eight fish fillets. Sprinkle with crumbled Ritz crackers and bake at 400° for about 20 minutes uncovered. Fish is done when it flakes easily with a fork.

Everyone loves fish cooked this way. We thank Becky McLeary for this recipe!

Special Vegetable Casserole

2 cups broccoli florets
2 cups cauliflower florets
2 cups small onions
1 cup sharp Cheddar, grated
1 cup mayonnaise
3 tablespoons Dijon mustard
½ teaspoon salt
¼ teaspoon pepper
2 cloves garlic, pressed
1 teaspoon parsley, chopped

Steam the vegetables individually. Make two complete layers of vegetables and cheese in a buttered, 2-quart casserole dish. Combine the mayonnaise, mustard, and seasonings. Spread over the vegetables. Preheat the oven to 350°. Bake for 20 minutes.

Avocado Salad with Lime Dressing

1 small head of leaf lettuce
1 large avocado
3 tablespoons fresh lime juice
1 medium cucumber, peeled and sliced
½ medium red onion, thinly sliced
½ cup pitted black olives
1 tablespoon wine vinegar
1 teaspoon sugar
¼ teaspoon dry mustard
Pinch of paprika
Dash of salt
Hot pepper sauce
⅓ cup corn oil

On a chilled serving platter, arrange the lettuce. Peel and slice the avocado and toss to coat with 1½ tablespoons of the lime juice. Arrange the avocado, cucumber, onion slices and olives on the lettuce. In a small bowl, combine the remaining 1½ tablespoons lime juice, the vinegar, sugar, mustard, paprika, salt and hot pepper sauce to taste. Gradually whisk in the oil until blended. Spoon the dressing over the salad.

Amaretto Cheesecake

1½ cups graham cracker crumbs
2 tablespoons sugar
1 teaspoon ground cinnamon
¼ cup plus 2 tablespoons butter, melted
3 8-ounce packages cream cheese, softened
1 cup sugar
4 eggs
⅓ cup amaretto
1 8-ounce carton sour cream
1 tablespoon plus 1 teaspoon sugar
1 tablespoon amaretto
¼ cup toasted sliced almonds
1 1.2-ounce chocolate candy bar, grated

Combine graham cracker crumbs, 2 tablespoons sugar, cinnamon, and butter; mix well. Firmly press mixture into bottom and ½ inch up the sides of a 9-inch springform pan. Beat cream cheese with electric mixer until light and fluffy. Gradually add 1 cup sugar, mixing well. Add eggs, one at a time, beating well after each addition. Stir in ⅓ cup amaretto; pour into prepared pan. Bake at 375° for 45 to 50 minutes or until set. Combine sour cream, 1 tablespoon plus 1 teaspoon sugar, and 1 tablespoon amaretto; stir well, and spoon over the cheesecake. Bake at 500° for 5 minutes. Let cool to room temperature; then refrigerate 24 to 48 hours. (Cheesecake is best when thoroughly chilled and flavors have time to ripen.) Garnish with almonds and the grated chocolate.
Serves 12 generously.

I always get a lot of requests for this recipe.

FIESTA!

SERVES EIGHT

Lime Tonic

Mexican Torte

Blue Corn Crepes with Beef Filling

Swiss Enchiladas   Mexican Rice

Tomato Marinate

Corn Savories

Caramel Flan

or

Frozen Mocha Mousse

Bordeaux Médoc

or

Italian Barolo

Lime Tonic

1 cup fresh lime juice
1 cup lime syrup (recipe below)
4 cups tonic
8 lime slices

In a pitcher combine the lime juice and the lime syrup and stir in the tonic. Pour the mixture into tall glasses filled with ice cubes and garnish each drink with 1 of the lime slices.

Makes 8 drinks.

Lime Syrup

2 cups sugar
the grated rind from 4 limes

In a saucepan combine the sugar with 2 cups water, bring the water to a boil over moderate heat, stirring until the sugar is dissolved, and add the lime rind. Cook the syrup, undisturbed, for 10 minutes. Let the syrup cool until it is lukewarm and strain it into a jar, pressing hard on the rind with the back of a spoon. The syrup keeps indefinitely, covered and chilled.

Makes about 2½ cups.

Make ANY excuse for a meal to become a celebration! Don't wait for just the obvious occasions. Let it be finding the first wildflower or a good report card (even better—a bad report card! focus the celebrating on the next one being better. It may not be, but your child will NEVER forget your vote of confidence!). The event isn't important but the pleasure that you will bring to your table for family or special friends will be treasured.

Mexican Torte

2 eggs, beaten
2 tablespoons flour
½ teaspoon salt
⅓ cup milk
1 4-ounce can chopped green chilies
1 cup Cheddar cheese, grated
1 cup Monterey Jack cheese, grated

Beat eggs, add flour, salt and milk; mix well. Add remaining ingredients and blend well. Pour into a greased 8×12 inch baking dish. Bake at 350° for 30 to 35 minutes. Cut into small squares and serve hot. May be frozen after baking. To serve, thaw and reheat.

My delightful daughter-in-law, Becky Hill Thompson, cooks wonderful Mexican food!

Blue Corn Crepes with Beef Filling

½ cup blue cornmeal (or yellow)
½ cup boiling water
3 eggs, beaten
½ teaspoon salt
½ cup flour
1 tablespoon melted butter
¾ cup milk

Combine cornmeal and boiling water, stir well and let cool. Add eggs, salt, flour and melted butter. Mix until smooth, then stir in milk. Use this batter to make 12 crepes. Set aside (crepes will freeze).

Filling

1 large onion, chopped
1 tablespoon vegetable oil
3 cloves garlic, crushed
2 cans chopped chilies
2 8-ounce cans tomato sauce
3 tablespoons chili powder
Salt and pepper to taste
¾ pound lean ground beef, cooked and drained (can also use chicken)
1½ cups sour cream
1½ cups mashed avocado
½ pound sharp Cheddar cheese, grated

Sauté onion in oil until soft; add garlic, chilies, tomato sauce and chili powder. Cook over low heat 1 hour. Adjust seasonings. Divide sauce into 2 bowls, stirring cooked beef into one. Correct seasonings again. Separate crepes on flat surface. Place equal amounts of beef mixture, sour cream, and avocado on each. Roll up. Place in greased 13×9 Pyrex dish. Cover with meatless portion of sauce and cheese. Bake at 325° for 30 minutes.

Blue corn meal may be found in specialty and gourmet shops. It only grows in a small area in New Mexico and is fun to use but certainly not necessary to create an excellent dish.

Swiss Enchiladas

1 onion, chopped
2 tablespoons vegetable oil
1 clove garlic, crushed
2 cups tomato purée
2 cans chopped green chilies
2 cups chicken, cooked and chopped (use breasts)
1 dozen either corn or flour tortillas
6 chicken bouillon cubes
3 cups heavy cream
½ pound Monterey Jack or Swiss cheese, grated
Avocado slices or ripe olice slices for garnish

Sauté onion in oil until soft. Add garlic, tomato purée, chilies, and chicken. Simmer 10 minutes. (Heat about 1 inch oil in frying pan. Heat each tortilla in hot oil about 45 to 60 seconds. Remove before they get crisp. Drain on paper towels.) Dissolve bouillon cubes in cream. Dip each tortilla in this, cover generously with chicken filling and roll up. Place each roll in greased 9×13 Pyrex dish and pour remaining cream mixture over. Top with grated chees. Bake at 350° for 30 minutes. Garnish with avocado and ripe olive slices. These do freeze.

Mexican Rice

1 cup uncooked rice
½ cup bacon drippings
½ cup chopped onion
1 clove garlic, minced
½ cup chopped green pepper
3 cups V-8 juice
Salt and cayenne pepper to taste

Sauté rice, onions, garlic and green pepper in drippings until rice is golden. Add V-8 juice. Cover and simmer for 30 minutes, or after adding juice, pour into greased 1½ quart Pyrex dish, cover and refrigerate. When ready to cook, bake covered at 350° for 45 to 50 minutes. Let sit few minutes, remove cover, stir with fork, add salt and cayenne pepper to taste. This rice freezes well after baking.

Tomato Marinate

6 medium fresh tomatoes
1 onion
1 green pepper
Salt and pepper to taste
2 tablespoons sugar
2 tablespoons vinegar
1 teaspoon dry mustard

Chop vegetables. Mix sugar, vinegar, mustard and salt. Pour over vegetables. Marinate in refrigerator several hours.

Corn Savories

6 tablespoons (¾ stick) butter
1½ cups buttermilk baking mix
1 8½-ounce can creamstyle corn

Preheat oven to 400° F. Melt butter in 11×17-inch jelly roll pan. Combine baking mix and corn in medium bowl. Drop biscuits onto pan by heaping teaspoons. Turn in butter to coat well. Bake until golden, 20 minutes. Serve hot. Makes about 3 dozen small biscuits.

Caramel Flan

½ cup sugar
4 eggs, beaten
1 can sweetened condensed milk
2 condensed milk cans filled with water
1 teaspoon vanilla

Melt ½ cup sugar in heavy saucepan over medium heat until caramel color liquid results. Pour into 6 cup Corning, Pyrex or gelatin mold to cover bottom of container. Beat eggs together with milk and water. Add vanilla. Do not beat more than two minutes. Pour mixture over cooled, melted sugar in container. Place mold in another container that is half filled with water. Bake, covered, at 350° for 1½ hours. Continue to bake an additional 30 minutes uncovered or until done. Test with a toothpick. A clean one means ready.

Frozen Mocha Mousse

1 pound semi-sweet baking chocolate
3 tablespoons instant coffee granules
½ cup boiling water
6 egg yolks
½ cup sugar
1 teaspoon vanilla
6 egg whites
1½ cups heavy cream, whipped
½ cup heavy cream
Chocolate curls

Melt chocolate over hot water. Dissolve coffee granules in boiling water and cool slightly. In a medium-sized bowl, beat egg yolks at high speed until foamy. Gradually beat in sugar and continue beating until mixture is very thick and pale yellow. Reduce speed and beat in vanilla, coffee and melted chocolate. With clean beater, beat egg whites in a large mixing bowl until they hold stiff peaks. Stir 1 cup of the beaten whites into chocolate mixture, then stir chocolate mixture into the remaining whites. Gently, but thoroughly, fold in 1½ cups whipped cream. Pour into an 8-inch springform pan and freeze. It will keep nicely in your freezer up to 1 month. To serve, remove the mousse from the freezer 20 to 25 minutes before dessert-time and remove springform sides. Whip ½ cup heavy cream and mound on top of mousse, garnishing with chocolate curls.

I get asked for this recipe more than any other, I think.

PATIO PARTY

FOR TEN

Ham and Cheese Log
Stuffed Artichoke Hearts
Arwin's Cheese Crackers (See Index)
Beef Tender
Deviled Potato Skins Vegetable Gelatin Salad
Double-Quick Dinner Rolls
Lemon Cheese Pie
Fumé Blanc

Ham and Cheese Log

4 ounces sharp Cheddar cheese, grated (1 cup)
8 ounces cream cheese, softened
1 4½-ounce can deviled ham
½ cup chopped ripe olives
½ cup chopped pecans

In small mixing bowl, beat cheeses until blended. Beat in deviled ham. Stir in olives and chill. Shape into two logs and roll in pecans. Chill before serving. Serve with crackers of your choice.

Makes 2 cups.

Stuffed Artichoke Hearts

1 can artichoke hearts, drained
½ cup seasoned bread crumbs
½ cup Parmesan cheese, grated
Wishbone Italian dressing

Mix bread crumbs and cheese. Moisten with Italian dressing till you can make small balls with it. Stuff the artichoke hearts with the mixture. Chill covered till time to serve. This is a good easy appetizer especially good in the summer. You may want to cut the artichoke hearts in half if they are too large for 1 or 2 bites.

Beef Tender

1 whole beef tender
Lemon pepper
Gobs of butter

Sprinkle beef tender generously with lemon pepper. Brown on hot barbecue fire on all sides for about 20 minutes. Put in shallow pan in 200° oven with gobs of butter on it. It will hold for hours and still come out pink. Can be done before guests arrive.

Deviled Potato Skins

5 tablespoons butter
2½ teaspoons Worcestershire sauce
4½ teaspoons Dijon-style mustard
Cayenne to taste
Skins from 10 baked russet (baking) potatoes, cut lengthwise into 1-inch-wide strips
Sour cream dipping sauce

In a small heavy skillet melt the butter with the Worcestershire sauce over low heat, remove the skillet from the heat, and stir in the mustard and the cayenne. Brush the insides of the skins with the mustard mixture, arrange the skins brushed side up on a buttered baking sheet, and sprinkle them with salt and pepper. Bake the skins in a preheated 450° oven for 5 to 10 minutes, or until they are golden and crisp, and serve them with the dipping sauce. Serves 10 as an hors d'oeuvre or side dish.

Sour Cream Dipping Sauce

2 cups sour cream
4 teaspoons Dijon-style mustard
4 scallions, minced
1 teaspoon Worcestershire sauce

In a small serving bowl combine the sour cream, the mustard, the scallions, and the Worcestershire sauce. Makes about 1 cup.

Vegetable Gelatin Salad

1 package (3 ounces) lime gelatin
1 cup boiling water
½ cup sour cream
3 tablespoons grated carrot
½ cup mayonnaise
½ cup condensed milk
1 carton cottage cheese
2 tablespoons grated onion
2 tablespoons green pepper, chopped

Dissolve gelatin in boiling water, cool slightly. Mix sour cream, mayonnaise, condensed milk and beat until smooth. Add to gelatin, then add the cottage cheese, onion, green pepper and carrot. Pour into mold and chill to set. Double this recipe to serve 10.

An especially good salad to serve with any meat, it came to me from Sharon Larson.

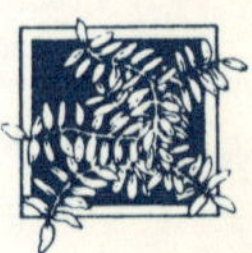

Double-Quick Dinner Rolls

1 package active dry yeast
1 cup warm water
2 tablespoons sugar
1 teaspoon salt
1 egg
2 tablespoons shortening
2¼ cups flour

Dissolve yeast in warm water in large mixer bowl. Add sugar, salt, egg, shortening and 1 cup flour. Beat until smooth. Stir in remaining flour; continue to stir until smooth. Scrape batter from side of bowl. Cover; let dough rise in warm place until doubled, about 30 minutes. Stir down batter. Spoon into 12 greased large muffin cups, filling each about ½ full. Let rise until batter reaches tops of cups, about 20 to 30 minutes. Heat oven to 400°. Bake 15 minutes.

Makes 1 dozen rolls.

Lemon Cheese Pie

1 9-inch pie shell
2 8-ounce packages cream cheese
4 tablespoons lemon juice
1 cup sugar
4 eggs

Prepare pie shell (see index) and bake at 450° for 8 to 10 minutes. Do not allow the crust to become too brown. Set aside. Mix cream cheese and sugar, add eggs and beat until all ingredients are well blended. Slowly add lemon juice and mix well. Pour into partially baked crust. Return to 350° oven for 15 to 20 minutes, until pie is slightly firm. Cool and then chill for at least 1 hour before serving. To serve, top with whipped cream and garnish with fresh strawberries, if desired. (The strawberries and whipped cream make the pie a little prettier, but it's just as good without them.) Make two to serve 10.

This is the pie that I like the very best. It is a recipe that I have used for such a long time that I have no idea where it came from, just that we always enjoy it.

DELTA DUCKS!

SERVES TWELVE

Caribbean Cheese Ring   Chicken Nut Puffs

Ducks

Garlic Cheese Grits   Gravy

Waldorf Salad or Creamy Burgundy Cherries

Green Bean Casserole

French Bread

Chocolate Cheesecake

Coffee

California Pinot Noir

Caribbean Cheese Ring

1 envelope unflavored gelatin
⅓ cup lemon juice
2 tablespoons water

Soften in small pan. Stir over low heat till gelatin is dissolved. In a large mixer bowl beat together:

4 8-ounce packages cream cheese
2 tablespoons finely snipped parsley
1 tablespoon sugar
1 teaspoon salt
Lemon peel
¼ teaspoon coarsely ground pepper

Beat till fluffy. Blend in gelatin mixture. By hand fold in 1 pound peeled and cleaned shrimp, cooked and finely chopped. Pour into 6½-cup ring mold. Chill till firm. To serve, unmold salad on lettuce lined plate. Combine plum preserves and Pickapeppa sauce. Drizzle over mold. Garnish with thin lemon slices and fill center with shrimp. (A spread for crackers.)

Chicken Nut Puffs

1 cup chicken broth
½ cup butter
2 teaspoons Worcestershire
1 cup flour
1 tablespoon parsley
2 teaspoons seasoned salt
½ teaspoon paprika
⅛ teaspoon pepper
4 eggs
1 5-ounce can boned chicken
¼ cup nuts

Bring to boil broth, butter, and Worcestershire. Mix together flour and seasonings, and add to boiling liquid. Cook, stirring 1 minute or until mixture forms a ball. Remove from heat; add eggs, one at a time, beating after each addition until mixture is smooth. Stir in chicken and nuts, mixing well. Drop by teaspoonful onto baking sheet. Bake at 400° 15 to 18 minutes. This can be frozen. After done, can split and fill with any type cheese filling.

Makes 7½ dozen.

Ducks

6 ducks, plucked
Lawry's Seasoned Salt
3 onions, quartered
3 apples, unpeeled, seeded and quartered
3 carrots, peeled and quartered
Parsley, chopped
Liquid shrimp boil (about ½ bottle)
Water to cover
Lawry's Brown Gravy Mix

Rub the ducks inside and outside with the seasoned salt. Stuff the cavities with the onions, apples, and carrots. Sprinkle with the parsley. Put in a large pot, add water and shrimp boil. Cover with a tight-fitting lid and bring to a boil. Lower heat and simmer ducks for 12 hours. Turn off heat and allow to cool in liquid. The meat will fall off the bones. Bone out and cut or tear meat into small pieces. If not serving immediately, wrap in foil and refrigerate until serving time. Reheat in foil in 300° oven 20 to 30 minutes until hot. Serve over Garlic Cheese Grits and top with Lawry's Brown Gravy, mixed as package directs.

This gravy is perfect for this dish and always gets raves. This is the one way even those who don't usually like ducks like it! Pam Lowery in Tupelo, Mississippi taught me how to cook ducks this way.

Garlic Cheese Grits

1 teaspoon salt
7 cups water
2 cups uncooked grits
1 6-ounce roll Kraft nippy cheese
1 6-ounce roll Kraft garlic cheese
1 cup butter, melted
4 eggs, well beaten
½ cup milk
Salt and pepper to taste

Add salt to boiling water and cook grits covered, on low heat, until done. Stir in cheese cut into small pieces, butter, eggs, milk, salt and pepper. Put in a 3-quart casserole and bake at 350° for 1 hour.

We KNOW everyone has cheese grits recipes, but this is the one to use with the ducks!!

Green Bean Casserole

3 cans French-style green beans, drained
½ cup butter
½ cup chopped onion
½ cup flour
4 cups milk
6 hard-boiled eggs
½ cup fine bread crumbs
Dash pepper and salt
½ teaspoon thyme
1 teaspoon Worcestershire sauce
1 tablespoon chopped parsley
1 cup grated Swiss cheese

Melt butter in saucepan, sauté onions until soft. Stir in flour, blending well. Slowly add milk and blend well. Cook over medium heat until thickened. Stir in salt, pepper, thyme, Worcestershire sauce and parsley, mixing well. Pour drained beans into greased 1½-quart casserole, slice eggs over and pour sauce over all. Combine bread crumbs with Swiss cheese and sprinkle over top. Bake at 375° for 20 minutes.

Creamy Burgundy Cherries

2 packages (8 ounces) cherry-flavored gelatin
2 cans (16 ounces each) pitted, dark sweet cherries, drained (reserve syrup)
4 cups boiling liquid (reserved syrup plus water)
2 packages (8 ounces each) cream cheese, softened
1½ cups Burgundy or dry red wine

Dissolve gelatin in boiling liquid. In large bowl, slowly add gelatin to cream cheese. Blend in wine. Chill until thickened but not set. Fold in cherries. Spoon into 12-cup fluted tube pan. Chill until firm. Garnish with sugared grapes and mint leaves for a pretty salad.
Serves 12 to 14.

(See Index for sugared grapes.)

Waldorf Salad

3 cups diced apple
3 cups diced celery
1 cup chopped walnuts
¾ cup mayonnaise
1 tablespoon lemon juice
4 tablespoons sugar

Combine apples, celery and walnuts. Mix mayonnaise, lemon juice and sugar. Fold in apple mixture. Chill. Serve on lettuce leaves.

French Bread

2 cups lukewarm water
1 package dry yeast
1 tablespoon sugar
2 teaspoons salt
4 cups flour
Melted butter

In large bowl, combine water, yeast, sugar, salt. Stir until dissolved. Stir in flour. Turn dough out onto floured surface. Knead slightly (4 or 5 times). Place in greased bowl. Cover and let rise in warm place 45 minutes or until doubled. Grease baking sheet. Divide dough into two equal parts. Shape into oblong loaves. Place both loaves on baking sheet. Let rise 20 to 30 minutes. Brush with part of melted butter. Bake at 425° for 10 minutes. Reduce temperature to 375° and bake additional 20 minutes. Remove from oven, brush with more melted butter. Serve hot. Will freeze.

This is our favorite French Bread and is good toasted, too.

Toss any leftover rolls or homemade bread into the workbowl of your food processor, add several slices of cold butter, and process until you have fine crumbs. Store in a plastic bag in the freezer and take out amount needed for any recipe calling for buttered bread crumbs as a topping. If you will add several shakes of paprika to the bag as you add the buttered crumbs, you will have the nice even color that makes a casserole so attractive and appealing.

Chocolate Cheesecake

3 cups graham cracker crumbs
1 cup butter, melted
1 12-ounce package semisweet chocolate morsels
4 8-ounce packages cream cheese, softened
2 cups sugar
4 eggs
1 tablespoon cocoa
2 teaspoons vanilla extract
1 16-ounce carton commercial sour cream
Whipped cream

Combine graham cracker crumbs and melted butter, mixing well; firmly press on bottom and sides of a 10-inch springform pan.

Place chocolate morsels in top of double boiler; bring water to a boil. Reduce heat to low; cook until chocolate melts.

Beat cream cheese with electric mixer until light and fluffy; gradually add sugar, mixing well. Add eggs, one at a time, beating well after each addition. Stir in melted chocolate, cocoa, and vanilla; beat until blended. Stir in sour cream, blending well. Pour into prepared pan. Bake at 300° for 1 hour and 40 minutes (center may be soft but will firm when chilled). Let cool to room temperature on a wire rack; chill at least 5 hours. Garnish each serving with whipped cream.

Yield: one 10-inch cheesecake.

Freezes well.

FESTIVE LAMB DINNER

SERVES TWELVE

Smoky-Cheese Squares
Oyster Crackers
Shrimp Canapés
Duxelles on Toast Points
Marinated Grilled Leg of Lamb
Black Cherry-Wine Mold
Spinach Stuffed Tomatoes with Blender Hollandaise Sauce
Alà Pilaf
Pita Bread, Split, Buttered and Toasted
Pineapple Pie
Cabernet-Sauvignon

Shrimp Canapés

- ½ pound shrimp, shelled, deveined, and cooked
- 1 stick butter, softened and cut into bits
- 3 tablespoons heavy cream
- 1 tablespoon lemon juice
- 2 teaspoons tomato paste
- 1 teaspoon anchovy paste
- 1 teaspoon salt
- 12 small shrimp, shelled, deveined, cooked and halved lengthwise
- 24 bread rounds, toasted

In food processor in batches, purée ½ pound shrimp, and butter. Add the cream, lemon juice, tomato paste, anchovy paste, and salt. Process until smooth. Have the 12 small shrimp split and place a half in each of 24 well buttered miniature muffin tins. Divide the purée evenly among the tins, filling each about ¾ full. Smooth the tops of each, cover the tins and chill at least 3 hours. With a 1½-inch round cutter, cut rounds from bread slices. Toast until lightly browned. Loosen the edge of each mold with tip of sharp knife and invert onto the toast rounds. Makes 24 small canapés.

Smoky-Cheese Squares

- 2 cups flour
- 1 teaspoon soda
- 1 teaspoon baking powder
- ½ teaspoon salt
- 1¼ cups sour cream
- 1 tablespoon chopped pimento
- 1 tablespoon chopped chives
- 2 teaspoons dried onion
- 1 tablespoon parsley

Sift dry ingredients into mixing bowl. Combine sour cream, pimento, chives, onion and parsley. Mix into dry ingredients, just until flour is moistened. Turn out onto floured surface, knead a few turns; roll out to ½ inch thickness. Cut into 16 squares. Place on greased baking sheet. Bake at 450° for 12 to 15 minutes. Remove from oven and spread with cheese topping. For cheese topping, blend together 1 5-ounce jar smoky cheese spread, 2 tablespoons sour cream, 1 teaspoon Worcestershire sauce. Return to oven just until topping melts. Serve hot.

Oyster Crackers

- 1 12-ounce package oyster crackers
- 1 package Hidden Valley Dry Milk Dressing (do not use the buttermilk dressing mix)
- ½ cup salad oil
- ½ teaspoon garlic powder
- ½ teaspoon dill weed
- 1 teaspoon lemon pepper

Empty crackers into a plastic bag. In separate bowl, mix remaining ingredients. Pour into bag with crackers and shake until crackers are well coated, about 5 minutes. Store in an airtight container. These will keep indefinitely and also freeze well.

Duxelles on Toast Points

Make melba toast by slicing thin sliced bread into desired shapes and baking in oven slowly at 300° till lightly browned. Set aside. In a pan sauté until fairly dry:

- ¼ cup butter
- ½ cup minced shallots or scallions
- 3 cups minced mushrooms
- ¼ to ½ cup vermouth
- Salt and pepper

Spread mixture on the toast points and sprinkle with grated Parmesan cheese. Heat briefly in 400° oven and serve.

I got this wonderful recipe at Pat Ross' cooking class in Vicksburg. Pat is a great cook and cooking teacher!

Marinated Grilled Leg of Lamb

½ cup Dijon mustard
2 tablespoons soy sauce
1 teaspoon rosemary or thyme
Dash garlic powder
¼ teaspoon ginger
2 tablespoons olive oil

Blend all ingredients together except the oil. Beat in the oil by drops. Paint the marinade onto the lamb with a spatula. Be sure all fat is trimmed off the lamb before you put the marinade on it. To have the leg of lamb ready for an 8:00 dinner, put the marinade on it before noon and put it in the oven at 4:00. Cook a 6 to 8 pound leg of lamb for 3 to 4 hours at 350°.

Black Cherry-Wine Mold

2 No. 303 cans dark sweet cherries, pitted
Water
2 3-ounce packages cherry-flavored gelatin
1 cup red wine

Drain cherries, saving syrup. Add enough water to make 2½ cups liquid. Bring to boil. Add to gelatin, stirring until gelatin is dissolved. Add wine. Chill and when slightly thickened, add cherries. Mold. Serve with sour cream dressing.

Serves 12.

Sour Cream Dressing

Mix 1 cup sour cream with 3 to 4 tablespoons sugar.

Roasted meats should be allowed, whenever possible, to stand for serveral minutes at room temperature before they are sliced or served. This will allow the internal juices to "settle" and slicing will be easier and more attractive.

Spinach Stuffed Tomatoes

4 boxes frozen spinach
1 cup water
1 teaspoon salt
12 tomatoes
1 cup red onion, chopped
1 tablespoon butter
¾ cup Parmesan cheese, grated
½ cup sour cream
Salt and red pepper to taste
1 package cracker crumbs
1 tablespoon melted butter

Cook spinach in water with salt for 5 minutes. Drain well till dry. Wash, but do not peel tomatoes. Cut off the tops and hollow out the pulp. Turn upside down to drain while you prepare the filling. Sauté the onion in butter until it is transparent. Add drained spinach, cheese and sour cream. Add pepper and salt. Mix well and stuff tomatoes with mixture. Top with crumbs and melted butter. Place in a shallow baking dish and cover the bottom with water. Bake 20 minutes at 350°.

Before serving top with a spoonful of Blender Hollandaise Sauce and run under the broiler just until sauce browns lightly and is bubbly. Watch it! This is a wonderfully easy but delicious Hollandaise. The tomatoes may be filled one day ahead of serving. Remove from refrigerator 1 hour before heating.

Blender Hollandaise Sauce

3 egg yolks
2 tablespoons lemon juice
¼ teaspoon salt
Dash cayenne pepper
1 stick butter, melted

Place yolks, lemon juice, salt and pepper in blender; mix on high only until well blended. Slowly add melted butter with blender running. Makes 1 cup sauce. This sauce will keep at room temperature for 1 hour before serving.

Alà Pilaf

2 tablespoons butter
½ cup chopped celery
1 medium onion, chopped
½ cup sliced fresh mushrooms
1 cup ala, uncooked
¼ teaspoon dill weed
¼ teaspoon oregano
½ teaspoon salt
¼ teaspoon pepper
2 cups beef or chicken bouillon
1 tablespoon chopped parsley
2 tablespoons chopped pimento

Melt butter in large skillet; add vegetables and ala. Stir constantly until vegetables are tender and ala is golden. Add seasonings and bouillon; cover and bring to boil. Reduce heat and simmer 15 minutes. Stir in parsley and pimento just before serving.

Pineapple Pie

1 9-inch pie shell, unbaked
4 eggs
1½ cups sugar
2 tablespoons flour
1 stick butter
1 small can crushed pineapple, well drained

Prepare pie shell (see index) and brush with a small amount of slightly beaten egg white. Set aside. Cream butter and sugar; add eggs, one at a time, beating well after each addition. Stir in flour. Add pineapple and mix until all ingredients are well blended. Pour mixture into pie shell and bake at 350° 30 to 40 minutes. Shake pan gently every few minutes during the last several minutes of baking time. The center should just be beginning to seem firm, but should still move. Remove from oven and set on a solid surface for pie to continue to set.

Make two to serve 12.

My aunt, Bonnie Robertson, is one of the most thoughtful ladies in the world. I couldn't count how many of these pies she has made and most of them were to fill the need of another. She always has one for my husband when we visit her.

LUCKY HUNTER'S DINNER

SERVES TWELVE

Elegant Hot Cheese Canapés

Toasted Pecans

Oyster Dip

Quail or Dove

Creative Casserole

Tomato Aspic with Cheese Balls

Refrigerator Rolls (See Index)

Mousse Amaretto

Beaujolais

Elegant Hot Cheese Canapés

- 3 cups New York Cheddar cheese (white) or Kraft's Coon Brand, grated
- 1 cup mayonnaise
- ½ cup chopped green onions
- 1½ cups chopped black olives

Mix all of the ingredients by hand. To serve, toast pita bread that has been split and halved and quartered and lightly buttered. When bread has cooled, put a dollop of cheese mixture on it and broil until the cheese melts. Serve hot.

Becky McLeary shared this recipe with us. It is our very favorite appetizer. It will keep covered in the refrigerator for two weeks.

Toasted Pecans

Soak 2 cups pecans in 2 cups water and ¼ cup salt for 3 hours. Drain and bake at 300° until done. (Small halves will take 1 hour.)

Oyster Dip

1 cup green onions, tops and bottoms, chopped
½ stick butter
2 pints oysters, drained
Dash Tabasco
1 stack pack Ritz crackers, crushed

Sauté onions in butter. Add oysters and chop and stir with two knives. Add Tabasco and cracker crumbs. Serve in chafing dish with potato chips.

Doves

2 dozen doves, dressed
Salt, pepper and garlic powder to taste
2 cups Wishbone Italian Dressing
2 to 3 tablespoons Worcestershire sauce
2 sticks melted butter
2 jars sliced mushrooms, undrained

Place doves, breast side up, close together in a large flat pan. Sprinkle lightly with salt, pepper and garlic powder; mix Wishbone dressing, Worcestershire and butter. Pour over birds, coating each. Add undrained mushrooms to bottom of pan. Cover pan tightly with lid or foil. Bake at 350° for 1½ hours.
Serves 12.

My father, Clyde H. Wilson, Sr., is an avid hunter who enjoys not only the hunt but cooking the game as well. The recipes that he shared with us have been enjoyed by many people at his game "cookins."

Quail

1 dozen quail, dressed
Salt and pepper
Flour
Crisco shortening
1 cup Wishbone Italian Dressing
½ cup melted butter
1 to 2 tablespoons Worcestershire

Mix salt, pepper, and flour. Lightly coat quail with mixture. Brown lightly in Crisco. Place birds in baking pan. Mix Wishbone dressing, melted butter and Worcestershire sauce. Pour over birds. Cover pan with lid or foil. Bake at 350° for 1 hour.
Serves 12.

Also good for domestic rabbit.

Creative Casserole

1 package frozen peas
1 package frozen lima beans
1 package frozen green beans
½ cup mayonnaise
⅓ cup minced onion
½ tablespoon Worcestershire sauce
1½ tablespoons salad oil
1 hard-boiled egg, grated
1 small jar chopped pimento

Preheat oven to 350°. Cook separately peas, lima beans, and green beans. Drain. Blend mayonnaise, onion, Worcestershire, salad oil, egg and pimento. Pour gently over vegetables. Bake about 15 minutes.

Serves 6 to 8.

Tomato Aspic with Cheese Balls

Aspic

1 can consommé
1 envelope gelatin
1½ cups V-8 juice
2 tablespoons cider vinegar
1 tablespoon sugar
2 teaspoons seasoning salt
1 teaspoon Worcestershire sauce
Dash hot sauce

Cheese Balls

½ pound cream cheese
½ cup chopped pecans
3 teaspoons horseradish
8 stuffed olives (slivered)

Soak gelatin in ½ cup consommé for about 5 minutes. While this is standing, heat the remaining can of consommé and pour over gelatin. Stir until the gelatin is well dissolved. Add V-8, vinegar, sugar, salt, Worcestershire sauce and hot sauce. Set bowl aside to cool until thick. Stir gently every now and then to keep the mixture from settling. Between stirs mix cream cheese, nuts, horseradish and slivered olives. Make into small balls and chill a bit. Place three balls in each individual mold and fill it with aspic. Serve on salad greens and garnish with mayonnaise.

This wonderful aspic recipe comes from our friend Zelda White in Indianola, Ms.

Mousse Amaretto

5 eggs, separated
½ cup sugar
Pinch salt
1 teaspoon vanilla
1 cup milk
1 package gelatin
2 tablespoons cold water
1 pint heavy cream, whipped

Beat yolks with sugar. Add salt. Add vanilla to milk and bring to boil. Add hot milk to yolks and mix well. Heat, stirring constantly, but do not boil. Soften gelatin in water. Add to milk. Stir. Cool in large bowl of ice water. Fold in whipped cream. Fold in stiffly beaten egg whites. Add 2 to 5 ounces of Amaretto. Pour into serving bowl. Chill. Put 1 tablespoon of Amaretto on each serving.

This recipe is from Jeanelle Street and is one of the best she has given me.

A WEST TEXAS TREAT

SERVES TWELVE

Dill Dip in a Bread Bowl

Pheasant

Apricot Salad

Wild Rice Casserole

Asparagus with Brown Butter Sauce

Hot Biscuits (See Index)

Chocolate Pie

Coffee

Chardonnay

Dill Dip in a Bread Bowl

1 pint Hellmann's mayonnaise
1 pint sour cream
3 tablespoons dill weed
3 tablespoons grated onion
1 tablespoon parsley flakes
1 teaspoon seasoned salt
3 drops green food coloring

Mix all ingredients and refrigerate for 24 hours. Hollow out the center of a round loaf of onion rye or pumpernickle bread. Break up the center into bite size pieces to be used for dipping. Place the "bread bowl" on a tray and pile the bread bites around it. Decorate the rim of the bowl with fresh parsley.

This is Jim's favorite dip. It's a hit with everybody at parties, because it is so pretty and delicious.

Pumpernickle Bread

- 3 packages dry yeast
- 1½ cups warm water
- ½ cup dark molasses
- 1 tablespoon plus 1 teaspoon salt
- 2 tablespoons caraway seed
- 2 tablespoons shortening
- 2¾ cups rye flour
- ¼ cup cocoa
- 2½ to 3 cups all-purpose flour

Dissolve yeast in warm water in large mixing bowl. Stir in molasses, salt, caraway seed, shortening, rye flour and cocoa. Beat until smooth. Stir in enough all-purpose flour to make dough easy to handle. Turn dough onto lightly floured surface, cover and let rest 10 to 15 minutes. Knead until smooth, 5 to 10 minutes. Place in greased bowl; turn greased side up. Cover; let rise until doubled, about 1 hour. Punch down dough; round up and let rise again until doubled, about 40 minutes. Punch down dough; divide in half. Shape each half into a round, slightly flat loaf. Place on greased baking sheets, cover and let rise 1 hour. Heat oven to 375°. Bake until loaves sound hollow when tapped. Remove from oven, brush tops with melted butter. Will freeze for several months.

Yield: 2 loaves

Pheasant

- 6 pheasants, separate legs from thighs and quarter each breast
- Salt, pepper and flour
- Crisco shortening
- 3 cups chopped green onion, tops and bottoms
- 3 cups sliced celery
- 1½ cups sliced fresh mushrooms
- 6 cloves garlic, minced
- 6 tablespoons Worcestershire sauce
- 6 cups Wishbone Italian Dressing

Dredge pheasant pieces in flour seasoned with salt and pepper until lightly coated. Brown in Crisco. When all pieces are lightly browned, remove from skillet and place in large, flat baking pan. Return skillet to medium heat and sauté vegetables and garlic. Mix Worcestershire and salad dressing; pour over birds and add sautéed vegetables to bottom of pan. Cover with lid or foil. Bake at 350° for 1½ hours.

Serves 12.

This delicious pheasant recipe was developed by Clyde Wilson, who hunts pheasant in West Texas, but cooks them at home in Ms.

Apricot Salad

1 can (29 ounces) apricots, drained and finely cut (save juice)
1 can (29 ounces) crushed pineapple, drained
2 packages orange gelatin
2 cups hot water
1 cup juice (from above)
¾ cup mini-marshmallows

Dissolve gelatin and add juice. Chill until slightly syrupy. Add fruit and marshmallows. Pour into mold and chill until firm.

Topping

½ cup sugar
3 tablespoons flour
1 cup apricot juice
1 egg, beaten
3 tablespoons butter

Mix all together and cook until thick. Cool.

Add 1 cup whipping cream, whipped last and folded in. Spread over gelatin and set. Serves 12.

Kitty Pegram, my sister, shared this delicious salad recipe with us.

Wild Rice Casserole

1 stick butter
1 cup wild rice
1 cup slivered almonds
3 tablespoons chopped chives, dried
1 7-ounce can mushroom stems and pieces, drained
3 cups chicken broth

Put all ingredients, except broth, in frying pan and cook over medium high heat until almonds brown, stirring often. Add chicken broth and stir. Put into a 2-quart baking dish. Cover and bake at 325° for 1½ hour. Can be made up to 2 days ahead and baked when needed.

This wild rice is available at gourmet or specialty food stores. Use all wild rice, not the mixed kind. The rice and this recipe were a nice welcome to Plainview from Cheryl Gebo.

Asparagus in Brown Butter Sauce

- 4 cups beef broth (preferably homemade)
- 1 medium carrot, thinly sliced
- 1 celery stalk, sliced
- 1 lemon, sliced
- ¼ cup chopped onion
- 4 parsley sprigs
- 1 teaspoon salt (reduce or omit if using canned broth)
- 4 packages frozen asparagus
- Lettuce leaves
- Brown Butter Sauce

Combine broth, carrot, celery, lemon, onion, parsley and salt in large skillet and bring to boil. Add asparagus. Cover and simmer until almost tender, about 5 minutes. Let cool (asparagus will continue to cook as it cools). Refrigerate asparagus in broth. (Can be prepared 1 day ahead.) Line platter with lettuce leaves. Drain asparagus well. Arrange atop lettuce. Serve with Brown Butter Sauce.

Brown Butter Sauce

- 1 cup (2 sticks) butter
- 4 egg yolks, room temperature
- 1 tablespoon Dijon mustard
- 1 tablespoon fresh lemon juice
- Salt and freshly ground pepper

Melt butter in heavy small saucepan over low heat. Continue cooking, swirling pan occasionally, until butter is rich chestnut brown, about 20 minutes. Let butter cool 15 minutes. Combine yolks, mustard and lemon juice in processor or blender. With machine running, pour in butter in slow, steady stream. Season sauce with salt and pepper. Refrigerate until ready to use. (Can be prepared 1 day ahead; whisk before serving if necessary.)

Makes 1½ cups.

Chocolate Pie

- 2 9-inch pie crusts, unbaked
- 1 cup sugar
- 4 tablespoons cocoa
- 4 tablespoons flour
- Dash salt
- 2 cups milk
- 4 egg yolks, beaten
- 1 teaspoon vanilla
- 1 tablespoon butter, melted

Mix together the sugar, cocoa, salt, and flour. Add the milk, egg yolks, vanilla and butter. Pour into 2 9-inch pie crusts. (See index for pie crust recipes.) Bake the pies at 350° for 30 to 40 minutes or until centers are firm. Make meringue according to recipe found in the index. Use 4 egg whites for your meringues for these two pies.

This is my mother's recipe and my son Marshall's favorite pie.

A GATHERING

BUFFET FOR SIXTEEN TO TWENTY

Broccoli Dip with Dippers
Hot Seafood Delight with Dippers
Cheese Spread
Smoked Turkey
Marinated Eye of Round
Salad Ribbon **Zucchini Salad**
Homemade Mayonnaise **Homemade Hot Mustard**
Best Baked Beans
Honey Whole Wheat Bread
Brown Sugar Cake with Caramel Sauce
Oreo Cheesecake
Dry Rosé

Broccoli Dip with Dippers

1 stick oleo
1 cup chopped onion
2 packages frozen broccoli
1 4-ounce can sliced mushrooms
2 rolls garlic cheese
1 teaspoon Accent
1½ cups slivered almonds
2 cans cream of mushroom soup
Tabasco, to taste
Worcestershire sauce, to taste

Melt ½ of the margarine and sauté the onions in it. Cook broccoli and drain well. Combine all of the ingredients and simmer one-half hour. Serve hot in a chafing dish. Makes 2 quarts. Freezes well. Serve with dippers.

Dippers

2 sticks butter
1 teaspoon garlic salt
1 teaspoon onion salt
1 teaspoon lemon pepper
1 teaspoon celery salt
1 teaspoon oregano
1 tablespoon parsley
1 package hot dog buns

Melt butter and add seasonings. Cut each hot dog bun into 12 pieces. Dip into seasoned melted butter. Put on cookie sheet. Bake 45 minutes at 300°. These keep well in tins.

Hot Seafood Delight with Dippers

2 10½-ounce cans cream of mushroom soup
1 10½-ounce can cream of shrimp soup
1 8-ounce package cream cheese
3 4½-ounce cans shrimp, drained and rinsed
3 8-ounce cans sliced mushrooms, drained
3 4½-ounce cans crabmeat, drained
2 8-ounce cans water chestnuts, sliced and drained
3 tablespoons Worcestershire sauce
½ cup sherry
2 teaspoons dry mustard
2 tablespoons chopped parsley
Salt and pepper to taste

Heat soups in saucepan. Stir in cream cheese, continue stirring until melted. Add remaining ingredients. Serve hot in chafing dish with Parmesan Dippers.

Parmesan Dippers

Thin sliced bread
Melted butter
Parmesan cheese, grated

Trim crust off bread. Cut each slice into 3 strips. Brush with melted butter and sprinkle with grated Parmesan cheese. Bake at 300° until dry and browned as desired.

Smoked Turkey

1 10 to 12 pound butter-basted turkey
Lawry's seasoned salt
10 pounds charcoal
Hickory chips

Thaw turkey completely. Remove the giblets. Rub the turkey generously inside and outside with Lawry's seasoned salt. Build fire in charcoal smoker using 10 pounds of charcoal and 6 to 8 hickory chips which have been soaked. Fill water pan in smoker. Put the turkey on the grill, cover the smoker and cook the turkey 10 to 12 hours. (Overnight usually works best.) Remove turkey when done. Chill and slice thinly.

Don't peek while turkey is smoking! My brother, C. H. Wilson, Jr. thinks this is THE way to cook a turkey! (So does anyone who has eaten one he has prepared!)

Cheese Spread

1 pound Velveeta
8 ounces cream cheese
1 cup pecans, chopped
1 teaspoon garlic powder
1 tablespoon Worcestershire sauce
5 drops Tabasco

Bring cheeses to room temperature. Mix all of the ingredients with your hands. Roll into a ball and roll in Gebhardt's chili powder. Wrap in wax paper and chill. You may put the mixture into a cheese crock and serve as a spread with crackers.

Marinated Eye of Round

5 pound eye of round roast
1 cup red wine
1 cup water
2 bunches green onions, tops and bottoms, chopped
4 fresh tomatoes, chopped
1 cup ripe olives, drained and chopped
2 green peppers, chopped
2 teaspoons salt
2 tablespoons wine vinegar
1 stick melted butter

Combine water and wine and pour over the roast in a heavy pan. Cover and bake at 325° about 3 hours until tender. While meat is cooking, combine the chopped vegetables, salt and wine vinegar. Mix well. When meat is done, remove from pan, slice in ¾-inch thick slices. Spoon marinated vegetables between slices and pour the melted butter over. Wrap tightly in foil and let stand 1 hour before serving.

This recipe is one of Pat Pierce's, a great cook in Vicksburg, Mississippi.

If you don't use a lot of different cheeses but like a few different ones on hand for certain recipes, grate the cheese, place in tightly closed plastic bags and keep in the freezer. All cheeses can be grated and frozen and will keep in the freezer for many months.

Salad Ribbon

- 2 3-ounce packages lime-flavored gelatin
- 2 cups boiling water
- 1½ cups cold water
- 2 3-ounce packages lemon-flavored gelatin
- 1 cup boiling water
- 2 cups miniature marshmallows
- 1 8-ounce package cream cheese
- 1 1-pound, 4-ounce can crushed pineapple, drained
- 1 cup pineapple juice
- ½ pint cream, whipped
- 2 3-ounce packages raspberry-flavored gelatin
- 2 cups boiling water
- 1½ cups cold water

Dissolve lime gelatin in 2 cups boiling water; add 1½ cups cold water. Pour into 14×10×2-inch pan. Chill until set. Dissolve lemon gelatin in 1 cup boiling water in top of double boiler. Add marshmallows and cream cheese, which has been cut in small pieces. Beat until well blended. Remove from heat and stir in pineapple and pineapple juice. Cool; then fold in whipped cream. Spoon over top of chilled lime gelatin. Chill until lemon layer is firm. Dissolve raspberry gelatin in 2 cups boiling water. Add 1½ cups cold water. Cool; then pour over chilled lemon layer. Chill until firm.

Serves 12 to 15.

Zucchini Salad

- 4 pounds zucchini, grated
- 2 teaspoons salt
- 6 tablespoons sour cream
- 6 tablespoons mayonnaise
- 3 tablespoons Dijon mustard
- 2 cloves garlic, mashed and minced
- Lettuce leaves and tomato quarters for garnish

In a colander, toss the zucchini with the salt, let stand, covered, for at least 1 hour. Squeeze in a cup-towel to remove as much moisture as possible. In separate bowl, combine sour cream, mayonnaise, mustard, garlic. Add the zucchini and mix well. Chill at least 30 minutes. Serve on inidividual lettuce leaves, garnished with tomato quarters. Salad may be prepared a day ahead of serving.

Homemade Mayonnaise

2 egg yolks
1 teaspoon prepared mustard
1 teaspoon salt
Juice of 1½ fresh lemons
1 pint oil, chilled

Put egg yolks, salt and mustard in small mixing bowl. Barely mix on slow speed. Start adding oil, by drops, very slowly, with mixer running. When mixture begins to thicken, add more oil, alternating with lemon juice in small amounts till all the oil and juice are used. I like to stir in a little red pepper when the mayonnaise is finished.

Homemade Hot Mustard

1 cup dry mustard (3 cans)
1 cup vinegar
3 eggs
1 cup sugar
Dash salt

Mix together mustard and vinegar, let stand overnight. Beat together eggs, sugar and vinegar. Add to mustard mixture. Mix and cook the entire mixture in a double boiler until thick.

Best Baked Beans

4 slices bacon
2 onions, chopped
1 cup bell pepper, chopped
1 cup parsley, chopped
1 cup celery, chopped
2 cloves garlic, pressed
2 large cans pork and beans
1 can Rotel tomatoes
1 can pimento, chopped
1 tablespoon prepared mustard
1 teaspoon chili powder
Salt and pepper to taste

Fry the bacon strips crisp, remove from drippings and set aside. Sauté all of the fresh vegetables in the bacon drippings until tender. Add beans, tomatoes, pimentos, seasonings and crumbled bacon. Place in a casserole or bean pot and bake at 300° for 1½ hours.

Serves 10 to 12.

These are a little different and you can increase the amount to easily feed a crowd.

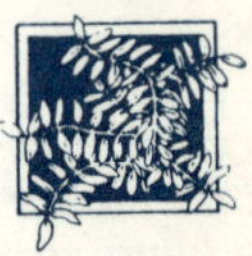

Honey Whole-Wheat Bread

- 2 packages yeast
- ½ cup warm water
- ⅓ cup honey
- ¼ cup shortening
- 1 tablespoon salt
- 1¾ cups warm water
- 3 cups whole-wheat flour
- 3 to 4 cups white flour

Dissolve yeast in ½ cup water. Stir in honey, shortening, salt, 1¾ cups water. Add whole-wheat flour. Stir until smooth. Mix in enough white flour to make easy to handle. Turn dough onto floured surface and knead until smooth. Turn into greased bowl, cover and let rise 1 hour. Divide and shape into 2 loaves. Brush with melted butter. Let rise until double (about 1 hour). Bake at 375° for 40 to 45 minutes. Brush again with melted butter.

Brown Sugar Cake with Caramel Sauce

Butter Cake

- 2 cups (4 sticks) butter, room temperature
- 2 cups firmly packed light brown sugar
- 6 eggs
- 4 cups all-purpose flour, sifted
- 1 teaspoon baking powder
- ¼ teaspoon salt
- ⅔ cup milk
- 2 cups pecans, chopped

Caramel Sauce

- 1 cup firmly packed light brown sugar
- ½ cup (1 stick) butter
- ½ cup whipping cream or half-and-half

For cake: Preheat oven to 325°. Grease and flour 10-inch tube pan. Beat 2 cups butter and sugar in large bowl until smooth and creamy. Add eggs beating well after each addition. Mix in flour, baking powder and salt. Gradually blend in milk. Add pecans. Pour batter into prepared pan, smoothing top with spatula. Bake until top is cracked and no longer moist, about 1½ hours. Invert cake onto rack and cool completely in pan. Meanwhile for sauce: Combine sugar, butter and cream in heavy-bottomed small saucepan over low heat. Cook, stirring constantly, until sugar is dissolved. Remove from heat and whisk 1 minute. Store caramel in jar with tight-fitting lid until ready to serve. To serve, cut cake into wedges. Spoon some sauce over each piece. Pass remaining sauce separately.

Don't be discouraged if a cake falls. Let it cool, make a boiled custard, break the cake into pieces, and place in small serving bowls. Pour the custard over the cake, maybe adding some fresh or canned fruit and you have a more elegant dessert than you intended in the first place!

Oreo Cheesecake

Oreo Crust

1¼ cups Oreo crumbs
⅓ cup butter, melted

Oreo Filling

2 pounds cream cheese, room temperature
1½ cups sugar
2 tablespoons all-purpose flour
4 extra-large eggs
2 large egg yolks
⅓ cup whipping cream
2 teaspoons vanilla
1½ cups coarsely chopped Oreo cookies
1 cup sour cream

Fudge Glaze

1 cup whipping cream
8 ounces semisweet chocolate, chopped
1 teaspoon vanilla

For crust: Blend all ingredients in bowl then press onto bottom and sides of 10-inch springform pan. Refrigerate crust until firm, about 30 minutes. For filling: Preheat oven to 425°. Beat cream cheese in large bowl of electric mixer on lowest speed until smooth. Beat in 1¼ cups sugar and flour until well blended. Beat in eggs and yolks until mixture is smooth. Stir in cream and 1 teaspoon vanilla. Pour half of batter into prepared crust. Sprinkle with chopped Oreos. Pour remaining batter over, smoothing with spatula. Bake 15 minutes. Reduce oven temperature to 225°. Bake 50 minutes, covering top loosely with foil if browning too quickly. Increase oven temperature to 350°. Blend sour cream, remaining ¼ cup sugar and remaining 1 teaspoon vanilla in small bowl. Spread over cake. Bake 7 minutes. Refrigerate immediately. Cover cake with plastic wrap and chill overnight. For glaze: Scald cream in heavy saucepan over high heat. Add chocolate and vanilla and stir 1 minute. Remove from heat and stir until all chocolate is melted. Refrigerate glaze 10 minutes. Set cake on platter and remove springform. Pour glaze over top of cake. Using pastry brush, smooth top and sides. Refrigerate cake until ready to serve.

YA'LL COME!

SERVES FIFTY

Cheddar Cheesecake (2 to 3 days ahead)
Spinach Squares (Made and frozen 1 month ahead)
Baked Ham with Hot Mustard Sauce (2 to 3 days ahead)
Fried Chicken (Half a day ahead if serving cold)
Tomatoes in Herb Vinaigrette (1 day ahead)
Potato Salad (1 day ahead)
Deviled Eggs (1 day ahead)

Pimento Cheese Sandwiches
(Make the spread 1 week ahead but spread on the bread 1 day before serving; wrap tightly and refrigerate)

Freezers of Homemade Ice Cream
(Make up to 1 month ahead — pack and keep in freezer until serving time.)
Peppermint Chocolate Fresh Peach

Cakes
(You will need at least 3 cakes for 50 people.)
Chocolate Pound Cake
Sour Cream Coconut Cake
Pineapple Pound Cake

This menu can be done by one because so much can be done ahead of time; however, it is an easy one to divide between your "what can I bring?" guests!

Cheddar Cheesecake

- 1½ tablespoons butter (for pan)
- ¼ cup fine breadcrumbs, lightly toasted
- ¼ cup finely grated sharp Cheddar cheese
- 6 ounces thinly sliced ham
- 1½ pounds cream cheese, room temperature
- ¾ pound sharp Cheddar cheese, grated
- 1 cup cottage cheese
- ¾ cup chopped green onion
- 4 eggs
- 3 tablespoons seeded and finely chopped jalapeño pepper
- 2 tablespoons milk
- 1 garlic clove, halved

Preheat oven to 325°. Butter 9-inch springform pan. Mix breadcrumbs and ¼ cup Cheddar. Sprinkle mixture into pan, turning to coat. Refrigerate. Dice about half of ham; reserve remaining slices. Mix diced ham with remaining ingredients in blender or processor until smooth. Pour slightly more than half of filling into prepared pan. Top with reserved ham slices in even layer. Cover with remaining filling. Set pan on baking sheet. Bake 1¼ hours. Turn oven off and cool cheesecake about 1 hour with door ajar. Transfer cheesecake to rack. Remove sides of pan. Cool cheesecake to room temperature before serving. Make 2 to serve 50.

Spinach Squares

- 2 10-ounce packages frozen chopped spinach, thawed
- 3 tablespoons butter
- 1 onion, chopped
- ¼ pound mushrooms, sliced
- 4 eggs, beaten
- ¼ cup bread crumbs
- 1 10½-ounce can cream of mushroom soup
- ¼ cup grated Parmesan cheese
- Dash pepper
- ¼ teaspoon oregano
- ⅛ teaspoon basil

Drain thawed spinach and press out all water possible. Sauté onion and mushrooms in butter just until onion is soft. Combine eggs, bread crumbs, soup, cheese, seasonings and spinach. Blend in onion mixture. Turn into greased 9-inch square Pyrex dish. Bake at 325° for 30 to 35 minutes. Cut into small squares. Refrigerate or freeze. May be served cold. If frozen, return to room temperature and reheat in 325° oven to serve hot. Make this recipe twice to serve 50.

Baked Ham

Pre-cooked, boned ham
Whole cloves
1½ cups brown sugar
2 cups pineapple juice
1 tablespoon prepared mustard
2 cups crushed pineapple (drain and use juice as part of above mentioned 2 cups)
Ginger ale

Score ham through layer of fat and stud with cloves. Mix sugar, juice, mustard and pineapple. Place ham in roasting pan. Pour mixture over ham. Bake at 350° for 1 hour. Reduce heat to 300° and cook 2 hours longer. As juice in bottom of the pan cooks down, add ginger ale. During last 2 hours of cooking, baste ham every 15 minutes, continuing to add ginger ale as needed. When ham is done, remove from pan, when cooled, slice and pour sauce from roasting pan over the ham. Refrigerate until ready to serve. Cook 2 hams to serve 50.

Mustard Sauce

1 regular size jar mustard
1 jar orange marmalade
1 small jar horseradish
1 jar apple jelly

Mix all ingredients. Will keep in tightly closed container in refrigerator indefinitely. Serve with cold ham or turkey. Delicious.

Fried Chicken

12 chickens, ready for frying
12 cups flour
6 teaspoons baking powder
3 cups milk
2 tablespoons salt
2 tablespoons pepper
Shortening to fry chicken in

In bowl combine 6 cups flour, baking powder, salt and pepper. In large brown paper bag, place remaining 6 cups plain flour. Drop several pieces of chicken into sack, shake well, coating each piece with flour. Remove one piece at a time, dip each in milk, then roll in seasoned flour mixture. Brown pieces in large skillet on both sides. As chicken is browned, place pieces on baking pans lined with brown paper bags. Bake each pan at 250° for 25 to 30 minutes. All grease will be gone and chicken very tender and crisp. Serve hot or cold.

Tomatoes in Herb Vinaigrette

3 cups fresh parsley
6 tablespoons fresh or dried tarragon
6 medium garlic cloves, minced
6 eggs, room temperature
3 cups vegetable oil
6 tablespoons red wine vinegar
3 teaspoons salt
Pinch of sugar
Freshly ground pepper
12 pounds tomatoes, cored and thinly sliced

Place parsley and tarragon in bowl. Add garlic. Add eggs, oil, vinegar, salt, sugar and pepper and mix 5 seconds. Arrange tomatoes in serving bowl or on rimmed platter. Pour dressing over. Adjust seasoning. (Can be made 2 hours ahead.)

Potato Salad

36 medium potatoes, boiled in skin until tender, peeled and diced
24 hard-boiled eggs, peeled and chopped
1 cup chopped parsley
3 4-ounce jars pimento, chopped
1½ cups green onions, tops and bottoms, chopped
6 tablespoons white wine vinegar
2 tablespoons melted butter
6 tablespoons sugar
1 tablespoon pepper
2 tablespoons salt

Peel the potatoes as soon as they are cool enough to handle but still warm. Mix the vinegar, butter, sugar, salt and pepper together and toss with the warm diced potatoes. Chill thoroughly. Stir in chopped eggs, parsley, pimento, and onions. Chill several hours or overnight. Mix together: 3 quarts mayonnaise and 3 5-ounce jars prepared horseradish. Stir into potato salad at least 1 hour before serving. Serve well chilled.

Deviled Eggs

4 dozen eggs, hard boiled
3½ tablespoons horseradish
3 tablespoons Worcestershire sauce
1 tablespoon cayenne pepper
3 tablespoons Dijon mustard
Enough mayonnaise to bind (about 5 to 6 tablespoons)

Place eggs in several pans, cover with water, bring to boil and cook 15 minutes. Pour off hot water, shake pan making sure egg shells crack. Cover with cold water, let sit several minutes. Eggs will peel easily. Slice eggs in halves lengthwise. Remove yolks and mash with remaining ingredients, using enough mayonnaise to bind all ingredients together. Spoon yolk mixture into egg halves; decorate each half with a slice of stuffed olive or sprig of parsley. Sprinkle with paprika.

Filling for Pimento Cheese

- 6 8-ounce packages sharp Cheddar cheese, grated
- ¾ to 1 cup mayonnaise
- 6 4-ounce jars chopped pimento
- 1 cup green onions, tops and bottoms, chopped
- 1 cup chopped pecans
- 3 4-ounce cans chopped ripe olives

Blend all ingredients, adding mayonnaise to desired thickness. Spread on slices of bread, top with another slice. Cut either in halves or thirds.

Peppermint Ice Cream

- 2 cups sugar
- 4 eggs
- 1 quart milk
- 1 pint whipping cream
- 1 pound peppermint stick candy, finely crushed (about 20 sticks)
- 1 teaspoon (about) peppermint extract or oil of peppermint

Mix well sugar, eggs, and milk. Cook over medium heat, stirring often, until mixture begins to thicken and coats spoon. Cool. This is basic boiled custard mixture for ice cream. When ready to freeze, combine remaining ingredients; add to custard. Pour into freezer can; add additional milk to fill can. Freeze.

Yield: 1 gallon.

(Candy may be pounded in heavy cloth bag with wooden mallet or crushed in food processor.)

Chocolate Ice Cream

- 1¼ cups sugar
- 8 egg yolks, beaten
- 4 ounces sweet chocolate, grated
- 1 quart milk, scalded
- 1 teaspoon vanilla extract
- 1 cup heavy cream

Mix the sugar, egg yolks, and chocolate in top of double boiler. Add milk and cook, stirring constantly, about 3 to 5 minutes. Cool. Add vanilla and cream. Chill. Pour into chilled freezer can and freeze.

Yield: ½ gallon.

Peach Ice Cream

- 1½ cups sugar
- 2 tablespoons flour
- ½ teaspoon salt
- 3 eggs, beaten
- 1 quart whole milk
- ½ pint whipping cream
- 1 tablespoon vanilla extract
- 6 cups chopped peaches, sweetened to taste
- 1 cup sugar

Combine the sugar, flour, and salt; add eggs and blend well. Add milk and cook slowly until slightly thickened. Let cool. Add the whipping cream, vanilla, and sweetened peaches. Pour into freezer and freeze.

Yield: 1 gallon.

Chocolate Pound Cake

- 1 cup butter
- ½ cup shortening
- 3 cups sugar
- 5 eggs
- 1 teaspoon vanilla extract
- 3 cups flour
- ½ teaspoon baking powder
- ½ teaspoon salt
- 4 tablespoons cocoa (may be heaping if desired)
- 1 cup milk

Cream together butter and shortening. Add sugar and mix well. Add eggs, one at a time, beating after each addition. Add vanilla. Combine dry ingredients and add alternately with milk to creamed mixture. Bake in greased 10-inch tube pan at 325° for 80 minutes. Will freeze.

This is the favorite cake of my son, Kevin—sometimes!

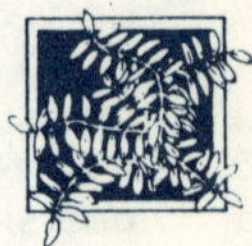

Never forget that you have the privilege of deciding what and how much alcohol will be served in your home. There has never been a dinner enhanced by too much food or drink being served during the cocktail time. Limit the kinds of drinks offered to that which best suits you and the type party you intend to have. Everyone will respond to your gracious yet firm decision in this matter. Too many hostesses forget that this is indeed their right.

Sour Cream Coconut Pound Cake

- 1 cup butter
- ½ cup margarine
- 3 cups sugar
- 6 eggs
- 3 cups flour
- ¼ teaspoon soda
- 1 carton sour cream
- 1 cup coconut
- ½ teaspoon coconut flavor
- ¾ cup sugar
- ¾ cup water
- 1 teaspoon almond flavor

Mix butter and margarine, add sugar and cream 10 minutes. Add eggs, one at a time, beating well. Sift flour with soda and add alternately with sour cream. Fold in coconut and coconut flavoring. Pour into tube pan and bake at 325° for 1½ hours. Freezes well.

Sauce

Combine ¾ cup sugar, ¾ cup water and almond flavoring. Boil 5 minutes. Pour over hot cake.

At other times, this cake is Kevin's favorite.

Pineapple Pound Cake

- ½ cup vegetable shortening
- ½ pound butter (2 sticks)
- 2¾ cups sugar
- 6 large eggs
- 3 cups sifted all-purpose flour
- 1 teaspoon baking powder
- ¼ cup milk
- 1 teaspoon vanilla extract
- ¾ cup undrained crushed pineapple and juice
- ¼ cup butter or margarine (½ stick)
- 1½ cups powdered sugar
- 1 cup crushed pineapple, drained

Cream shortening, butter, and sugar. Add eggs, one at a time, beating thoroughly after each addition. Add flour sifted with baking powder, alternately with milk. Add vanilla; stir in crushed pineapple and juice and blend well. Pour batter into well-greased 10-inch tube pan. Place in cold oven. Turn oven to 325° and bake for 1½ hours or until top springs back when touched lightly. Let stand for few minutes in pan. Run knife around edges and remove carefully to rack. Combine butter, powdered sugar, and about 1 cup drained pineapple. Pour over cake while hot. Freezes well.

My Aunt, Mildred Ashby, gave me this recipe and it has been our "take-to-the-lake" cake.

Elegant
Events
"Celebrations for
Every Occasion"

Elegant Events
CELEBRATIONS FOR EVERY OCCASION

New Year's Day Brunch
New Year's Day Dinner
Valentine's Day Tea
St. Patrick's Day Coffee
Easter Dinner
Derby Day Party
Memorial Day Cookout
Summertime Down South
Father's Day
4th of July Bash
He Cooks for Her Birthday
Labor Day Picnic
Kick-Off Dinner
Thanksgiving Feast — Mississippi Style
Christmas Galore
- **Yuletide Open House**
- **Christmas Morning**
- **A Texas Christmas Dinner**

New Year's Day Brunch

SERVES TWELVE

Fresh Orange Juice

Early Riser's Punch

Mushroom Bites

Individual Dishes of Fruit with

(Sliced apples, pears, pineapple chunks)

Romanoff Sauce Spooned Over

Cinnamon Crisps

Eggs in a Nest

Artichoke Quiche and Spinach Stuffed Tomatoes (See Index)

Glazed Canadian Bacon

Hawaiian Coffee Ring or Cranberry Coffee Cake

Coffee

New Year's Brunch

Bright colors should set the mood for this party as well as the coming year. Use your brightest and most varied linens. For the centerpiece, fill a basket with multi-colored balloons, having a ribbon of contrasting color going from the balloons to each plate. Attach a small scroll to each ribbon with an appropriate wish for each guest in the coming year.

A "Set Sail for the Coming Year" theme is fun. Let invitations read like a passport or visa card, giving the host's address as the Port of Call, "departure" date and time, etc. The centerpiece could be a "bon voyage" basket of fruit and champagne. Have a piece of a cut-out map, depicting an exotic place, beside each plate. Each guest must tell how their life will be arranged during the year to make possible a visit to this "spot". The basket used as center piece would make a suitable "prize" for the best idea.

Limericks are another good place card idea. Write a suitable limerick for each guest, place at every plate and have your guests decide which is their appropriate place.

There once were two ladies who wrote
A cookbook most worthy of note;
Their husbands despair
The ladies don't care
Their lunch in a sack they now "tote"!

Early Riser's Punch

4 cups cranberry juice cocktail
1 cup water
½ of a 6-ounce can (1/3 cup) orange juice concentrate
6 inches stick cinnamon
1 750-milliliter bottle champagne, chilled

In a large saucepan combine cranberry juice cocktail, water, orange juice concentrate, and cinnamon sticks. Bring to boiling; boil, uncovered, for 5 minutes. Strain; cover and chill. Just before serving, pour cranberry mixture into a small punch bowl. Gradually pour the chilled champagne down the side of the bowl, stirring gently with an up-and-down motion.

Makes 18 (1/2 cup) servings.

Mushroom Bites

- 1 large onion, chopped
- ¾ pound mushrooms, chopped
- 1 tablespoon butter
- ¼ teaspoon salt
- Dash pepper
- 12 ounces cream cheese, softened
- ½ teaspoon Worcestershire sauce
- ¼ teaspoon garlic powder
- Dash Tabasco
- 1 loaf thin-sliced bread, crust trimmed
- Melted butter

Sauté onion and mushrooms in butter 2 minutes. Add salt and pepper. Set aside. Mix cream cheese in bowl, stir in onions and mushrooms, mixing until smooth. Add seasonings. Correct to taste. Let mixture sit at room temperature 1 hour. Flatten each slice of bread with rolling pin. Spread mushroom mixture on each slice and roll up tightly. Cover rolls and chill. Slice into bite-size pieces. Brush each slice with melted butter. Bake at 350° for 15 minutes.

These freeze wonderfully, reheat, if desired, before serving.

Romanoff Sauce

- 2 cups raisins
- 1 cup sour cream
- Vanilla
- 2 tablespoons brandy
- 1½ cups brown sugar
- 2 tablespoons cinnamon

Grind raisins. Stir in sour cream, brown sugar, vanilla, cinnamon. Mix well. Fold in 1 cup whipped cream. Serve over fresh fruit (sliced apples, pears, and pineapple chunks).

Gloria Tunnell shared this recipe with me and it is always a welcome treat.

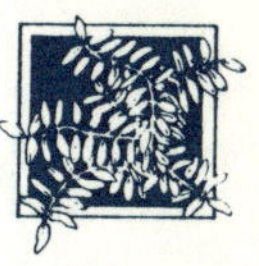

Cinnamon Crisps

1 cup butter
¾ cup sugar
2 cups flour
1 egg yolk and reserved white
4 teaspoons cinnamon
1 teaspoon vanilla
1 cup chopped pecans

Cream butter and sugar; stir in flour, egg yolk, cinnamon and vanilla. Mix well. Pat out on greased cookie sheet to ¼ inch thickness. With a fork, whip egg white just until foamy, spread over top of dough. Sprinkle chopped nuts over all and firmly press into dough. Bake at 350° for 30 minutes.

Remove from oven, allow to cool slightly and cut into fingers or bars while still warm. Store in tightly covered container. Will keep 2 weeks.

Makes 3 dozen.

Eggs in a Nest

2 pounds Cheddar cheese, grated
12 eggs
½ cup whipping cream
¼ cup Dijon mustard
Salt and cayenne pepper to taste

Butter a 3-quart casserole. Place cheese in dish, making a "nest" to hold each egg. Break eggs into nests. Mix cream, mustard, salt and pepper. Spoon mixture over each egg, coating well. Bake at 325° for 20 minutes.
Serves 12.

This can be assembled a day before baking and refrigerated. Return to room temperature before baking.

Artichoke Quiche

1 10-inch pie shell, baked 8 minutes
½ cup green onions, tops & bottoms, chopped
3 6½-ounce jars marinated artichoke hearts, drained and cut into pieces
4 eggs
1½ cups whipping cream
Dash nutmeg
Dash white pepper
1 teaspoon salt
½ teaspoon cayenne pepper
½ cup Swiss cheese, grated
6 tablespoons butter, divided

Prepare pie shell (see index) and bake 8 minutes. Set aside. Sauté onions in 2 tablespoons butter. Set aside. Beat eggs, cream and seasonings. Stir in onions and artichoke pieces. Correct seasonings. Pour into quiche shell. Sprinkle grated cheese over top and dot with remaining butter. Bake at 375° 25 to 30 minutes.

This quiche can be made ahead and frozen. Thaw completely and reheat 10 to 12 minutes.

Glazed Canadian Bacon

3 pounds Canadian bacon
½ cup brown sugar
1 tablespoon flour
½ teaspoon dry mustard
Dash of ground cloves
2 tablespoons water

Remove outer casing from bacon, if necessary. Place bacon in baking pan; bake, uncovered, at 350° 1½ hours. Combine sugar, flour, mustard and cloves; mix well. Stir in water. Brush half of mixture over bacon; bake at 350° 10 minutes. Brush with remaining glaze; bake an additional 5 minutes.
Serves 12.

Often leftover wine is not good for drinking, but is excellent for cooking. Refrigerate and use as needed.

Hawaiian Coffee Ring

1 package yeast
½ cup warm water
¼ cup butter
¼ cup sugar
2 eggs
½ cup evaporated milk
¼ cup warm water
1 teaspoon salt
3½ to 4 cups flour

Mix yeast and ½ cup warm water. Cream butter and sugar. Beat in eggs, milk, water and yeast mixture. Add 1½ cups flour, beat well. Let rise 30 minutes.

Add 2 to 2½ cups flour. Knead until smooth. Let rise 45 minutes. Divide dough in half. Press ¾ of one half into bottom of greased ring. Top with ½ of filling. Make roll of remaining ¼ dough. Press onto filling. Repeat with other half. Let rise 1 hour. Bake 350° for 30 minutes. Glaze while warm.

Filling

Combine ⅔ cup sugar, ½ cup coconut, ½ cup pecans, ½ cup soft butter, 2 tablespoons evaporated milk, 1 teaspoon vanilla and ½ teaspoon cinnamon.

Glaze

Combine 1½ cups powdered sugar, ½ teaspoon vanilla, ¼ cup nuts, 1 to 2 tablespoons evaporated milk.

A delicious recipe from Wanda Carter.

Cranberry Coffee Cake

1 cup butter (2 sticks)
1 cup sugar
2 eggs
2 cups flour
1 teaspoon baking powder
1 teaspoon soda
½ teaspoon salt
1 carton sour cream
1 teaspoon almond extract
1 can cranberry sauce
½ cup nuts

Cream butter, sugar and eggs; stir in dry ingredients alternately with sour cream. Spoon ½ mixture into greased tube pan. Spoon ½ of cranberry sauce over, repeat layers. Top with nuts. Bake at 350° for 1 hour. Drizzle glaze over the cake. For glaze mix together ¾ cup powdered sugar, ½ teaspoon almond extract and water to make desired thickness.

New Year's Day Dinner

SERVES TWELVE

Bourbon Punch

Mississippi Caviar (See index)

Nancy's Guacamole

Jalapeño Cheese Log

Cold Citrus Pork

Broccoli with Lemon Butter

Black Beans

Buttermilk Aspic

Mayonnaise Biscuits (Double recipe for twelve)

Hot Apple Cake with Caramel Rum Sauce

New Year's Day should be relaxed and fun for everyone. With this do-ahead menu (Except for the quick-to-prepare biscuits) the hostess can begin the New Year with a smile, too!

New Year's Dinner

Football dominates the day in most households! Cut a piece of green felt to fit your table. With white spray paint, mark off lines to resemble the yard lines on a football field. Place a bowl of large mums in center of the table in a brass or copper bowl. Use streamers to represent competing teams' colors. Paint the name of each guest on a miniature football to be used as "place cards".

Invitations could be in the form of a ticket. Cut different colored cardboard slightly larger than a college game ticket, using a variation of that wording (i.e., Admit Two — Kickoff time — address of hosts as "playing field," etc.)

Bourbon Punch

- ½ cup sugar
- 5 whole cloves
- 1 cinnamon stick
- 1 liter bourbon
- 1 cup apple brandy, such as applejack
- 1 cup orange liqueur, preferably Grand Marnier
- 1 tablespoon aromatic bitters
- 2 seedless oranges, cut in half and then into thin slices
- 1 lime, thinly sliced
- 1 apple, cut into 1-inch cubes
- ½ cup strong, hot black tea
- 2 cups club soda

In a small saucepan, combine the sugar with 1 cup of water. Bring to a boil over moderately low heat and cook, stirring to dissolve the sugar, for 5 minutes. Add the cloves and cinnamon stick, remove the syrup from the heat and let cool.

In a large punch bowl, combine the bourbon, apple brandy, orange liqueur, bitters, orange slices, lime slices, apple cubes and tea. Add the syrup and let stand, covered, for 30 minutes, or until cooled to room temperature. Before serving, add ice and pour in the soda.

20 Servings.

Nancy's Guacamole

- 8 ounces cream cheese
- 8 ounces sour cream
- 2 large or 4 small avocados, mashed
- 1 package Taco Seasoning
- 1 tablespoon picante sauce
- Dash Tabasco
- Dash garlic powder
- Dash onion salt

Mix above ingredients and spread on a platter. Top with shredded lettuce, chopped tomatoes, cheese and ripe olives, sliced. Serve with Doritos, etc. for dipping.

Nancy Lamberson served this when we visited in her home in Memphis, TN. It is excellent.

Take care to properly store and refrigerate all dressings and sauces, as well as other cooked foods. It takes only a short time for bacteria to form that can be much more costly than throwing away any food that you suspect of having been improperly refrigerated!

Jalapeño Cheese Log

¾ cup grated very sharp Cheddar cheese
¾ cup creamed pimento cheese
¾ cup creamed English cheese
6 ounces cream cheese
1 tablespoon grated onion
3 canned jalapeño peppers, chopped
1 clove garlic, crushed
1 cup chopped pecans

Leave sharp cheese and cream cheeses at room temperature until each is soft. Blend all ingredients well except nuts. Stir in nuts last and form into a log. Seal in wax paper and refrigerate for 2 days. Remove from refrigerator 3 hours before time to serve.

Cold Citrus Pork

2 cups sherry
2 cups fresh orange juice
1 cup fresh lemon juice
1 cup olive oil
4 teaspoons grated lemon peel
4 teaspoons dried marjoram, crumbled
2 teaspoons cumin seed
2 teaspoons ground ginger
4 bay leaves
4 boneless pork tenderloins (to equal 6½ pounds total)
Salt and freshly ground pepper
4 tablespoons (½ stick) butter
4 tablespoons red currant jelly
4 teaspoons Dijon mustard

Combine first 9 ingredients in large dish or plastic bag. Add pork and marinate 2 to 3 hours in refrigerator, turning pork over frequently. Preheat oven to 325°. Pat pork dry with paper towels (reserve marinade). Sprinkle with salt and pepper. Melt butter in Dutch oven or heavy roasting pan over medium heat. Add pork and brown on all sides, about 20 minutes. Add reserved marinade. Cover and bake, basting often, about 1¼ hours. Remove pork from cooking liquid and cool to room temperature. Wrap tightly in foil and refrigerate up to 2 days. Strain cooking liquid. Transfer to small covered dish and refrigerate. Just before serving, discard fat from surface of cooking liquid. Bring to simmer over medium heat. Stir in currant jelly and mustard. Remove from heat. Slice chilled pork and arrange on platter. Pour warm sauce over and serve.

Serves 12.

Broccoli with Lemon-Butter

2 bunches of broccoli
4 tablespoons butter
2 tablespoons fresh lemon juice
⅓ teaspoon salt
¼ teaspoon freshly ground pepper

Separate the broccoli into spears. Steam until crisp-tender, 8 to 10 minutes. In a small saucepan, warm the butter, lemon juice, salt and pepper over moderate heat, stirring until the butter melts. Transfer the broccoli to a serving bowl and pour the hot sauce over the broccoli.

The broccoli may be steamed a day ahead of serving and placed in a covered dish in the refrigerator. It is quickly re-heated in a microwave or heat in a saucepan, covered, without additional liquid just until hot. Sauce may also be made ahead and re-heated.

Black Beans with Sour Cream

1 pound dried black beans
1½ cups onion, coarsely chopped
2 large cloves garlic, minced
3 stalks celery, coarsely chopped
1 medium carrot, scraped and coarsely chopped
1½ tablespoons salt
½ teaspoon black pepper, freshly ground
2 bay leaves
¼ teaspoon oregano
1 tablespoon parsely, chopped
Dash cayenne
4 tablespoons butter
4 ounces dark rum

Rinse beans and pick over. Place in large kettle, add water to cover. Cover and bring quickly to full boil. Remove from heat and let stand, covered, for 1 hour. Add next 9 ingredients and more water to cover, bring back to a boil and simmer, covered, over low heat for 2 hours, stirring occasionally. Correct seasoning and if desired, a bit of cayenne can be added.

Remove bay leaves and turn bean mixture into a 3 quart casserole. Stir in butter and 2 ounces dark rum. Mix thoroughly. Cover and bake in preheated 350° oven for 1 hour or more, until beans are thoroughly tender. Remove from oven and stir in 2 ounces dark rum. Serve with side dish of sour cream as topping.

Serves 12.

Buttermilk Aspic

- 2 envelopes unflavored gelatin
- ½ cup cold water
- ½ cup boiling water
- 2 cups buttermilk
- 2 teaspoons salt
- 1 tablespoon lemon juice
- 2 teaspoons sugar
- ½ teaspoon Worcestershire sauce
- 1 cup catsup
- 1 tablespoon grated onion
- 1 cup finely chopped celery

Soften gelatin in cold water for 5 minutes. Add boiling water and stir until gelatin is dissolved; then cool to room temperature. Combine the buttermilk, salt, lemon juice, sugar, Worcestershire sauce, catsup, and onion. Add gelatin and blend well. Chill to consistency of honey; fold in chopped celery. Spoon into a 1½-quart ring mold; chill until firm.

Mayonnaise Biscuits

- 1 cup sifted, self-rising flour
- 3 tablespoons mayonnaise
- ½ cup milk

Preheat oven to 450°. Combine all of the ingredients and stir until moistened. Spoon into well-greased muffin tins. Fill ⅔ full. Bake 10 to 15 minutes. Butter tops and insides.

Makes 6 to 8.

Educate your taste buds! Learn to detect special flavors in a dish. The benefit is twofold: you will recognize a spice or distinctive flavor and be able to add it to a like dish that you want to prepare and you will also be able to adjust the amount of a particular ingredient to better suit your taste. Let young children learn about spices, too. If they are encouraged to grow some herbs in the kitchen window, are given the responsibility of cutting the amount needed in a recipe, and allowed to stir them in, you will be amazed at their willingness to try new tastes.

Hot Apple Cake with Caramel Rum Sauce

Cake

- 1 cup (2 sticks) butter, room temperature
- 1 cup sugar
- 2 eggs, beaten
- 1½ cups all-purpose flour
- 1 teaspoon freshly grated nutmeg
- 1 teaspoon cinnamon
- 1 teaspoon baking soda
- ½ teaspoon salt
- 3 medium-size tart apples, cored and finely chopped
- ¾ cup chopped walnuts
- 1 teaspoon vanilla
- Vanilla ice cream (optional)

Preheat oven to 350°. Grease 10-inch pie plate and set aside. Cream butter with sugar in large bowl. Add eggs and beat well. Sift flour, spices, soda and salt. Blend into butter mixture. Add apple, nuts and vanilla and mix thoroughly. Pour into prepared pie plate. Bake until lightly browned, about 45 minutes. Serve warm topped with vanilla ice cream and Caramel Rum Sauce.

Make two cakes and sauce to serve twelve.

Rum Sauce

- ½ cup sugar
- ½ cup firmly packed brown sugar
- ½ cup whipping cream
- ½ cup (1 stick) butter
- ¼ cup rum

Combine sugars and cream in top of double boiler. Set over gently simmering water and cook 1½ hours, replenishing water in bottom of double boiler as necessary. Add butter and continue cooking 30 minutes. Remove from heat and beat well. Add rum and blend thoroughly. Serve warm. Cake and sauce can be prepared ahead and reheated before serving.

Makes 1 cup.

When flattening bread slices for appetizers or party sandwiches, steam slices of bread in a colander over boiling water for a few minutes or heat briefly in microwave oven. Bread will roll easily without tearing.

VALENTINE TEA

SERVES THIRTY

Hot Spiced Wine or Wine Punch

Sweetheart Punch

Coffee

Ham-filled Sandwiches

Chicken-Almond Sandwiches

Celery Swirls

Avocado-Stuffed Cherry Tomatoes

Minted Pecans or Deviled Pecans

Silver Tray filled with

White Chocolate Cake Squares

Red Cake Squares

or

Sno-Ball Cake

(Make Three)

Valentine Tea

Sweetheart roses, Baby's breath and Violets in a large cut glass bowl will set an elegant air for this tea. Surround the bowl with heart-shaped boxes of any size or material—from treasured candy boxes to fine antiques.

A lace cloth is always appropriate and paper napkins in the colors of the flowers will complete a beautiful table.

If you know far enough in advance that you will be giving this tea, arrange with your florist for a branch of a flowering tree to be forced into bloom. Set the branch into a thick piece of Styrofoam and place in a silver or crystal bowl. Crush a piece of velvet, in a color to compliment your table to cover the Styrofoam. You may want to add tiny velvet bows and hearts (cut from cardboard and covered with the velvet) if the blooms are too scattered.

Hot Spiced Wine

8 cups water
2 cups sugar
24 whole cloves
12 whole allspice
8 1-inch sticks cinnamon
1 teaspoon ground ginger
Rind of 2 oranges
Rind of 2 lemons
4 cups orange juice
2 cups lemon juice
2 bottles (750ml) Burgundy wine

In saucepan, combine water, sugar, spices and rinds. Bring to boil, stirring until sugar dissolves. Simmer 15 minutes, remove from heat and let stand 1 hour. Strain and add juices and wine. Reheat before serving. May be made several days ahead.

Serves 30.

Cold Wine Punch

Cranberry juice, chilled
Chablis wine, chilled
Ginger ale, chilled

Use equal parts of juice, wine and ginger ale. Pour into punch bowl as needed.

Sweetheart Punch

½ gallon raspberry sherbet
½ gallon lime sherbet
4 29-ounce bottles ginger ale, chilled
1 28-ounce bottle club soda, chilled
1 46-ounce can pineapple juice, chilled
1 6-ounce bottle maraschino cherries

Mix all ingredients together in large container. Make ice ring by freezing some of punch in ring mold. When ring is partially frozen (still slushy) arrange more maraschino cherries and cover with small amount of punch. Freeze solid.

Filling for Ham Sandwiches

½ pound ground ham
1 8-ounce package cream cheese
4 tablespoons mayonnaise
1 tablespoon chopped green onion, tops and bottoms
1 tablespoon Dijon mustard
Whole wheat bread
Additional mayonnaise
Chopped parsley

Mix all filling ingredients, adding enough mayonnaise to bind filling. With biscuit cutter, cut 50 rounds from thin-sliced whole wheat bread. Spread filling on half of rounds, top with remaining rounds. Stack 4 or 5 sandwiches together. Spread sides evenly with additional mayonnaise. Roll sides of stack in chopped parsley. Separate into individual sandwiches. Chill until serving time.

Filling for Chicken Sandwiches

½ pound cooked chicken, ground or finely chopped
2 ribs celery, minced finely
Dash curry powder
Salt and pepper to taste
4 tablespoons mayonnaise
Thin-sliced white bread
Additional mayonnaise
1 cup toasted almonds, finely chopped

Mix all filling ingredients, adding enough mayonnaise to bind filling. With biscuit cutter, cut 50 rounds from thin-sliced white bread. Spread filling on half of the rounds, top with remaining rounds. Stack 4 to 5 sandwiches together. Spread sides evenly with mayonnaise. Roll sides of stacks in chopped almonds. Separate into individual sandwiches. Chill until serving time.

Celery Swirls

3 bunches celery
3 8-ounce packages cream cheese
1½ cups sharp Cheddar cheese, grated
3 tablespoons green onion, tops and bottoms, chopped
3 cloves garlic, minced
Salt and cayenne pepper to taste
3 tablespoons half-and-half

Separate celery into ribs; cut all ribs into 3 inch pieces. Combine remaining ingredients and blend thoroughly. Fill each rib of celery with mixture. Press 3 filled ribs together with cheese toward center. Secure each bundle with a rubber band. Chill overnight. When ready to serve, remove rubber banks, slice each bundle into ½ inch slices.

Serves 30.

Avocado Stuffed Cherry Tomatoes

30 large cherry tomatoes
Salt
2 ripe avocados
2 tablespoons sour cream
2 tablespoons chopped parsley
4 teaspoons lime juice
2 teaspoons lemon juice
2 teaspoons chopped chives
½ teaspoon salt
¼ teaspoon Tabasco
¼ teaspoon sugar

Carefully slice tops off tomatoes and scoop out seeds and pulp. (A small melon-baller works well for this.) Sprinkle inside of shells with salt, invert and drain on paper towels 45 minutes to 1 hour. Mash avocados with remaining ingredients, blending well. Fill tomato shells with avocado mixture. Cover with plastic wrap and chill until serving time. Double this recipe to serve 30.

Serves 15.

Minted Pecans

1 cup sugar
¼ cup water
3 tablespoons plus 1 teaspoon white Karo
2 tablespoons butter
6 large marshmallows, cut in pieces
¼ teaspoon peppermint extract
3 cups pecan halves

Combine sugar, water, Karo and butter in saucepan. Bring to boil over medium heat, cook to soft ball stage. Remove from heat, stir in marshmallows and extract. Stir until creamy. Stir in pecans until well coated. Pour out onto greased cookie sheet. Using two forks, separate pecans as quickly as possible.

Allow to cool. Store in freezer when dry.

Deviled Pecans

½ cup butter, melted
3 cups pecan halves
2 tablespoons Worcestershire sauce
½ teaspoon Tabasco
1 teaspoon salt
Garlic powder to taste

Combine all ingredients and bake 20 minutes at 350°, stirring often. Drain on paper towels.

White Chocolate Cake

- ⅓ cup white chocolate, cut in small pieces
- ½ cup hot water
- 1 cup butter
- 1½ cups sugar
- 4 egg yolks, unbeaten
- 1 teaspoon vanilla extract
- 2½ cups sifted cake flour
- 1 teaspoon baking soda
- 1 cup buttermilk
- 4 egg whites, stiffly beaten

Melt white chocolate in hot water; allow to cool. Cream butter and sugar together until light and fluffy. Add egg yolks, one at a time, beating well after each addition. Add melted white chocolate and vanilla.

Sift flour and baking soda together and add alternately with buttermilk to creamed mixture. Gently fold in stiffly beaten egg whites. Pour into 3 greased and floured 9-inch layer pans. Bake 30 to 35 minutes in preheated 350° oven. Cool

White Chocolate Frosting

- ½ cup plus 2 tablespoons sugar
- 6 tablespoons evaporated milk
- ¼ cup butter
- 2 cups white chocolate, cut into small pieces
- 1½ teaspoons vanilla extract
- Slivered toasted almonds or other nuts for garnish

Combine sugar, milk, and butter in a saucepan. Bring mixture to full rolling boil and boil 1 minute. Remove from heat and add white chocolate and vanilla. Stir until candy is melted; beat until smooth and of spreading consistency. Frost cake and garnish with nuts.

Red Cake

½ cup butter
1½ cups sugar
2 whole eggs
1½ ounces red food coloring
2 level tablespoons cocoa
1 scant teaspoon salt
1 teaspoon soda
2½ cups cake flour
1 cup buttermilk
2 tablespoons vanilla extract

Cream the butter and sugar; add the eggs, and cream until well blended. Mix the food coloring and cocoa and add to the creamed mixture. Sift salt, soda, and cake flour. Add dry ingredients and liquids alternately to creamed mixture. Fold; do not beat. Bake in 3 9-inch greased and floured cake pans at 350° for 30 to 35 minutes. Cool.

Icing

6 tablespoons flour
1 cup water
1 cup butter
1 cup granulated sugar
1 teaspoon vanilla extract
⅛ teaspoon red food coloring, if desired

Cook the flour and water until slightly clear. Cool completely. Cream the butter, sugar, and vanilla, and add to cool flour mixture. Beat with electric beater until light and fluffy. Add food coloring if desired. Frost the cake.

White Chocolate and Red Cakes

Mix each batter as recipes direct but bake each in sheet cake pans. When cool, spread with frostings. Cut each cake into small squares when ready to serve and arrange alternately on serving platter.

You may freeze the squares after cutting. Thaw completely before serving.

Sno-Ball Cake

1 large angel food cake, broken in pieces
2 packages unflavored gelatin
4 tablespoons cold water
1 cup sugar
1 cup boiling water
1 #2 can crushed pineapple, undrained
1 bottle maraschino cherries, well drained and chopped
1 teaspoon lemon juice
1 cup chopped pecans
1 cup coconut
2 packages Dream Whip
1 additional package Dream Whip
Additional coconut

Soften gelatin in cold water; add boiling water and stir until dissolved. Mix in separate bowl: sugar, pineapple, cherries, lemon juice, coconut, and pecans. Stir in dissolved gelatin. Chill until thickened but not set. Mix 2 packages of Dream Whip as package directs and fold into chilled gelatin mixture. Put ½ of the pieces of angel food cake into a tube pan with a removable bottom. Pour ½ of gelatin mixture over, repeat layers. Chill several hours or overnight until cake is set. Remove from pan and place on serving plate or tray. Whip the remaining package of Dream Whip and frost cake. Sprinkle with additional coconut. Return to refrigerator, covered, until serving time. Will freeze up to 3 months.

This is a beautiful dessert to serve for a party and is especially nice because it can be made several days (or months, if freezing) ahead of serving. Its main attraction for me, however, is because it was given to me by Faye Ashby, my delightful step-mother.

ST. PATRICK'S DAY COFFEE

SERVES TWENTY

Melon Magic   Delta Mint Tea

Avocado Fingers

Mock Cheese Blintzes (Tint the Cheese Green)

Crunchy Cheese Ball
(Use pistachio nuts for this party)

Shamrock Dip with Assorted Crackers

Bunches of Green Grapes with
Dishes of Sour Cream and Brown Sugar
for dipping

Green Peppermint Meltaways
Butterscotch Shortbread
Coffee

St. Patricks Day Coffee

Cut shamrocks from green felt. On half, glue green glitter over the surface. Glue one plain and one "jeweled" shamrock together, placing a small green stick between each. Attach it with glue to one of the halves before sticking down the other. When glue has dried, stick the shamrocks into a piece of Styrofoam, cut to fit a brass bowl. You can find a mossy-type filler at the florist shop to cover the Styrofoam.

Melon Magic

1 gallon vanilla ice cream
1 cup Midori melon liqueur
¾ cup white crème de cacao

Combine liqueurs and ice cream in blender in batches. Blend until smooth. Serve in small punch cups or in stemmed glasses. If honeydew melons and fresh strawberries are available, skewer a chunk of melon and a strawberry and serve as garnish for each glass.
Serves 20.

Delta Mint Tea

8 tea bags
12 sprigs mint
Rind of 3 lemons
8 cups boiling water
Juice of 7 lemons
2 cups sugar
8 cups cool water

Steep tea, mint and lemon rind in boiling water for 12 minutes. Remove from water. Add juice and sugar. Strain, add cool water. Makes 1 gallon. Garnish with fresh mint.

Avocado Fingers

1 ripe avocado
¼ teaspoon salt
⅛ teaspoon paprika
1 teaspoon lemon juice
Toast strips
Bacon strips

Mash avocado; add salt, paprika, and lemon juice. Spread on 1×3-inch toast strips. Place narrow strips of bacon over avocado. Broil until bacon crisps.

Serves 24.

Mock Cheese Blintzes

2 loaves very thin-sliced white bread
1 pound cream cheese
2 egg yolks
½ cup sugar
¾ cup melted butter
6 tablespoons brown sugar
1½ teaspoon cinnamon

Trim crusts from bread and roll very thin. Cream the cheese, egg yolks, and ½ cup sugar. Spread each flattened slice of bread with cheese mixture; roll like a jelly roll. Combine melted butter, brown sugar and cinnamon. Dip each roll in this mixture and place in buttered baking dish. Bake at 350° for 20 minutes.

May be made ahead and reheated.

Crunchy Cheese Ball

1 package (8-ounce) cream cheese, softened
¼ cup mayonnaise
2 cups ground cooked ham
2 tablespoons chopped parsley
1 teaspoon minced onion
¼ teaspoon dry mustard
¼ teaspoon hot pepper sauce
½ cup chopped peanuts or pistachio nuts

Beat cream cheese and mayonnaise until smooth. Stir in next 5 ingredients. Cover; chill several hours. Form into ball; roll in nuts to coat. Serve with crackers.

Shamrock Dip

1 cup sour cream
1 cup mayonnaise
1 tablespoon onion
1 tablespoon dill weed
1 tablespoon parsley
1 teaspoon Beau Monde

Mix together until well blended. Chill. Serve with assorted crackers.

Green Peppermint Meltaways

1 cup butter
½ cup sifted powdered sugar
1 teaspoon peppermint extract
2¼ cups cake flour
Dash salt
Few drops green food coloring

Mix butter, powdered sugar and peppermint. Add flour and salt, mixing well. Drop by teaspoonfuls on ungreased baking sheet. Bake at 400° 7 to 8 minutes.

Yield: 5 dozen.

Butterscotch Shortbread

1 cup butter
½ cup brown sugar
¼ cup granulated sugar
2¼ cups flour
1 teaspoon salt

Mix butter and sugars thoroughly. Stir in flour and salt. Mix well. Roll out on floured surface ¼ inch thick. Cut in desired shaped. Place on ungreased cookie sheet. Bake at 300° 20 to 25 minutes.

Yield: 7 dozen.

EASTER DINNER

SERVES SIXTEEN

Zucchini Squares
Cold Blueberry Soup
Glazed Ham
Delux Vegetables
Baked Corn Pudding
Wined Fruit
Jiffy Rolls
Fresh Coconut Cake

Easter Dinner

Spray a small branch white or any suitable, soft color. Let dry completely. Cut a piece of Styrofoam that is thick enough to hold the branch into a large rectangle. Stick the branch firmly into the Styrofoam. Cover with green "Easter egg grass". With cardboard, glue, and bits of lace, material and trim, create variously shaped and decorated tiny hats. This is an excellent project for children 6 to 10 and you will be amazed at the different "designs" that you will have. Attach a piece of thread to each hat and hang it on the branch.

Zucchini Squares

3 cups shredded zucchini squash
1 cup Bisquick
¾ cup chopped onion
¾ cup grated sharp Cheddar cheese
¼ cup Parmesan cheese
2 tablespoons parsley
½ teaspoon salt
½ teaspoon seasoned salt
½ teaspoon oregano
Pepper to taste
½ cup oil
4 eggs slightly beaten
2 cloves garlic, grated

Mix all ingredients well. Bake in a 9×11 baking dish at 350° for 30 to 35 minutes.

Melinda Thompson Hampton, my daughter, shared this excellent recipe. It freezes wonderfully and the squares can be reheated.

Cold Blueberry Soup

6 cups blueberries
5 cups water
1 cup sugar
2 medium lemons, thinly sliced
1 3-inch cinnamon stick
½ teaspoon freshly grated nutmeg
¼ teaspoon allspice
4½ cups sour cream
1 cup dry red wine

Combine blueberries, water, sugar, lemon and spices in large saucepan and bring to boil over high heat. Reduce heat to medium-low and simmer for 15 minutes.

Strain mixture into large bowl, discarding cinnamon stick and lemon peel. Cover and chill thoroughly. Just before serving, whisk in sour cream and wine.

Glazed Ham

8 to 10 pound fully cooked, boneless ham

Cook ham as label directs. 30 minutes before ham is done, spread with ½ of glaze. Bake 15 minutes. Baste again, return to oven for final 15 minutes, basting every 5 minutes, using all of glaze.

Glaze

1 cup bourbon
1 cup brown sugar, firmly packed
¼ teaspoon cloves
1 teaspoon grated orange peel

Combine all ingredients, stirring until sugar is dissolved.

Serves 16.

Delux Vegetables

- 4 cups Italian breadcrumbs
- 2 cans artichoke hearts, drained and cut up
- 2 cans French-sliced green beans, drained
- 4 hard boiled eggs, chopped
- 1 cup Romano or Parmesan cheese, grated
- 2 cups Wishbone Italian Salad Dressing

Combine all ingredients, mixing well to moisten bread crumbs. Place in 2 greased Pyrex dishes and bake, uncovered, at 350° for 20 minutes.

Can be frozen; thaw before baking.

Serves 16.

Baked Corn Pudding

- 3 17-ounce cans whole kernel corn, drained
- 3 cups milk
- 4 eggs, beaten
- 1 teaspoon salt
- ½ teaspoon pepper
- 4 tablespoons sugar
- 1 stick butter

Combine all ingredients except butter. Place in a well-greased shallow baking dish. Butter should be dotted on top. Bake at 375° for 30 to 35 minutes. Serve hot.

Serves 16.

Wined Fruit

1 6-ounce and 1 3-ounce package raspberry gelatin
3 cups boiling water
1½ cups port wine
1 large can crushed pineapple, drained
¾ cup pecans, chopped
1½ cups celery, chopped

Dissolve both packages gelatin in boiling water. Cool until slightly thickened, stir in remaining ingredients. Pour into large mold that has been greased with mayonnaise or into 9×13-inch Pyrex dish. Chill until firm. Serve on lettuce leaves. If you use the Pyrex dish you will need to cut smaller squares to serve 16; however, this is a very rich salad and a small serving is adequate.

Serves 16.

Jiffy Rolls

2 packages dry yeast
1 cup warm water
⅓ cup salad oil
1½ tablespoon sugar
2 teaspoon salt
1 egg, well beaten
3 to 3½ cups flour

Soften the yeast in warm water. Stir in oil, sugar, salt, and egg. Stir in flour, one cup at a time, until soft dough is formed. Turn out onto lightly floured surface and knead until smooth, adding a small amount of flour as needed to keep dough from being sticky. Cover dough with clean towel and let rest 15 minutes. Roll dough out into rectangle, brush surface with melted butter, and roll up as jelly roll and slice into pieces about 1 inch thick. Place each piece in buttered muffin tins, cover and let rise 30 minutes. Bake at 400° 10 to 12 minutes or until lightly browned. Take pans from oven and brush with melted butter.

Yield 1½ to 2 dozen.

This is about the quickest and most successful roll recipe I've used. The dough doesn't hold well like a refrigerator roll, but this one is excellent for a make-and-serve roll.

Fresh Coconut Cake

1 cup butter
2 cups sugar
5 eggs
1 teaspoon soda
Dash salt
2¾ cups cake flour
1 teaspoon baking powder
1 cup buttermilk
1 teaspoon vanilla extract
½ to ¾ teaspoon coconut flavoring
White Frosting Supreme - recipe doubled
2 cups fresh grated coconut

Cream butter and sugar until perfectly smooth (about 15 minutes on electric mixer). Add eggs, beating well after each addition. Sift dry ingredients together and add to creamed mixture alternately with buttermilk. Stir in vanilla and coconut flavoring. Bake in 3 or 4 greased and floured round 9-inch layer cake pans (number you use will depend on whether you like 3 thick layers or 4 thinner layers). Bake at 350° for about 25 minutes or until layers test done. Cool and frost. Sprinkle with coconut.

We also like this cake with the lemon filling between the layers. See Index or Memorial Day Cookout.

White Frosting Supreme

½ cup water
2¼ cups sugar
3 tablespoons white Karo
3 egg whites
2½ tablespoons powdered sugar

In large saucepan, mix water, sugar, and Karo. Bring slowly to a boil over medium heat, stirring constantly, until sugar is dissolved. Cook to 238° on candy thermometer or soft ball stage, without stirring. While syrup is cooking, beat egg whites until stiff but not dry. Slowly add syrup to beaten whites, continuing to beat as you pour. Beat until the mixture is the consistency of whipped cream. Add the powdered sugar and beat until well blended.

This recipe doubles easily for large cakes. It is the best and most successful white icing I have every used—tastes just like divinity! It adapts to any additional flavoring you might want to use which may be added with the powdered sugar.

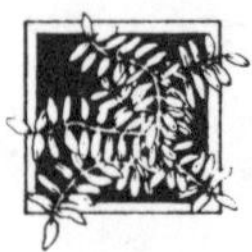

DERBY DAY PARTY

FRIENDS GATHER TO WATCH THE KENTUCKY DERBY

SERVES THIRTY

Avocado Logs
Cocktail Cheese Cake
Exotic Chicken Balls
Curried Catfish Stuffed Eggs
Fresh Strawberries with Powdered Sugar

Assorted Fresh Vegetables
with Curry Dip
and/or Zucchini Dip

Cheese Logs
Salted Pecans
Good Luck Tarts
Mint Juleps

Derby Day Party

The mood of this early May afternoon party is one of informality and fun. For an interesting centerpiece, either make or purchase a topiary horse. He can be "planted" with greenery either before or after the party because you will enjoy him on the porch or patio all year long. Before placing him on the table, put a "winner's circle" of red roses (real or silk) around his neck. Stand him on a runner or tray that coordinates with your serving trays, plates, and napkins.

Invitations can be like a racing form, listing the hosts as Stable Owners; for the address use "Track Name"; Starting Time; list of horses running (these are usually found in the newspaper well ahead of Derby Day), and any other information necessary, using track or racing terms whenever possible. If more than one couple is hosting the party, and these are listed as "Stable Owners", give one phone number as "Bookie to Contact" for R.S.V.P.'s. Your local printer can do these on different colored "flier" sheets of paper like are used at the races.

Avocado Logs

1 cup mashed avocado
1½ cups dry-roasted cashew nuts, chopped
8 ounces cream cheese, softened
½ cup sharp Cheddar cheese, grated
2 teaspoons lime juice
1 garlic clove, crushed and minced
½ teaspoon Worcestershire sauce
½ teaspoon salt
Dash Tabasco
Paprika

Combine all ingredients except paprika, and mix well. Cover mixture and refrigerate 30 minutes. Divide mixture in half and shape each into roll. Sprinkle waxed paper with paprika, turning roll to cover with paprika. Wrap each roll in foil and refrigerate until ready to serve. Slice and serve with crackers.

May be made up to 2 days ahead of serving.
Yield: 2 logs

Cocktail Cheese Cake

¼ stick butter, melted
¾ cup Ritz crackers, crushed
½ cup pimento stuffed green olives, chopped
2 ribs celery, chopped
4 green onions, tops and bottoms, chopped
2 tablespoons lemon juice
1 teaspoon salt
1 teaspoon Worcestershire sauce
2 cups sour cream
1 pound cream cheese, softened
Dash Tabasco

Mix the cracker crumbs with the butter and press mixture into greased 9-inch spring-form pan, reserving ¼ cup for topping. Combine remaining ingredients and mix until well blended. Spread mixture over cracker crust. Sprinkle remaining crumbs over top. Cover and refrigerate overnight. When ready to serve remove spring-form and place cake, still on pan bottom, on serving platter. Garnish with lettuce leaves or parsley. Serve with asssorted crackers.
Serves 30.

Exotic Chicken Balls

8 ounces cream cheese, softened
1 cup chicken, chopped fine
1 cup almonds, chopped fine
2 tablespoons mayonnaise
1 tablespoon chutney
1 tablespoon curry powder
½ teaspoon seasoned salt
Coconut or parsley

Mix all ingredients and form into small balls. Chill mixture. Roll in grated coconut or parsley. Chill until ready to serve, covered. These may be made 2 to 3 days in advance.
Yield: 52.

Curried Catfish Stuffed Eggs

3 cups flaked catfish
12 hard-cooked eggs
1 cup mayonnaise or salad dressing
2 tablespoons cider vinegar
¼ cup sweet pickle relish
2 tablespoons finely minced onion
½ teaspoon curry powder
1 teaspoon salt
Chopped parsley

Combine mayonnaise, vinegar, pickle relish, onion, curry powder and salt. Blend well. Fold in flaked catfish. Cut eggs in half lengthwise and remove yolks. Put egg yolks through sieve. Blend yolks with fish mixture. Place fish mixture in egg whites. Garnish with chopped parsley. Makes 24 canapés.

Flaked Catfish

1½ pounds catfish fillets, fresh or frozen
1 quart boiling water
1 tablespoon salt

Boiled:
Thaw frozen fillets. Place fillets in boiling salted water. Cover and return to the boiling point. Reduce heat and simmer for 10 minutes or until fish flakes easily when tested with a fork. Drain and flake.

Steamed:
Thaw frozen fillets. Place fillets on a rack over boiling water; sprinkle with salt. Cover and steam for 10 minutes or until fish flake easily when tested with a fork. Drain and flake.

You won't believe how good these are until you've tried them. Any firm fish can be used but catfish is best.

Assorted Fresh Vegetables

Line a round basket with red-tipped lettuce leaves. Put fresh mushrooms, bell pepper strips, cherry tomatoes, carrot sticks, celery sticks, fresh broccoli and fresh cauliflower cut into flowerets on the lettuce. Alternate colors. Put one or two hollowed-out bell peppers in the center to hold the dip or dips.

Curry Dip for Fresh Vegetables

- 2 cloves garlic, minced
- 1 pint mayonnaise
- 6 tablespoons catsup
- 2 tablespoons Worcestershire sauce
- 3 teaspoons curry powder
- 3 teaspoons minced onions
- ½ teaspoon salt
- 2 teaspoons Tabasco
- 2 teaspoons horseradish

Combine all ingredients thoroughly and chill. Serve with assorted vegetables to dip. Will keep covered in refrigerator 2 weeks.

Zucchini Dip for Fresh Vegetables

- 1 cup grated sharp Cheddar cheese
- 1 cup grated zucchini
- ¾ cup mayonnaise
- ½ cup chopped pecans
- 1 teaspoon fresh lemon juice

Combine cheese, zucchini, mayonnaise, pecans and lemon juice in medium bowl. Refrigerate 1 hour or overnight. Transfer to serving dish.

Cheese Logs

- 1 8-ounce package very sharp New York cheese, grated
- 1 8-ounce package Cheddar cheese, grated
- 1 8-ounce package cream cheese
- 1 6-ounce package Old English Cheese
- 1 6-ounce roll garlic cheese
- ½ teaspoon cayenne pepper
- ½ teaspoon salt
- 2 tablespoons mayonnaise
- 1 clove garlic, minced

Have all ingredients at room temperature. Mix all ingredients well. Shape into four 5-inch logs. Sprinkle paprika heavily on waxed paper. Roll logs in paprika until completely covered. Wrap logs tightly in foil and refrigerate. Serve with assorted crackers.

Yield: 4 Logs.

The logs may be frozen for one month or refrigerated in plastic bags for one week.

Good Luck Tarts

Crust

1½ cups flour
½ cup shortening
Dash salt
1 teaspoon sugar
⅓ cup ice water
1 egg yolk

Mix flour, salt and sugar. Cut shortening into dry mixture with a pastry cutter. Beat egg yolk with ice water and add to mixture 1 tablespoon at a time. Put into miniature muffin pans.

Filling

½ cup flour
1 cup sugar
2 eggs, beaten
1 stick butter, melted
½ cup pecans
1 cup chocolate chips
1 teaspoon vanilla
Bourbon

Mix flour and sugar, add the eggs, then the melted butter. Add the pecans, chocolate chips, and vanilla. Pour into shells and bake at 350° for 20 minutes. Brush tarts with bourbon while hot.

Yield: 36 miniature tarts.

Mint Juleps

1 ounce mint syrup
2 ounces bourbon

Mix syrup and bourbon in a julep cup. Add crushed ice and stir till glass frosts. Garnish with fresh mint.

Makes 1 Mint Julep.

Mint Syrup

2½ cups water
2 cups sugar
6 lemons, juiced
2 oranges, grated peel and juice
4 large handfuls of mint

Wash and clean mint well. Dissolve sugar in water and boil together for ten minutes. Pour hot syrup over fruit juices and mint. Cover and let steep several hours. Strain. Pour in jars and refrigerate. This keeps well several weeks. Use in iced tea, mixed drinks, or freeze to a slush and serve in sherbet glasses.

Makes 30 Mint Juleps.

MEMORIAL DAY COOKOUT

SERVES EIGHT

Mexican Spread

Smoked Chicken Halves

Stuffed Potatoes

Green Bean Casserole

Raspberry Salad

Cheese-Filled Bread

Chocolate Cake

or

Lemon Tarts

Memorial Day Cookout

Hurricane lamps twined with English ivy will provide a lovely atmosphere for this party. Use basket holders, but instead of paper plates have foil pie plates. The green bean casserole and the raspberry salad can be made using the individual foil containers that would fit on the pie plates. Have a variety of colored hand towels, folded in long rolls, standing upright in a basket, to be used for napkins.

Mexican Spread

1 can refried beans
3 chopped green chilies
3 chopped green onions
2 chopped tomatoes
1 cup grated Cheddar cheese
1 can guacamole frozen dip
8 ounces sour cream

Layer the above ingredients on a plate or platter. Serve with tortilla chips.

This is another of Becky McLeary's good appetizer recipes. It is one she used a lot while living in Memphis, TN.

Smoked Chicken

8 chicken halves
Lawry's seasoned salt

Wash the chicken halves and season generously with Lawry's seasoned salt. Refrigerate overnight. Cook on an outdoor smoker using 10 pounds of charcoal, a full pan of water, and 4 to 6 hickory or mesquite chips which have been soaked in water for one hour. Cook for 4 hours. Don't peek!

Serves 8.

This is Jim Corder's very favorite recipe for outdoor cooking. He always gets raves when we serve this. We reommend using the smallest chickens your butcher has, preferably ones that have never been frozen. Everybody will eat a chicken half, so have plenty!

Stuffed Baked Potatoes

6 baking potatoes
1 stick butter
4 ounces sharp Cheddar cheese
3 pods garlic, minced
1 cup light cream
½ cup green onions, chopped

Bake potatoes at 400° for 1 hour. While potatoes bake, make a sauce of butter, cheese, garlic and cream. Cut potatoes in half lengthwise and scoop out. Put potatoes in mixer bowl and mash with the sauce. Add green onions. Put mixture back in the potato shells and bake at 350° until hot. These freeze well.

Serves 12.

Jo Wilson, my sister-in-law, gave me this recipe, which is a favorite in her family.

Green Bean Casserole

2 cans French cut green beans
1 can sliced water chestnuts
1 can mushroom soup
1 roll Kraft Jalapeño cheese
Dash Worcestershire sauce
1 can French fried onion rings

Heat soup and cheese and stir together until the cheese melts. Mix all ingredients except onion rings and bake at 350° for 30 minutes. Top with onion rings and bake 10 more minutes.
Serves 8.

This recipe was given to me by my sister, Kitty Pegram, when she was a new bride. It has become a family favorite of ours.

Raspberry Salad

2 packages frozen red raspberries
2 packages red raspberry gelatin
2 tablespoons lemon juice
½ cup applesauce

Dissolve gelatin in 2 cups boiling water. Pour over frozen raspberries. Stir until thawed and slightly thickened. Stir in lemon juice and applesauce. Pour into mold or Pyrex dish and refrigerate until set. (1 cup chopped nuts or celery may be added with applesauce.) Before serving top with dressing.

Dressing

Mix 1 cup minature marshmallows with 1 cup sour cream. Allow to stand in refrigerator several hours, stirring frequently, until marshmallows have dissolved.

Mrs. Janice Dinkins, from Charleston, MS is a wonderful cook as well as a popular baby nurse in the Mississippi Delta.

Bread

1 package dry yeast
¼ cup warm water
½ cup melted butter
1 cup scalded milk
⅓ cup sugar
1 teaspoon salt
2 eggs, well beaten
5 to 5½ cups flour

Soften yeast in warm water. Scald milk; add butter, sugar, and salt. Cool to lukewarm. Stir in eggs and yeast mixture. Stir in flour, one cup at a time, to form a fairly stiff dough. (You should never add more flour than the dough can absorb. This is one cause for tough bread. If the dough is too sticky, correct by adding more flour as you are kneading.) Turn out onto a lightly floured surface and knead until dough is smooth. Place in greased bowl and turn to grease top. Cover and let rise in warm place until doubled in bulk, about 1 hour. Punch down dough and divide in half Shape into two loaves, place in greased loaf pans, cover and let rise again until almost doubled, about 30 to 45 minutes. Bake 30 minutes at 350°. Remove from oven, brush tops with additional melted butter.

This bread freezes well and is also excellent toasted. I have used this bread recipe more than any other and it is always dependable.

Cheese-Filled Bread

1 recipe of Bread dough
Melted butter
¼ cup mayonnaise
2 cups grated cheese; Cheddar, Monterey Jack, or combination both
½ cup green onion, tops and bottoms, chopped
1 small can chopped ripe olives, well drained
1 small can chopped green chilies, well drained
1 small clove garlic, minced
About 1 cup additional cheese, same choices as above, reserved

Make bread as directed, allow to rise in bowl, punch down and divide dough in half. Working with one half at a time, roll out into rectangle, about 12×8. Brush with melted butter. Mix remaining ingredients and spread half of mixture over dough, leaving a clear border all around. Starting with one of the short sides, roll up tightly and tuck in ends, forming a nicely shaped loaf. Place loaf in well-greased loaf pan (9×5×3 inches) With a sharp knife, make a deep slit down center of loaf. Stuff ½ of the additional cheese in slit. Cover and allow to rise 30 minutes. Bake 30 to 35 minutes at 350° (repeat with remaining dough). Remove loaves from oven, brush with melted butter.

This is the bread that started the cookbook! When the Corders moved to Plainview, I took a loaf of Cheese-Filled Bread to them. Suzanne called the next day for the recipe and we have been trading recipes ever since. You may not end up writing a cookbook, but we promise that you will love this bread!!

Chocolate Cake

3 1-ounce blocks unsweetened chocolate, melted
1 cup boiling water
1¼ teaspoons baking soda
½ cup butter
1 teaspoon vanilla extract
2 cups sugar
3 eggs, separated
2½ cups sifted cake flour
½ teaspoon salt
1 cup thick sour cream
1 teaspoon red food coloring

Combine chocolate and water, cool slightly; add soda. Work butter in a mixing bowl until creamy; add vanilla. Stir in 1½ cups of the sugar gradually, then beat until fluffy. Add egg yolks and beat well. Sift flour and salt together. Add flour mixture alternately with sour cream, beating after each addition until smooth. Add chocolate mixture and food coloring and blend thoroughly. Whip egg whites until soft peaks form. Add remaining ½ cup sugar gradually, whipping well after each addition. Continue whipping until stiff peaks form. Fold into first mixture. Pour into two 9-inch round pans lines with waxed paper. Bake in a moderate oven, 350°, 40 to 45 minutes. Cool in pans 5 minutes; remove from pans and peel off paper. Cool completely before frosting.

Chocolate Frosting

¼ cup butter
2 1-ounce blocks unsweetened chocolate
Dash of salt
1 teaspoon vanilla
1 pound (3½ cups) confectioner's sugar
5 tablespoons evaporated milk

Melt butter and chocolate in a quart saucepan over very low heat of hot water. Stir in salt and vanilla. Blend in sugar, and enough milk for smooth spreading. Will cover tops and sides of two 9-inch layers.

This is the first recipe I remember receiving compliments on and it is still my favorite chocolate cake recipe.

Lemon Filling for Tarts

2 eggs
2 egg yolks
½ cup butter
1 cup sugar
Juice and grated rind of 2 lemons

Prepare pastry (see index) and fit into desired size pans. Bake as recipe directs.

In saucepan or top of double boiler, beat eggs and yolks together until well blended.

Add remaining ingredients and mix well. Cook over low heat (or simmering water if using double boiler), stirring with wooden spoon until consistency of mayonnaise.

Store in covered jar in refrigerator until ready to use. Keeps several weeks. Will fill 12 tarts, 72 tartlets.

Also delicious over angel food or pound cake slices or as filling for white or yellow cake layers. It is very good as the filling for the coconut cake on the Easter Menu (see Index).

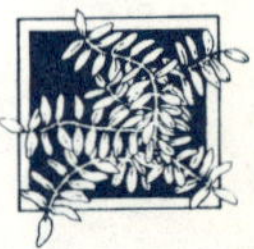

SUMMERTIME DOWN SOUTH

ARWIN'S PARTY

Shrimp Deluxe

Hanky Panky **Layered Cheese Ring**

Assorted Crackers

Relish Tray

Platter of Homemade Candies

Indianola, Mississippi has long been as noted for its abundance of good cooks as for its Indian mounds. This was never more evident than on a trip the Thompson's and the Corder's made to Mississippi. We were entertained royally in both Vicksburg and Indianola. Arwin Corder gave one of her delightful cocktail parties and asked everyone to bring a favorite recipe. The results follow!

Summertime Down South

The bonus of having this party in the summer is the abundance of fresh flowers. Make a grapevine wreath large enough to hold a shallow glass container. Float fresh magnolia blossoms in the container.

If magnolias are not available, use the summer flowers of your choice.

A nice addition to your permanent collection of party supplies is an eyelet cloth bound by a ruffle and an assortment of polished cotton undercloths in varied colors. (You may also want to make napkins to match undercloths.) These work well for any luncheon, tea, coffee, or buffet. This way you can change your color scheme with a minimum investment.

Shrimp Deluxe

4 pounds raw shrimp
4 pints French dressing
1¾ cups vinegar
2 cups oil
4 tablespoons Creole mustard
9 drops Tabasco
12 tablespoons chopped parsley
12 green onions (tops and bottoms), chopped
8 ribs celery, chopped fine
4 cloves garlic, mashed
salt
pepper

Boil shrimp your way (peeled and deveined either before or after cooking) and have still hot from cooking. To the French dressing add all the rest of the ingredients, except shrimp, and shake well. Add hot shrimp, and let marinate overnight. Serve with picks as an hors d'oeuvres.

Serves 24.

Hanky Panky

1 pound ground beef
1 pound hot sausage
1 pound Velveeta cheese

Brown meats, drain and add cheese. Cook till cheese melts. Then add:

1 tablespoon Worcestershire sauce
1 teaspoon oregano
Salt and pepper to taste
Garlic powder to taste

Spread on party rye bread. It will be enough for 2 loaves. Freezes well. Heat at 350° til bubbly.

Delicious as an appetizer!

Arwin Corder

Layered Cheese Ring

1 package (8-ounce) cream cheese, softened
1 cup grated Tybo cheese
3 drops Tabasco sauce
2 tablespoons chopped parsley
2 tablespoons chopped pimento
⅓ cup chopped almonds
1 tablespoon sesame seeds
1½ cups grated extra-sharp Cheddar
1½ cups grated hickory-smoked cheese
⅓ cup sour cream
1 teaspoon Dijon mustard
1 teaspoon Worcestershire sauce
1 teaspoon onion powder
¼ teaspoon dill weed
⅓ cup chopped almonds

Mix cream cheese, Tybo, Tabasco, parsley and pimento. Add nuts and sesame seeds. Mix. Pack into 6-inch ring mold. Refrigerate. Combine remaining ingredients. Mix. Pack over first layer. Chill. Serve with crackers.

Written as we listened to her play the piano.

Arwin Corder

Homemade Candies

Iced Almonds

1 cup whole blanched almonds
½ cup sugar
2 tablespoons butter
½ teaspoon vanilla extract
¾ teaspoon salt

Heat almonds, sugar, and butter in heavy skillet over medium heat, stirring constantly, until almonds are toasted and sugar is golden brown (about 15 minutes). Stir in vanilla. Spread almond mixture on a sheet of aluminum foil; sprinkle with salt. Cool; break into 2 or 3 nut clusters.

Pecan Brittle

2 cups sugar
1 cup white Karo

Boil 7 minutes after it comes to rolling boil, add 2 cups pecans, boil 7 minutes. Add 1 teaspoon vanilla, ½ stick butter, 2 teaspoons soda. Beat and dump.

White Velvet Coconut Creams

3 cups sugar
1½ cups cream
6 tablespoons butter
Salt

Bring to boil and lower heat. Cook until it reaches 234°. Remove pan from heat and let stand 5 minutes. Pour onto large buttered plate. Let cool.

Add 1 teaspoon vanilla. Beat until thick and creamy.

Add 1½ cups coconut and continue to beat.

Pour into pan and sprinkle ½ cup coconut over top. Chill overnight.

Brown Sugar Fudge

1 pound light brown sugar
2 cups white sugar
Dash of salt
6 tablespoons cocoa
¼ teaspoon cream of tartar
3 tablespoons light corn syrup
1 cup milk
3 tablespoons butter or margarine
2 teaspoons vanilla extract

Mix brown sugar, white sugar, salt, cocoa, and cream of tartar in a heavy aluminum 4-quart saucepan. Add corn syrup and milk. Stir well until sugar dissolves. Bring to boil and cook to soft ball stage (234°). Remove from heat. Add butter and vanilla extract. Beat until glossy and beginning to thicken. Pour into a buttered 11×7×1 ½-inch pan to cool. Cut into squares.

Yield: 2½ to 3 pounds.

Mississippi Caviar

4 cups cooked blackeye peas
Thinly sliced onions
Cracked pepper
1 cup oil
2 cloves garlic
¼ cup wine vinegar
Parsley
⅛ teaspoon Tabasco
½ teaspoon salt
1 can (2¼ ounce) pitted ripe olives
2 jalapeño peppers, seeded and sliced
6 slices crisp bacon, crumbled

Put the oil, garlic, vinegar, parsley, Tabasco, and salt in the blender. Mix at high speed. Pour over drained peas. Add onions and pepper. Marinate overnight. Add the olives and peppers. Cover with crumbled bacon.

This keeps in the refrigerator over a week. It may be served as a vegetable side dish or as an appetizer with crackers.

Rebecca Barrett

Oyster Spread

2 8-ounce packages cream cheese, softened
¼ cup milk
2 to three tablespoons mayonnaise
1 tablespoon lemon juice
1 tablespoon Worcestershire
Dash of hot sauce
Salt to taste
2 cans smoked oysters, minced
Paprika
Chopped parsley

Combine all ingredients except oysters, paprika and parsley; blend well. Stir in oysters, and refrigerate several hours. Sprinkle with paprika and parsley before serving.
Yield: about 3 cups.

Martha Vaught

Olive Tomato Dip

1 can Rotel tomatoes and juice
16 ounces cream cheese
½ cup stuffed green olives, chopped
Dash Worcestershire sauce
Lawry's seasoned salt, to taste
Pepper, to taste
½ teaspoon lemon juice

Mix and serve chilled with crackers.

A good dip for an afternoon of bridge. Sue Terney, another good cook from the Mississippi Delta served this one to our club.

"Cheese" Crackers

2 stacks saltines
8 ounce package sharp cheese, grated
½ stick oleo
red pepper to taste

Spread crackers with oleo and place on large cookie sheet. Sprinkle grated cheese and red pepper (to your taste) over crackers. Place under broiler until bubbly. Remove from oven and when oven is cool, set at 150° and bake crackers for 8 hours.

Delicious! Eat like popcorn. I put all the crackers on two trays and brush oleo on with a pastry brush.

Arwin Corder

Cheese Ball

2 8-ounce packages cream cheese
1 small jar chopped ripe olives
1 jar Armour dried beef, (cut up with scissors)
1 small can mushrooms (cut up)
4 green onions (cut up)
2 tablespoons Accent

Soften cream cheese. Add other ingredients. Serve with Ritz crackers.

Kaye Buchanan

My Favorite Tex-Mex Dip

2 can jalapeño bean dip
8 ounces sour cream
3 medium sized ripe avocados
3 tablespoons lemon juice
½ teaspoon salt
¼ teaspoon pepper
1 package taco seasoning mix
½ cup mayonnaise
1 cup chopped green onions
3 medium tomatoes, chopped
2 cans ripe olives, chopped
1 8-ounce package sharp Cheddar cheese, grated

Mix the bean dip with the sour cream. Make this your first layer. Mash the avocados with the lemon juice, salt and pepper. Layer this next. Mix the taco seasoning mix with the mayonnaise. Layer this. Then layer the onion, chopped tomatoes, chopped olives and cheese.

Lynn Baker

Jimmy's Shrimp Rémoulade

1 pint Hellmann's or Kraft mayonnaise
¼ cup horseradish
1 teaspoon anchovy paste (more if needed)
2 tablespoons mustard
1 stick celery, chopped fine
1 onion, chopped fine
Salt to taste

Mix all ingredients well, being sure anchovy paste is well blended. Serve over shrimp, well chilled.

This specialty of Jim's dad, James Corder, is always a welcome treat.

Eggplant Lusco

1 medium egg plant, peeled and diced
1 can Rotel tomatoes with hot peppers
2 bay leaves
1 tablespoon olive oil
Garlic powder
½ tablespoon sweet basil
Black pepper and salt

Cook eggplant, drain. Heat tomatoes and seasonings in small skillet. Add eggplant and heat. Serve with tortilla chips.

Marion and Claiborne Barnwell

Lusco's is in Greenwood, MS. Traditionally it is the place to meet and enjoy dinner after Ole Miss and MS state games!

Tortellini Ala Sanno

- 1 box tortellini
- 1 4-ounce wedge Parmesan cheese, grated
- ½ pint whipping cream
- ½ stick butter
- 1 can quartered artichoke hearts
- 10 to 12 fresh mushrooms sliced and sautéed in garlic butter
- 2 sliced and sautéed zucchini

Cook tortellini by package directions. Drain. Add butter, grated Parmesan, and toss until melted. Then add cream, hearts, mushrooms and zucchini.

Natalie Peeler

Anne Gorton's Vermicelli Salad

- 16-ounce package vermicelli (cook and drain)
- ½ chopped purple onion
- ½ chopped bell pepper
- 2 chopped tomatoes
- 1 can sliced ripe olives

MARINADE — (mix well)

- 8-ounce bottle Wishbone Italian dressing
- ½ bottle salad supreme
- 1 package Good Seasons salad dressing

Toss and chill overnight.

Different and delicious!

Sandra Crosthwait

Fresh Broccoli Salad

- 1 bunch broccoli spears, fresh
- ⅔ cup olives, chopped fine
- 1 small onion, chopped fine
- 4 hard-boiled eggs, chopped fine
- ⅔ cup mayonnaise
- 1 tablespoon lemon juice
- ½ teaspoon sugar
- Salt and pepper
- Fresh mushrooms, sliced (for garnish)

Cut broccoli including stalks into cubes. Toss with olives, onions and eggs. Combine mayonnaise, lemon juice, sugar, salt and pepper. Toss with broccoli mixture and garnish with fresh mushrooms.

I fix the salad and dressing the day before serving and refrigerate separately. Then combine them 1 hour before serving.

Camille Corder Towery

Cheese Casserole

- 1 pound Velveeta, cubed
- 8 ounces sharp Cheddar cheese, grated
- 8 ounces cottage cheese
- 1 stick butter, melted
- 4 eggs
- 1 tablespoon flour

Mix cottage cheese, butter, eggs and flour. Pour over Velveeta and Cheddar. Bake at 350° for 30 minutes. Use a 9×13 dish and grease it well.

This recipe comes from Laura Gresham, from Indianola, MS. She served it to our supper club there and got raves!

Doe's Broiled Shrimp

- 2 pounds raw shrimp, peeled
- Kourico Creole Seasoning
- 3 cloves minced garlic
- ½ stick butter
- ⅛ cup olive oil
- ⅛ cup peanut oil
- Juice of 3 lemons
- 1 tablespoon Worcestershire sauce
- 1 tablespoon paprika
- 1 tablespoon creole seasoning
- ½ teaspoon red pepper
- Tabasco to taste

Sprinkle shrimp with Kourico Creole Seasoning. Make a basting sauce of the remaining ingredients. Broil the shrimp quickly on both sides basting frequently with the sauce. Serve the remainder of the sauce with the shrimp.

Marion and Claiborne Barnwell

Doe's Eat Place is a famous restaurant in Greenville, MS. People come from all over the Southeast to eat their delicious steaks and shrimp.

Chocolate Almond Mousse

Crust

1 cup flour
¼ cup brown sugar
½ cup butter
1 cup toasted almonds, chopped

Combine sugar and flour. Cut in butter. Pat firmly into lightly greased 9×13 pan. Bake at 350° for 12 to 15 minutes, but do not allow to brown. Sprinkle chopped almonds over crust. Set aside to cool.

Filling

2 envelopes unflavored gelatin
1½ cups milk, divided
1½ cups sugar
¼ teaspoon salt
2 egg yolks
8 tablespoons butter
¾ cup cocoa
1 cup whipped cream

Sprinkle gelatin over ½ cup of the milk to soften. In saucepan, mix sugar, salt, yolks, butter and cocoa. Stir in remaining 1 cup milk. Cook over medium heat until all ingredients are well blended. Remove from heat, stir in softened gelatin. Return to heat and cook, stirring, until gelatin is dissolved. Chill until mixture begins to thicken — about 45 minutes. Fold in whipped cream. Pour into prepared crust. Chill until firm. Spread with topping.

Topping

1 carton sour cream
1 cup powdered sugar
1 cup toasted almonds, chopped

Mix sour cream and powdered sugar until smooth. Spread over mousse. Sprinkle almonds over top.

Evelyn Roughton

A nice addition to this delicious dessert is a raspberry sauce passed separately.

Raspberry Sauce

2 10-ounce packages frozen raspberries
2 tablespoons cornstarch
1 cup sugar

Thaw and drain raspberries, reserving juice. Mix cornstarch and sugar. Blend in reserved juice. Cook, stirring over medium heat until sauce is thick and clear. Stir in raspberries. Chill.

Mississippi Mud

2 sticks melted oleo
4 tablespoons cocoa
2 cups sugar
1½ cup flour
4 eggs
1 teaspoon vanilla
1 cup nuts
1 jar marshmallow cream

Mix well together. Pour into a 9×13 pan. Bake 350° for 20 to 25 minutes. when done, cover cake with marshmallow creme. Let melt. Ice cake.

Icing

4 tablespoons cocoa
1 stick melted oleo
4 tablespoons evaporated milk
1 box powdered sugar

Mix and pour over marshmallow creme.
Serves 15

Lois Robertson

Father's Day

SERVES FOUR

Cream of Asparagus Soup
Lamb Chops Dijon or Lamb Shanks in Wine
Mint Sauce
Orange Brussels Sprouts
Potato Puff
Wined Mushrooms
Salad Greens with Dressing Eleanor
Royal Triangles
or
Parmesan Breadsticks
Peach Cobbler

Father's Day

Use a large model sailboat set on a blue cloth. Fold white napkins in pleats and place between the plates and the sailboat to create the suggestion of waves — with the napkins being picked up and used as dinner is served.

A Captain's hat will mark "Dad's" place, to be worn throughout the dinner. A list of "Privileges of the Captain" can be presented, read aloud or laid beside his plate.

Cream of Asparagus Soup

1 10-ounce package frozen asparagus spears
1 cup water
¼ cup chopped onion
2 tablespoons butter
2 tablespoons all-purpose flour
1 cup milk
1 cup half-and-half
½ teaspoon white pepper
Croutons (optional)

Combine first 3 ingredients in a saucepan; bring to a boil. Separate asparagus with a fork; cover, reduce heat, and simmer 5 minutes or until tender. Drain well. Place asparagus in container of electric blender, and process until smooth.

Melt butter in a heavy saucepan over low heat; add flour, stirring until smooth. Cook 1 minute, stirring constantly. Gradually add milk and half-and-half; cook over medium heat, stirring constantly, until mixture is thickened and bubbly. Stir in asparagus purée, salt, and pepper; cook until thoroughly heated. Garnish with croutons, if desired.

Yield: 4½ cups

Soup may be served cold. Add additional milk for a thinner soup.

Lamb Chops Dijon

8 ¾ inch thick loin lamb chops
2 cloves garlic, peeled
1 cup olive oil
1 cup brandy
2 tablespoons rosemary
2 teaspoons seasoned pepper
2 tablespoons garlic powder
4 cloves garlic, minced
4 tablespoons Italian breadcrumbs
2 tablespoons butter, melted
1 cup Dijon mustard, divided
Additional rosemary

Rub chops with peeled garlic and place in shallow dish. Combine and mix well, olive oil, brandy, rosemary, pepper, garlic powder, minced garlic. Pour over chops. Cover and marinate in refrigerator at least 8 hours, turning chops several times.

Remove chops from marinade, and place on broiler pan. Combine breadcrumbs, butter, and ½ cup mustard; mix well and spread on top of chops. Sprinkle each chop with additional rosemary. Broil 11 inches from heat for 10 minutes. Remove from oven, brush tops of chops with remaining mustard. Return to oven and broil additional 10 minutes. Let stand 5 minutes before serving. Allow 2 chops per serving.

Serves 4.

Mint Sauce

1½ tablespoons powdered sugar
3 tablespoons water
⅓ cup mint leaves, finely chopped
½ cup white wine vinegar

Heat water, stir in sugar to dissolve; add mint leaves and vinegar. Make at least one day ahead of serving.

Yield: 1 cup

Many recipes call for fresh lemon juice. Keep this mixture in your refrigerator for several weeks for a handy supply: slice and seed 1 lemon. Place in blender or food processor. Add 3 Tablespoons water. Process until well blended. Store in tightly covered jar.

Lamb Shanks in Wine

4 lamb shanks
¼ cup butter
1 onion, grated
1 clove garlic, grated
1 cup red wine
1 carrot, minced
2 stalks celery, minced
Herb bouquet (tied in bag together — parsley, thyme, bay leaf)
Salt and freshly ground pepper

Dust shanks in seasoning and flour; brown in butter with onion and garlic; remove to casserole. Rinse the pan with the wine. Pour over the shanks, add carrot, herb bouquet and celery and cook in covered casserole 1½ to 2 hours at 350°. If sauce remaining in casserole is too thin, thicken with kneaded rolls of butter and flour in small balls. Remove herb bouquet before serving.

Serves 4.

This excellent dish is from Mary Louise Gee and was one of her mother's.

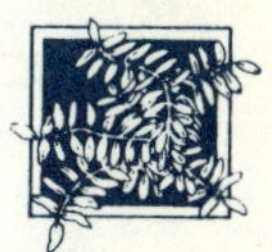

Orange Brussels Sprouts

1 pound fresh brussels sprouts
1 small orange, unpeeled and cut into wedges
⅓ cup fresh orange juice
1 tablespoon white wine vinegar
1 tablespoon butter or margarine, melted
1 teaspoon sugar
½ teaspoon salt
½ teaspoon dried whole dillweed

Wash brussels sprouts thoroughly; drain. Combine brussels sprouts and remaining ingredients in a saucepan; bring to a boil. Cover, reduce heat, and simmer 8 to 10 minutes or until tender.

Serves 4.

Potato Puff

- 5 tablespoons freshly grated Parmesan cheese
- 2 cups freshly cooked mashed potatoes
- 1 teaspoon salt
- ¼ teaspoon pepper, freshly ground
- ⅛ teaspoon nutmeg, freshly grated
- ½ cup light cream or half-and-half, scalded
- 4 eggs, separated

Preheat the oven to 325°. Butter a 6-cup soufflé dish. Sprinkle in 2 tablespoons of the cheese and tilt to coat the bottom and sides of the dish; tap out any excess. Refrigerate while you prepare the soufflé. In a large bowl, combine the potatoes with the salt, pepper and nutmeg. Beat in the light cream until blended and smooth. Stir in the remaining 3 tablespoons cheese. Add the egg yolks, one at a time, beating thoroughly after each addition. Beat the egg whites until stiff, but not dry. Stir one-fourth of the beaten egg whites into the potato mixture; gently but thoroughly fold in the remaining whites. Scrape the mixture into the prepared soufflé dish; smooth out the top. Place the dish into a baking pan and fill the pan with enough hot water to reach ½ inch up the side of the dish. Bake in the middle of the oven for 1½ hours, or until the potatoes are golden brown on top. Serve hot.

Note: 4 or 5 medium potatoes will yield 2 cups mashed.

Wined Mushrooms

- 6 tablespoons butter
- ½ pound mushrooms, sliced
- 2 medium onions, finely chopped
- 1 clove garlic, minced
- 2 tablespoons chili sauce
- ½ teaspoon flour
- Pinch dried marjoram
- Pinch dried thyme
- 4 drops Tabasco sauce
- 2 dashes Worcestershire sauce
- 5 ounces dry red wine
- 1 bouillon cube, dissolved in ¼ cup water
- Salt and freshly ground pepper to taste
- Minced parsley

Melt butter in a large skillet. Add the mushrooms, onions, and garlic. Sauté until the onions are soft. Add remaining ingredients and mix well. Barely simmer for about 10 minutes. Serve hot with a sprinkling of minced parsley.

Salad Dressing Eleanor

½ cup fresh lemon juice
1¼ cup salad oil
2½ teaspoons (rounded) salt
Juice of ½ garlic pod

Blend in blender or shake in jar and refrigerate until chilled. The fresh lemon juice is the secret.

Eleanor Davis' recipe is Jim's most favorite salad dressing. It is very tangy and delicious especially on a fresh spinach salad.

Royal Triangles

8-ounce can Refrigerated Crescent Dinner Rolls
½ cup spicy French dressing

Heat oven to 375°. Lightly grease cookie sheet. Separate dough into 8 triangles; cut each in half lengthwise to form 16 triangles. Place on prepared cookie sheet. Brush lightly with French dressing. Bake at 375° for 10 to 12 minutes until puffed and golden brown.

Parmesan Breadsticks

1 package active dry yeast
⅔ cup warm water (105 to 115°)
1 tablespoon sugar
1 teaspoon salt
¼ cup salad or olive oil
2 to 2¼ cups flour
Salad oil or olive oil
1 egg white
1 tablespoon water
Parmesan cheese

Dissolve yeast in warm water in large mixing bowl. Stir in sugar, 1 teaspoon salt, ¼ cup oil and 1 cup of the flour. Beat until smooth. Stir in enough remaining flour to make dough easy to handle.

Turn the dough onto lightly floured surface; knead until smooth and elastic, about 5 minutes. Shape dough into uniform roll 10 inches long. Cut into 32 equal parts. Roll each part into a pencil-like rope, 8 inches long for thicker breadsticks, or 10 inches long for thinner breadsticks. Place 1 inch apart on greased baking sheets. Brush lightly with oil. Cover; let rise in warm place 20 minutes.

Heat oven to 350°. Beat egg white and 1 tablespoon water slightly; brush over sticks. Bake until breadsticks are golden brown, 20 to 25 minutes. Remove from oven and sprinkle with Parmesan cheese.

Peach Cobbler

1 large can sliced peaches
1 box Duncan Hines pudding recipe yellow cake mix (Lemon cake mix may be used.)
1 cup pecans, finely chopped
2 sticks oleo margarine, cut in slices
¾ cup light brown sugar
Cinnamon, clove and nutmeg powder
Salt

Put undrained peaches in bottom of well buttered casserole (13×9×3 approx.) Spread the brown sugar over the peaches. Then shake salt, cinnamon, clove and nutmeg powder over the brown sugar (generously). Over this, spread the cake mix. Do not mix water or milk with the cake mix. Put the sliced oleo over the top of the cake mix. Then, sprinkle pecans over all. Cook 50 minutes to 1 hour in oven at 350°. (Ovens vary so the last half you may have to put foil over the top.) Serve this warm with ice cream, whipped cream or Cool Whip.

Five grandchildren to do one ingredient each, except spices, makes this cobbler very good!

Our Aunt Elaine Corder, always lets the children make this when they visit her in Greenville, MS.

Fourth of July Bash

SERVES TWELVE TO FOURTEEN

Vodka Slush
Iced Tea Cooler
Mexican Cheesecake
Herbed Dip in Red Cabbage Bowl
Marinated Mushrooms
Barbeque Strings in Bread Rounds
Corn on the Cob
Potato Salad Mold
Blueberry Salad
Supreme Bean Salad
Dilled Cucumbers on Tomatoes
Coconut-Macadamia Nut Cookies
Brownies
Special Fruit Sherbet

Fourth of July Bash

Set up tables for 4, each covered with a piece of red, white, or blue oilcloth. Use red, white, or blue ribbon for a napkin ring, holding white napkins. On the serving table, covered with strips of each color of the oilcloth, using either a white or blue enamel washpan as the container, arrange daisies and geraniums. (You can also find the small blue enamel bowls or cups and make smaller arrangements of the same flowers for each table.) Add small flags and long sparklers. Runners of English Ivy make a nice filler with the daisies and geraniums.

Iced Tea Cooler

6 cups strong tea
1 cup sugar
2½ cups pineapple juice
1 6-ounce can frozen lemonade
4 6-ounce cans ice cold water
Mint to garnish, lemon slices

Dissolve sugar in hot tea. Add other ingredients except mint and mix well. Serve over ice in tall glasses, garnished with mint and lemon slices.

Serves 12 to 14.

Vodka Slush

1 6-ounce can frozen orange juice thawed
1 12-ounce can frozen lemonade, thawed
2 6-ounce cans frozen limeade, thawed
1 cup sugar
3½ cups water
2 cups vodka
2 32-ounce bottles lemon-lime carbonated drink

Combine all ingredients except lemon-lime drink. Mix well and freeze. Spoon ¾ cup of frozen mixture into tall glass, fill with lemon-lime drink, to serve.

Serves 12 to 14.

Mexican Cheesecake

Mix 2 cups crushed corn chips with ¼ cup melted butter. Press on bottom and sides of 9-inch springform pan. Bake at 350° 8 to 10 minutes; cool. Layer the dip ingredients as follows.

2 16-ounce cans refried beans
1 package taco seasoning
1 jar Marie's Avocado dressing
1 pint sour cream
1 can ripe olives, chopped
1 layer chopped tomatoes
2 cans green chili peppers, chopped
8 ounces grated Monterey Jack cheese with peppers

Mix the beans and taco seasoning. Beginning with the bean mixture, layer all of the ingredients. Chill several hours before serving.

Herbed Dip in Red Cabbage Bowl

1 cup mayonnaise
½ tablespoon lemon juice
½ teaspoon salt
¼ teaspoon paprika
¼ cup chopped parsley
1 tablespoon chopped green onion
1 tablespoon chopped chives
⅛ teaspoon curry powder
½ teaspoon Worcestershire
Garlic powder to taste
1 tablespoons capers
½ cup sour cream

Mix all ingredients and fold in sour cream. Make 1 to 2 days before serving. When ready to serve spoon into large red cabbage that has been hollowed out to form bowl. Serve with assorted raw vegetables for dippers.

Marinated Mushrooms

- ¾ cup salad oil
- 3 tablespoons soy sauce
- ⅛ cup Worcestershire sauce
- 1 teaspoon salt
- 3 tablespoons lemon juice
- ¼ teaspoon garlic powder
- 1 teaspoon pepper
- ⅓ cup red wine
- 3 cans button mushrooms

Cook about 15 minutes. Refrigerate several hours before serving.

These are really good to keep on hand in your refrigerator.

Barbeque Strings

- 4 to 5 pounds eye of round roast, cut into cubes
- 1 green pepper, chopped
- 2 medium onions, chopped
- 1 8-ounce can tomato sauce
- 2 tablespoons vinegar
- 2 tablespoons Dijon mustard
- 2 tablespoons Worcestershire sauce
- 2 tablespoons brown sugar
- 2 tablespoons chili powder
- 1 tablespoon soy sauce
- 1 teaspoon liquid smoke
- 1 to 2 cups water

In large pan, brown meat on all sides. Add onions, green pepper and water. Cover and cook slowly 5 hours or until meat shreds into strings easily. Add remaining ingredients, simmer 30 minutes longer, adding water as necessary.

Serve on buns.

Note: When meat mixture is done use two forks to shred meat into "strings".

This is really better made at least one day ahead and kept covered in refrigerator until ready to serve. Reheat and spoon into bread rounds. May use toasted buns. Will freeze beautifully.

Serves 12 to 14.

Bread Rounds

2 cups warm water (105 to 115°), divided
2 teaspoons sugar
1 package dry yeast
About 6½ cups all-purpose flour, divided
1½ teaspoons salt
3 tablespoons vegetable oil

Combine ¼ cup warm water, sugar, and yeast; stir until yeast dissolves. Combine 4½ cups flour and salt; add oil, yeast mixture, and remaining 1¾ cups water, stirring until smooth. Add enough of remaining flour to form a moderately stiff dough, stirring well.

Turn dough out onto a lightly floured surface, and knead 8 to 10 minutes until smooth and elastic. Place in a greased bowl, turning to grease top. Cover and let rise in a warm place (85°), free from drafts, 1 hour or until doubled in bulk.

Divide dough into 12 equal portions; shape each portion into a smooth ball. Pat each ball into a 5-inch circle. Place circles on lightly greased baking sheets.

Let rise, uncovered, in a warm place, free from drafts, 1 hour or until doubled in bulk. Bake at 500° for 4 to 6 minutes or until lightly browned.

Note: You may use 3 cups whole wheat flour for part of flour, mixing all of it in first addition of flour (i.e. use 3 cups whole wheat and 1½ cups white). Finish recipe with white flour.

1 dozen

Blueberry Salad

- 2 3-ounce packages raspberry gelatin
- 1 cup boiling water
- 1 15-ounce can blueberries, undrained
- 1 8-ounce can crushed pineapple, well drained

Dissolve gelatin in hot water. Stir in undrained blueberries and drained pineapple. Pour mixture into a flat 2 quart Pyrex dish. Chill until set firmly. Before serving, spread with topping:

Topping

- 1 8-ounce package cream cheese
- ½ cup sugar
- 1 cup sour cream
- 1 teaspoon vanilla
- 1 cup chopped nuts

Combine cream cheese, sugar, sour cream, and vanilla in bowl and mix until well blended. Stir in nuts. Spread mixture over salad, cover with plastic wrap and refrigerate until ready to serve. This salad is better made a day ahead of serving.

Dale McWilliams brought this salad to us with the recipe when we moved to Indianola. We always enjoy it.

Potato Salad Mold

- 20 medium potatoes
- 1 envelope unflavored gelatin
- ¼ cup cold water
- ½ cup olive juice drained from olives, adding enough water if olives don't yield enough
- ½ cup vinegar
- ¼ cup dill pickle juice
- 2 medium onions, chopped
- 2 large peppers, chopped
- 2 celery stalks, chopped
- 1 large bottle olives, chopped
- 1 cup chopped pickles
- ¾ cup mayonnaise

Boil potatoes in jackets. Peel when cool, and chop in large bowl. Dissolve gelatin in cold water. Bring olive juice, vinegar, and dill pickle juice to a boil and pour over gelatin. Stir until dissolved. Cool. Place in refrigerator until slightly congealed. Add onions, peppers, celery, olives, and chopped pickles to potatoes. Add gelatin preparation and blend in mayonnaise. Put salad in mold and refrigerate overnight.

20 servings

Supreme Bean Salad

- 2 pounds small white navy beans
- 2 cups olive oil
- 1¼ cups lemon juice
- ½ cup white vinegar
- 3 cups finely chopped celery
- ½ cup plus 1 tablespoon finely chopped green bell pepper
- ½ cup chopped parsley
- 2 tablespoons finely chopped onion
- 4½ teaspoons salt
- ¼ teaspoon thyme

Soak and cook beans according to package directions but do not overcook. They should retain their shape.

Marinate in the reamining ingredients, tightly covered, 8 hours or more, stirring occasionally.

Serves 24.

Dilled Cucumber on Tomatoes

- 2 large cucumbers, peeled and thinly sliced
- ⅔ cup vegetable oil
- 6 tablespoons vinegar
- 3 teaspoons minced fresh dillweed or 1 teaspoon dried dillweed
- 1 teaspoon salt
- ½ teaspoon sugar
- ¼ teaspoon pepper
- Bibb lettuce leaves
- 6 medium tomatoes, sliced

Place cucumber in a shallow bowl, and set aside.

Combine next 6 ingredients, and mix well with a wire whisk; pour over cucumbers, tossing gently. Cover and chill at least 6 hours.

Arrange lettuce leaves on a serving platter, and top with tomato slices. Spoon cucumber mixture over tomatoes.

Serves 12.

Brownies

- 2 cups sugar
- 1/3 cup cocoa
- 2 sticks butter
- 4 eggs, well beaten
- 2 teaspoons vanilla
- 1 cup flour
- 2½ cups chopped pecans

Mix sugar and cocoa in saucepan, add butter and cook over medium heat, stirring, until butter melts. Remove from heat and allow to cool slightly. Add vanilla; stir in eggs, mixing well. Stir in flour, mixing until all ingredients are well blended. Stir in pecans. Pour into a greased and floured 9×13 baking pan. Bake at 350° 25 to 30 minutes or until brownies pull away from sides of pan. Let cool in pan before cutting into squares. You may frost or dust with powdered sugar — but why? They are wonderful! These freeze well.

This is the brownie recipe I've used since I was a bride. It was given to me by my sister-in-law, Jeanelle Street. Both she and the brownies are the best to be found.

Coconut Macadamia-Nut Cookies

- 1 cup butter
- ½ cup sugar
- 1 cup coconut
- 1 cup chopped macadamia nuts
- 2 cups flour
- 1 teaspoon vanilla

Cream butter and sugar; add coconut, macadamia nuts, flour and vanilla. Mix well. Form into small balls. Place on cookies sheets. Flatten with bottom of small glass dipped in sugar. Bake at 300° 9 to 10 minutes.

Watch carefully to keep from getting too brown.

There is a large store in Dallas that sells wonderful cookies and their Coconut Macadamia-Nut are the best. This is the closest I could come to their delicious ones and I think they're pretty good!

Special Fruit Sherbet

- 3 cups sugar
- 1 cup lemon juice
- 1 6-ounce can frozen orange juice
- 1 small can crushed pineapple, undrained
- 2 quarts milk

Mix all ingredients, pour into ice cream freezer and freeze as directed.

He Cooks for Her Birthday

SERVES FOUR TO EIGHT

Frisky Sours

Canapés

Grilled Steaks with Herb Butter

Garlic Cheese Potatoes

Kahlua Baked Beans

Crispy Onion Rings

Tossed Green Salad with Creamy Garlic Dressing

Toasted French Bread

Quick Chocolate Mousse

All of these recipes serve four but are easily doubled to serve eight.

He Cooks for Her Birthday

This menu is designed for a man — even one unfamiliar with the kitchen — to successfully create. You may want to order her very favorite flowers for the center-piece, making certain that you know what that flower is and not sending again what you think she likes! Use candles, and the prettiest linens and serving pieces you have. And —part of this unique gift should be — you, sir, wash the dishes!

Frisky Sours

1 6-ounce can frozen grapefruit-orange juice concentrate
1 6-ounce can frozen lemonade concentrate
1½ cups (2 juice cans) whiskey
1½ cups (2 juice cans) cold water

In blender container combine the grapefruit-orange juice concentrate, the lemonade concentrate, the whiskey, and the cold water. Cover and blend just till combined. Pour into serving glasses. Garnish with lemon slices, if desired.

Canapés

1 8-ounce package cream cheese
1 egg yolk
1 teaspoon grated onion

Combine all ingredients and mix well. Spread on crackers and broil. The canapés puff up and turn golden brown.

Yield: enough for 2 dozen crackers

Grilled Steaks

½ cup Burgundy wine
¼ cup Worcestershire sauce
1 clove garlic crushed
¾ cup soy sauce
1 tablespoon lemon pepper
2 teaspoons dry mustard
4 New York Strip steaks (or Ribeye steaks or Top Club steaks)

No mistake — don't add salt!

Make marinade of first six ingredients. Marinate steaks several hours or overnight, turning often. (I use a large zip-lock bag and keep turning it). Allow meat in marinade to return to room temperature before cooking. Cook on grill until desired doneness. Serve with generous dab of Herb Butter on each steak.

Serves 4.

This is the marinade that Gayle Thompson has used for many years and steaks! All the Thompson family agree that this is their favorite meal.

Herb Butter

½ cup butter, softened
1 tablespoon lemon juice
½ teaspoon salt
⅛ teaspoon pepper
2 tablespoons chopped parsley
1 tablespoon chopped chives
½ teaspoon tarragon leaves

Cream butter. Blend in remaining ingredients until smooth.

Garlic Cheese Potatoes

- 3 pounds frozen hash browns
- 2 sticks butter
- 2 rolls Kraft Garlic Cheese Rolls
- 1 cup grated Cheddar cheese
- 1 pint half-and-half

Place hash browns in a 9×13 baking dish. In a saucepan melt butter and cheeses. Stir in half-and-half. Pour over potatoes. Let stand at room temperature 1 hour. Bake at 350° for 1 hour.

Serves 12.

Quick, good and always many requests for the recipe.

Kahlua Baked Beans

- 1 pound can oven baked beans
- ¼ cup Kahlua
- 1 tablespoon chili sauce
- 1 teaspoon prepared mustard
- 1 teaspoon molasses

Mix all ingredients, refrigerate 4 hours or overnight before baking. Bake at 375° 30 to 40 minutes.

Crispy Onion Rings

- ⅔ cup all-purpose flour
- ⅓ cup cornstarch
- ¼ teaspoon salt
- 1 cup ice water
- Vegetable oil, for deep frying
- ½ teaspoon baking soda
- 2 medium onions, sliced crosswise into ¼ inch thick rounds and separated into rings

Sift the flour and cornstarch into a medium bowl. Add the salt and ice water and whisk rapidly to form a smooth batter; cover and refrigerate for at least 1 hour.

Preheat the oven to 250°. In a wok, deep fryer or heavy saucepan, heat about 2½ inches of oil to 375°.

Remove the batter from the refrigerator and whisk in the baking soda. Coat a few of the onion rings in the batter at one time and drop them, one by one, into the hot oil. Fry until crisp and golden brown, about 1 minute. Remove with tongs or a slotted spoon and drain on paper towels. Lightly sprinkle with salt. Keep warm in the oven while remaining onion rings are fried; serve hot.

4 servings

Creamy Garlic Dressing

2 cups mayonnaise
1 cup buttermilk
1 teaspoon Accent
1½ teaspoons garlic salt
1 teaspoon onion salt
1 teaspoon parsley flakes
1 teaspoon oregano
⅛ teaspoon celery salt
1 teaspoon dried chives

Mix all ingredients well. Refrigerate. This will keep for a month.
Makes 3 cups.

Great on salad or baked potato.

Toasted French Bread

(Buy the French Bread that comes several sticks to a package. This recipe will fill two of these loaves and will double easily if serving eight.)

2 cups Mozzarella cheese, grated
6 to 8 slices bacon, fried, drained and crumbled
¼ cup melted butter

Slice bread, but not through bottom of crust. Mix bacon and cheese and stuff generously between slices. Slowly pour butter over tops of bread. Wrap tightly in foil and bake at 350° 20 to 25 minutes.
Serves 4.

Quick Chocolate Mousse

6 ouce package chocolate bits (semi-sweet)
2 eggs
3 tablespoons very strong coffee
2 tablespoons rum or orange flavored liqueur
¾ cup scalded milk
Whipped cream to garnish

Combine all ingredients except whipped cream in blender. Blend mixture at high speed for 2 minutes. Pour mousse into dessert cups and chill. Top with whipped cream when ready to serve.
Makes 4 large servings.

Labor Day Picnic

SERVES TWENTY-FOUR

Chilled Tomato Soup

Cheese Roll and Crackers (Make 2)

Frosted Lemon Chicken

Hobo Salad

Pickled Eggs

Don't Tell the Kids It's Healthy Sandwich Spread

Pumpernickel Bread (see Index)

Fresh Fruit

Prune Cake

Pineapple Spice Cake

Two Nut Toffee

Caramel Fudge Balls

Pecan Pralines

Iced Tea

Labor Day Picnic

Write out invitations on Big Chief tablets in crayon. Fold them over, address and stick with the colored or "gold" stars. Have a large free-standing black board with various competitions listed and have guests "sign-up" as they arrive. (You might even have jacks and hop scotch!) Have a child's red wagon filled with crushed ice to serve drinks and the soup from. If enough quilts aren't available, find patchwork material and cut cloths and napkins with pinking shears. Your florist will sell enough boxes for you to "pack" the food into. Tie the boxes with strips of the patchwork material. Have all the desserts set up on one large table and call a "recess" somewhere between the games.

If you don't have school-aged children at home, borrow some textbooks and use these, along with various "school supplies" grouped with bright red apples for the centerpiece.

Chilled Tomato Soup

2 36-ounce cans tomato juice
2 cartons (8 ounces) sour cream
½ cup chopped green onion, tops and bottoms
½ teaspoon basil
½ teaspoon curry
½ teaspoon ginger
½ teaspoon nutmeg
2 teaspoons salt
2 teaspoons sugar
4 tablespoons lemon juice
6 tablespoons catsup

Mix all ingredients until well blended. Chill overnight. Serve cold. Can be made days ahead.
Serves 24.

Cheese Roll

1 package (8 ounces) cream cheese
1 glass (5 ounces) American cheese
1 glass (5 ounces) Bleu cheese
1 small jar minced onion (flakes)
1 clove garlic pressed (or garlic powder)
½ cup chopped nut meats

Cheese must be at room temperature. Beat together until well blended all ingredients except nut meats. Chill. Roll into a ball or a roll then roll in nuts. Can be frozen. (Make two for 24.)

Frosted Lemon Chicken

24 boneless halves of skinned chicken breasts
4 cups white wine
8 cups water
4 cups lemon juice
2 cups mayonnaise
2 cucumbers, peeled, seeded and finely chopped
3 tablespoons grated lemon rind
2 teaspoons salt
2 teaspoons pepper
4 lemons thinly sliced

In a large pan, combine wine, water and lemon juice. Bring to a boil. Add chicken pieces, cover and cook over medium heat 30 minutes or until chicken is done. Allow to cool in liquid.

Mix mayonnaise, cucumber, rind, salt and pepper.

Drain chicken and spread mayonnaise mixture over each piece in a thin layer. Top each breast with one or two slices of lemon. Wrap individually in foil and chill thoroughly. Serve in foil packet.
Serves 24.

Hobo Salad

- 4 cans pork and beans, drained as much as possible
- 8 green onions, tops and bottoms, chopped
- 2 green peppers, sliced in thin rings
- 2 cups mayonnaise
- 1 cup catsup
- 4 cups Cheddar cheese, cubed
- 2 cups Monterey Jack cheese, cubed
- 3 cups celery, sliced
- 4 tablespoons Dijon mustard
- 1 cup brown sugar

Mix all ingredients together. Chill overnight before serving.

Pickled Eggs

- 2 dozen hard-boiled eggs, peeled and left whole
- 2 cups white vinegar
- 2 tablespoons sugar
- 2 tablespoons salt
- 4 teaspoons pickling spice
- 2 cloves garlic, cut in slivers
- 2 slices lemon
- 1 teaspoon cayenne pepper
- Beet juice to color

Simmer vinegar, sugar, salt, spice, garlic, lemon and cayenne. Remove from heat and add enough beet juice to make desired depth of red. Pour over eggs, cover and refrigerate 1 to 2 weeks.

Don't Tell the Kids It's Healthy Sandwich Spread

- ½ cup finely chopped celery
- ½ cup green onion, tops and bottoms, chopped
- 1½ cups grated carrot
- ½ cup chopped green pepper
- 2 8-ounces cream cheese, softened
- 2 tablespoons lemon juice
- ½ teaspoon white pepper
- Pumpernickel bread

Chop vegetables and drain well. Beat cream cheese with lemon juice until smooth; stir in vegetables and pepper. Spread on pumpernickel bread. Cut and wrap sandwiches. Refrigerate until serving time.

Prune Cake

½ cup butter
1¼ cups sugar
2 eggs
2¼ cups flour
1 teaspoon soda
1 cup chopped pecans or walnuts
¼ teaspoon salt
½ teaspoon each: cloves, allspice, cinnamon
1 cup cooked prunes, mashed
1 cup buttermilk

Cream butter and sugar. Beat in eggs one at a time. Sift together all dry ingredients. Mix prunes into batter and add dry ingredients alternately with buttermilk until blended. Stir in nuts. Pour batter into greased and floured tube pan. Bake at 350° for 1 hour or until done. When cake has cooled slightly, remove from pan, pour frosting over cake while warm.

Frosting

1 cup sour cream
1½ cups sugar
1 tablespoon white corn syrup
2 tablespoons butter
1 teaspoon vanilla

Mix sour cream, sugar and corn syrup in saucepan. Bring to boil, stirring, reduce heat and cook without stirring to soft ball. Remove from heat, add butter and vanilla, beating until blended. Pour over hot cake.

An old recipe from my mother-in-law, Ruth Thompson. It is a wonderfully moist cake and freezes well.

Beat together 1 cup Crisco, 1 cup salad oil, and 1 cup flour. Store in covered container and use on all pans that recipe calls for a greased and floured pan.

Two Nut Toffee

- 2¼ cups sugar
- 1¼ cups butter (2½ sticks)
- ½ cup water
- 1 teaspoon salt
- 1½ cups chopped blanched almonds (½ pound)
- 6 ounces semisweet or milk chocolate, melted
- 1 cup chopped walnuts (6 ounces)

Generously butter 9×13-inch baking dish and set aside. Combine sugar, butter, water and salt in 3-quart saucepan and bring to boil over medium-high heat. Continue cooking, stirring constantly with wooden spoon, until mixture registers 325° on candy thermometer. Stir in almonds and ½ cup walnuts. Pour into prepared pan, spreading evenly. Let cool. Spread with melted chocolate and sprinkle with remaining walnuts. Break toffee into pieces before serving.

Toni Jenkins gave me this wonderful recipe. It is special and so is she!

Caramel Fudge Balls

- 1 cup walnuts
- ¼ cup butter
- 1 cup brown sugar, packed
- 1 cup granulated sugar
- ¼ teaspoon salt
- ¾ cup dairy sour cream
- 1 teaspoon vanilla

Chop ½ cup of walnuts to medium-size pieces. Chop remaining walnuts into fine pieces for coating fudge balls. Melt butter in heavy 2-quart saucepan. Add sugar, salt and sour cream. Cook over low heat, stirring until sugars dissolve. Cover; boil slowly 5 minutes. Uncover; cook rapidly without stirring to 236° (soft ball stage). Remove from heat; cool to lukewarm. Add vanilla; beat until mixture is creamy and begins to hold its shape. Stir in medium-size walnut pieces.

Drop by rounded teaspoonfuls onto waxed paper. Quickly shape into balls. Roll in finely chopped walnuts. Let stand until firm.

Put into small muffin papers.

Makes 24 balls.

Pineapple Spice Cake

- 2/3 cup butter
- 1 cup drained crushed pineapple
- 1 cup sugar
- 3 eggs
- 6 tablespoons sour cream
- 1 teaspoon cloves
- 1 teaspoon soda
- 1 teaspoon allspice
- 3 cups flour

Cream butter and sugar; add eggs and pineapple. Mix soda in sour cream. Sift cloves, allspice and flour. Add flour and cream alternately. Bake in 2 layers at 375°, 30 minutes or until done.

Filling

- 2 eggs
- 1 tablespoon flour
- 1½ cups sour cream
- 1½ cups sugar
- 1 tablespoon butter
- 1 cup pineapple

Cook until thick. Cool before filling cake. Spread filling between layers and on top of cake. No icing is needed.

This cake from Ernestine Bain gets better as it sits a day or two — the trick is to keep it that long!

Pecan Pralines

2 cups sugar
1 teaspoon soda
1 cup buttermilk
⅛ teaspoon salt
2 tablespoons butter
3 cups pecan halves

In large, heavy saucepan combine sugar, soda, buttermilk and salt. Cook over high heat for five minutes, stirring frequently and scraping the bottom of the pan. Add butter and pecans. Continue cooking, stirring constantly scraping bottom and sides of pan until candy reaches soft ball stage. Remove from heat and cool slightly. Beat until thick and creamy. Drop from a tablespoon onto waxed paper and let cool.

Makes about 18 2-inch pralines.

My mother Sue Wilson, loves to bake and make candy. Of all the praline recipes, we still like this one best.

Kick-Off Dinner

SERVES SIXTEEN

Apricot Glogg

Cinnamon Cider

Hot Cheese and Jalapeño

Vegetable Beef Soup

Miniature Swiss Quiches

Cheese and Corn Muffins

Applesauce Cake with Streusel Topping

Now Hurry To the Game!

Kick-Off Dinner

A large crock or earthenware pot filled with multi-colored mums will carry out this theme. Burlap cut to fit the serving table, small pumpkins and decorative gourds will complete the colorful centerpiece. Use napkins of the appropriate teams' colors.

Another "container" idea is to punch holes in a pumpkin and fill the holes with gold or multi-colored mums.

Apricot Glogg

12 whole cloves
2 pieces stick cinnamon
6 whole allspice
3 cups water
½ cup sugar
6-ounce can orange juice concentrate
6-ounce can lemonade concentrate
2½ cups apricot nectar
1½ cups apricot brandy
3½ cups white wine

Tie cloves, cinnamon and allspice in small piece of cheesecloth. In large saucepan, (4 quarts) combine spice bag, water, sugar concentrates and nectar. Heat to simmering; add brandy and wine. Allow to steep 10 minutes. Remove spice bag. Serve warm. If desired, garnish with orange slices and cinnamon stick stirrers.

Serves 16.

Cinnamon Cider

8 cups (2 quarts) apple juice or cider
½ cup cinnamon red hot candies

In saucepan, combine juice or cider and candies; bring to a boil. Reduce heat and simmer 4 minutes or until candies dissolve. Serve hot or cold. If desired, garnish with apple wedge or cinnamon stick stirrer.

Serves 16.

Hot Cheese and Jalapeño

1 cup fine fresh bread crumbs
1 cup milk
½ pound Monterey Jack, grated
2½ ounces sharp Cheddar, grated
1 tablespoons Dijon-style mustard
1 teaspoon Worcestershire sauce
3 tablespoons minced fresh parsley leaves
4 teaspoons seeded and minced canned pickled jalapeño peppers, or to taste
Corn tortilla chips, crackers or toast

In the top of a double boiler set over simmering water, combine the bread crumbs, the milk, the Monterey Jack, and the Cheddar and cook the mixture, stirring, until the cheeses are melted. Stir in the mustard, the Worcestershire sauce, the parsley, and the jalapeño peppers and serve the sauce hot with tortilla chips.

Makes about 2 cups.

Vegetable Beef Soup

1 can tomato paste
2 pounds round steak
1 medium onion, chopped
1 medium potato, chopped
1 cup chopped celery
1 cup chopped okra
1 can Veg-all, if desired
1 can tomatoes or 2 fresh, chopped
1 teaspoon garlic powder
1 teaspoon salt
1 teaspoon pepper
1 teaspoon lemon pepper
1 teaspoon Italian seasoning
1 teaspoon oregano
1 teaspoon onion salt
2 bay leaves
1 can chicken broth

Put tomato paste into large pan or dutch oven. Add chicken broth and 1½ quarts water. Bring liquids to a boil. Meanwhile, cut steak into bite-size pieces and brown it in a small amount of oil in a skillet. Add to liquid mixture. Add all vegetables and seasonings. Simmer 3 to 4 hours. Add more water if needed. Freezes beautifully.

This is my daughter, Kendall's very favorite winter food and probably my most original recipe!

Miniature Swiss Quiches

- 1 (3-ounce) package cream cheese, softened
- ½ cup butter
- 1 cup flour
- 1 cup Swiss cheese, grated (Cheddar or Monterey Jack may be used)
- 1 egg, slightly beaten
- ½ cup milk
- Dash salt
- Paprika

Cream the cream cheese and butter; add flour and mix well. Shape dough into a ball. Wrap in plastic wrap and chill. When ready to bake, divide dough into 24 small pieces. Press into greased miniature muffin tins. (Unfilled shells may be frozen at this point and filled when ready to serve.) Divide the grated cheese evenly in each shell. (If shells are frozen there is no need to thaw before filling.) Beat egg, milk and salt together and carefully pour over the cheese. Sprinkle with the paprika. Bake at 350° 20 to 30 minutes. (These may also be frozen after they are baked. To serve, allow quiches to come to room temperature and warm in a 300° oven.)

Cheese and Corn Muffins

- ½ cup cornmeal
- 1 cup flour
- 3 teaspoons baking powder
- 1 tablespoon sugar
- ½ teaspoon salt
- ¾ cup milk
- 1 egg, well beaten
- 1 tablespoon melted butter
- 1 tablespoon chopped green pepper
- 1 teaspoon chopped onion
- ½ cup shredded Cheddar cheese

Combine dry ingredients. Add milk gradually and mix well. Add other ingredients. Turn into greased muffin pans and bake at 375° for 25 minutes. May be frozen for one month.

Applesauce Cake with Streusel Topping

Cake

½ cup butter
1½ cup flour
¾ cups brown sugar, firmly packed
1 teaspoon allspice
1 teaspoon soda
2 teaspoons cinnamon
½ teaspoon salt
1 teaspoon vanilla
1 cup applesauce
1 egg
½ cup chopped dates or raisins

Preheat oven to 350°. Melt butter in saucepan. Add all other ingredients for cake and mix well. Pour into well-greased 9-inch cake pan.

Topping

¼ cup sugar
¼ cup brown sugar, firmly packed
¼ cup flour
¼ teaspoon cinnamon
¼ teaspoon nutmeg
¼ cup soft butter
¼ cup chopped nuts

Combine all ingredients for topping in mixing bowl and mix well. Sprinkle over cake batter. Bake for 40 to 50 minutes or until top springs back when lightly touched in center.

A THANKSGIVING FEAST - MISSISSIPPI STYLE

SERVES 12

Artichoke Cheese Puffs

Roast Turkey

or

Smoked Turkey (See Index)

Cranberry Sauce

Oyster Dressing

Frozen Fruit Salad

Sweet Potato Casserole

Celery and Water Chestnut Casserole

Refrigerator Rolls

Mississippi Pecan Pie

Pumpkin Pie (See Index)

Thanksgiving Feast - Mississippi Style

Beacuse Thanksgiving is primarily a family event, let the children decide on and make the centerpiece and the placards. They might also write a brief Thanksgiving play, litany of thanks or other suitable ``production''. If there are no children, use a cornicopia filled with Indian corn, fresh vegetables (red and green bell peppers, cauliflower, squash, etc.) and flowers. For the cloth, use ecru or warm brown linen to suggest the earth and its bounty. A copper bowl of fall leaves and pyracantha will add a warm glow.

Artichoke Cheese Puffs

12 baked patty shells (miniature)
2 8-ounce plus 1 3-ounce packages cream cheese with chives, room temperature
1 teaspoon Tabasco
6 tablespoons softened butter
3 eggs
2 tablespoons Worcestershire
3 cans artichoke hearts, drained
(Set aside 12 whole artichoke hearts, finely chop remaining hearts and add to cream cheese mixture.)

Place baked shells on baking sheets. Beat cheese with butter, eggs and seasonings. Spoon ½ of mixture into bottom of each shell. Place an artichoke heart in center of mixture and top with remaining cheese mixture. Bake 20 to 30 minutes at 475° until the cheese puffs slightly and is brown on top.

Roast Turkey

Wash turkey in cold running water and pat inside dry with paper towels; leave outside of bird moist. Stuff turkey (wrap any leftover stuffing in foil and place in oven during last hour turkey is roasted). Fasten neck skin to body with skewer. Push legs under band of skin at tail, or tie to tail. Place turkey, breast side up, on rack in shallow open roasting pan. Insert meat thermometer in thigh muscle or in thickest part of breast; thermometer must not touch bone. Place loose covering or "tent" of aluminum foil over turkey. Roast in slow oven (325°) according to timetable. Remove foil last half hour to brown turkey. When turkey is done, the thermometer should read 180° to 190°.

Basic Roast Turkey Timetable

Ready-To-Cook Weight (pounds)	Approximate Time (hours)
6 to 8	3½ to 4
8 to 12	4 to 4½
12 to 16	4½ to 5½
16 to 20	5½ to 6½
20 to 24	6½ to 7

Since turkeys vary in type, roasting periods are approximate. You may have to decrease or increase indicated times.

Oyster Dressing

- 5 to 6 cups breadcrumbs
- ½ cup melted butter
- ½ cup chopped onion
- ⅛ teaspoon black pepper
- 1 egg, beaten
- 1 teaspoon salt
- ½ cup cold water to moisten
- ¼ teaspoon thyme
- 1 teaspoon sage
- ½ to 1 pint oysters

Combine all ingredients. Pour into greased 3-quart casserole. Bake at 350° for 1 hour. Serves 8 to 10.

Frozen Fruit Salad

1 large can crushed pineapple
¼ pound cream cheese
1 cup mayonnaise
2 tablespoons powder sugar
1 small bag miniature marshmallows
1 cup whipping cream, whipped
1 small jar maraschino cherries, chopped

Put marshmallows in mixing bowl. Add pineapple, sugar, cherries and juice. Mix cream cheese and mayonnaise and add to mixture. Fold in whipped cream last. Put in mold or muffin tins and freeze.

This the girls' favorite salad. It is a good salad to take to friends who are ill. My friend, Pam Lowry gave me this one.

Sweet Potato Casserole

7 medium sweet potatoes
2 sticks butter
2 eggs
1 teaspoon baking powder
1 teaspoon vanilla
2 teaspoons cinnamon
1 cup sugar
¾ cup buttermilk
1½ cups pecans, chopped
Miniature marshmallows

Cook potatoes, peel and put in mixer bowl. Add all of the ingredients except marshmallows and mix well. Put mixture into casserole dish and bake at 350° for 20 minutes. Top with miniature marshmallows. Bake 10 minutes more.
Serves 12.

Celery and Water Chestnut Casserole

- 4 tablespoons flour
- 4 tablepsoons butter
- ¾ cup milk
- 1½ cup chicken broth (homemade preferred)
- 5 cups celery, sliced
- ½ teaspoon salt
- ½ cup slivered almonds
- 1 can sliced water chestnuts, drained
- 1 can sliced mushrooms, drained
- ¾ cup freshly grated Parmesan cheese
- ¾ cups cheese crackers, crushed
- 4 tablespoons melted butter

Melt 4 tablespoons butter. Stir in flour and cook until bubbly. Add milk and chicken broth, stirring until thick. Cover celery with water, add salt and cook over medium heat, covered, for 5 to 7 minutes. Drain well. Add almonds, water chestnuts and musthrooms. Combine with cream sauce. Pour into well-greased 2-quart casserole. Mix Parmesan cheese, cheese crackers and 4 tablespoons butter. Sprinkle over top of casserole. Bake at 350° for 30 to 35 minutes. Make be made 1 day ahead of serving. Serves 12.

Refrigerator Rolls

- 2 packages yeast
- 1 cup warm water
- 1 cup boiling water
- ⅔ cup sugar
- 1 stick butter
- ½ cup salad oil
- 1½ teaspoons salt
- 2 eggs, well beaten
- 6 cups flour

Mix yeast in warm water, stirring until dissolved. Let stand for 5 minutes. In separate bowl, combine boiling water, sugar, butter, salad oil, and salt. Stir until butter melts. Let cool. When mixture cools, stir in beaten eggs. Mix with mixer until well blended. Add yeast mixture and continue to mix until all ingredients are thoroughly blended. Mix in 3 cups of the flour one cup at a time, mixing well after each addition. By hand, stir in enough of the remaining flour to make a stiff dough. Turn dough into well-greased bowl, turning to grease top. Cover with plastic wrap and refrigerate at least 2 to 4 hours before using. (Dough will keep in refrigerator up to 5 days.) When ready to use, turn as much of dough as needed out onto lightly floured surface and knead until smooth. Roll out and cut. Fold rounds in half and place in lightly greased pans. Cover and let rise until doubled in size, about 1 hour. Bake at 375° 12 to 14 minutes until brown. Remove from oven and immediately brush each roll with melted butter.

This simple and easy roll recipe is my family's favorite. My sister uses this recipe for her catering business.

Mississippi Pecan Pie

1 9-inch pie crust, unbaked
1/8 teaspoon salt
1 teaspoon vanilla
1 cup sugar
1 cup light corn syrup
3 eggs, lightly beaten
2 tablespoons butter, melted
1½ cups pecan halves

See index for pie crust recipe. Mix the ingredients together except pecans. When well mixed add pecans and stir. Be sure pecans are well coated. Pour into pie crust. Bake at 400° for 15 minutes. Reduce heat to 350° and bake another 30 to 35 minutes. Make 2 pies to serve 12.

A YULETIDE OPEN HOUSE

SERVES TWO HUNDRED

Overnight Eggnog (Make 6 times)
Cranberry Punch or Wassail Bowl
Coffee Appetizer Trees (Make 10)
Smokers
Curried Shrimp Spread

Trays of:
Sesame Wafers (Make 5 times)
Holiday Delight (Make 6)
Spicy Pecans (Make 6)
Marinated Cheese (Make 5 times)

Combined Sandwich Trays of:
Spinach Sandwiches Deviled Pimento Sandwiches
Cucumber Sandwiches Artichoke Spread

Trays of:
Nut Crickle Almond Brittle
Chocolate Divinity Heavenly Hash Squares

Large bowl of
Brandied Cherries

Trays of Assorted Cookies:
Fruitcake Bars
Cookie Logs Brandied Wreaths
Ginger Strips Toffee Squares

Trays of:
Eggnog Tarts (Make 150 to 200)
Rum Cake (Make 4)
Bourbon Pound Cake (Make 4)

This party is ideal for five or six couples to host during the holiday season.

A Yuletide Open House

This party deserves your very best and will require some advance thought and preparation, especially if you are doing it alone. The cookies, candies, tarts, cakes, nuts, sesame wafers, marinated cheese and brandied cherries can be made a month or more ahead and frozen or kept as the recipe suggests. The sandwiches can be frozen 2 weeks ahead or made early in the week of the party, tightly wrapped, and kept in the refrigerator. Don't leave anything for "last minute" that can be done early.

If you don't have a special Christmas Cloth, consider making one of green velvet. The green is usually a good color to blend or contrast with any other colors you might choose for your Christmas decor and will be usuable for many years. A crocheted runner down the center of the table, or wide bands of gaily colored silk ribbons can be used. Fill a large silver, crystal or brass bowl, depending on the other table appointments, with the prettiest Christmas balls you can find, adding live stems of holly or pine. The glow of candles on either side of the bowl will complete the effect.

Overnight Eggnog

6 dozen egg yolks
9 cups bourbon
4½ cups sugar
12 quarts milk
6 dozen egg whites
6 quarts whipping cream

Beat egg yolks until lemon colored. Add bourbon slowly, a jigger at a time. Add sugar slowly; then add milk and beat well. Cover bowl and set in refrigerator overnight. Just before serving, beat egg whites until stiff and fold into yolk-milk mixture. Beat cream until stiff and add nutmeg. Pour over mixture. Ladle into cups so that each cup is topped with a layer of whipped cream and nutmeg.

200 servings.

This eggnog is so rich that one recipe will serve 200 if you have another beverage that you are serving, too. It is delicious but one small cup is usually all one person wants.

Cranberry Punch

3 quarts cranberry juice cocktail
6 quarts strained orange juice
6 cups water
10 cups strained lemon juice
12 cups pineapple juice
12 cups sugar

Combine ingredients and blend well. Chill in refirgerator. Pour into a punch bowl with an ice ring and lemon slices.

Plastic holly frozen into a clear ice ring is a pretty addition to the punch bowl. Do Not *use fresh holly!*

Wassail Punch

4 gallons apple cider
4 quarts orange juice
4 cups lemon juice
4 quarts pineapple juice
60 cloves
16 sticks cinnamon
4 cups sugar

Mix all ingredients and simmer for 10 minutes. Remove cinnamon and cloves. Serve warm in punch cups.

Yield: 3 gallons. Serves 150 to 200.

For a festive punch bowl, float small oranges that have been precooked about 10 minutes. Stick several cloves in each orange.

Appetizer Tree

2 small heads curly endive, leaf lettuce, red tipped leaf lettuce or 2 bunches parsley
1 plastic foam craft cone (12 inches high)
5 cups assorted vegetable dippers (cherry tomatoes, caulifloweret, carrot curls, celery fans, radish roses, zucchini sticks, cucumber slices)

Thoroughly wash and dry endive, lettuce or parsley. Attach greens to cone, starting from bottom and working upwards, with toothpicks or common pins. Attach assorted vegetables to toothpicks and insert in tree for decorations. Arrange remaining vegetable dippers on serving plate around base of tree. Refrigerate until serving time. Serve with Curried Taragon Dill Dip.

For 200 you will need to make 10 of these trees. May be made one day ahead.

Curried Tarragon Dill Dip

2 cups mayonnaise
2 teaspoons garlic salt
1 teaspoon curry powder
2 teaspoons tarragon vinegar
2 teaspoons chopped green onion
2 teaspoons horseradish mustard
2 teaspoons dill weed

In small bowl, combine all ingredients; blend thoroughly. Chill. Serve with vegetable dippers. Refrigerate leftovers.

Makes 2½ cups.

Smokers

20 pounds tiny smoked sausage
10 16-ounce jars raspberry jam
10 tablespoons cider vinegar
Cayenne pepper to taste

Broil all sausages until browned. Combine jam, vinegar and cayenne in large pan. Bring to boil. Remove from heat. Add sausages and marinate overnight. When ready to serve, reheat sausages in marinade and fill chafing dishes. Serve hot.

Serves 200.

Curried Shrimp Spread

48 6-ounce cans shrimp, drained and chopped
32 ribs celery, diced
8 bell peppers, chopped
80 green onions, tops and bottoms, chopped
6 cups mayonnaise
2 cups cream style horseradish
¾ to 1 cup curry powder, to taste
Tabasco to taste
Paprika

Mix all ingredients except paprika. Chill several hours or overnight. Serve with Ritz Crackers.

Serves 200.

Sesame Wafers

¾ cup all-purpose flour
½ teaspoon baking powder
½ teaspoon salt
8 ounces sharp cheddar cheese, grated (2¼ cups)
¼ cup butter, room temperature
½ teaspoon ground red pepper
2 dashes hot pepper sauce
½ cup sesame seed (2 ounces)

Sift flour, baking powder and salt. Combine cheese and butter in large bowl and mix until smooth. Add flour mixture, red pepper and pepper sauce and blend with fingertips or pastry blender to form smooth dough. Shape dough into 2 logs about 1 inch in diameter. Roll in sesame seed. Wrap in waxed paper and refrigerate until firm. Preheat oven to 425°. Cut dough into ⅛-inch thick slices. Arrange on ungreased baking sheets, spacing ¾ inch apart. Bake until edges are lightly browned, about 8 to 10 minutes. Serve warm or at room temperature. Store remaining wafers in airtight container.

Make this recipe five times to serve 200.

Holiday Delight

12 ounces Philadelphia cream cheese
1 stick butter
½ cup sour cream
½ cup sugar
1 envelope plain gelatin
¼ cup cold water
½ cup white raisins
1 cup slivered almonds, toasted
Grated rinds of two lemons
Saltine crackers

Let cream cheese, butter, and sour cream come to room temperature. Cream well and add sugar. Soften envelope of gelatin in ¼ cup cold water. Dissolve over hot water. Add to cream cheese mixture. Then add raisins, slivered almonds, and lemon rind. Put in one-quart mold in refrigerator. When firm unmold and serve with saltine crackers.

Make 6 of these. This will freeze; thaw before serving.

Spicy Pecans

- 3 tablespoons butter or margarine
- 2 teaspoons salt
- 1 pound pecans
- 3 tablespoons Worcestershire sauce
- ¼ teaspoon cayenne pepper
- ½ teaspoon cinnamon
- Dash Tabasco

Preheat oven to 275°. Melt butter in heavy baking dish. Stir in salt. Add pecans and toss well until thoroughly coated. Add Worcestershire sauce, cayenne pepper, cinnamon and Tabasco. Toss again. Roast in oven 45 minutes, stirring frequently until nuts are slightly burned and crisp. Turn off oven and leave in closed oven for another ½ hour. Makes 4 cups.

Make 6 times this amount to serve 200.

These will keep or freeze.

Marinated Cheese

- 1 pound firm cheese (use Swiss, Cheddar or Monterey Jack or all three)
- ½ cup olive oil
- ¼ cup wine vinegar
- ¼ teaspoon oregano
- 4 to 5 thin slices onion
- Salt and pepper to taste

Cut cheese in cubes. Mix remaining ingredients. Pour over cheese. Marinate overnight. Pour off marinade. Serve at room temperature. May be made up to 1 week ahead.

Spinach Sandwiches

- 2 10-ounce packages frozen chopped spinach, thawed, but not cooked
- 1 8-ounce can water chestnuts, drained and chopped
- ½ cup sour cream
- 1 teaspoon lemon pepper
- 1 teaspoon salt
- ½ teaspoon cayenne pepper
- 6 green onions, tops and bottoms, chopped
- 4 tablespoons mayonnaise
- 2 loaves thin-sliced bread, crust trimmed

Squeeze water from thawed spinach. Mix with remaining ingredients, except bread. (More sour cream may be added, if necessary.) Spread mixture on half the bread slices, top with remaining slices of bread. Cut diagonally twice (4 small triangles). Each recipe should yield about 4 dozen small sandwiches.

Serves 200.

Deviled Pimento Spread

8 ounces cream cheese
1 small carton pimento cheese
1 large can deviled ham

Cream all together. Spread on white bread with a little mayonnaise.

Make this four times.

Cucumber Sandwiches

1 8-ounce package cream cheese
1 teaspoon lemon juice
1 tablespoon milk
1 teaspoon salt

Mix to spreading consistency, adding more lemon juice if necessary.

Spread on bread. Slice cucumbers thin and put on bread.

Make this four times.

Artichoke Spread

10 cans artichoke hearts, drained and chopped fine
10 packages Hidden Valley Ranch dressing mix
2½ cups mayonnaise (more if necessary)

Mix all together. Spread on whole wheat bread.

This can easily be converted to a dip by adding 8 ounces of cream cheese and 1 cup sour cream. Omit the mayonnaise.

Nut Crickle

2 cups salted cashews, toasted
2 cups sugar
⅔ cup light corn syrup
½ cup water
3 tablespoons butter
1 teaspoon vanilla
½ teaspoon soda

Butter 15×10-inch jelly roll pan. In large heavy saucepan, heat sugar, corn syrup and water to boiling. Stir constantly until sugar is dissolved. Cook, without stirring, over medium heat, until candy thermometer registeres 300° or hard crack stage. Remove from heat. Stir in butter, vanilla and soda. Add cashews. Pour mixture into prepared pan. When cooked, break into pieces.

Yield: 1¾ pounds

Almond Brittle

1 stick butter
1 cup sugar
2 tablespoons water
1 small package slivered almonds

Heat all in iron skillet. Cook over medium-high heat, stirring all the time. When light brown, turn out on lightly salted aluminum foil. Spread thin quickly. Let cool, break into pieces.

I have had this recipe of Nancy Spaulding's so long it calls for a 39¢ package of almonds!

Chocolate Divinity

2½ cups sugar
½ cup light Karo
½ cup water
¼ teaspoon salt
2 egg whites
2 squares melted chocolate
1 teaspoon vanilla
1 cup nuts

Mix sugar, Karo, water and salt together in pan. Cook over medium heat to boil; reduce heat. Cook without stirring to 248°.

Beat egg whites until stiff.

Pour about ½ of syrup slowly over whites, beating constantly. Cook remaining ½ syrup to 272°. Add slowly to first mixture, continue beating 5 minutes.

Add melted chocolate and vanilla.

Beat until mixture holds shape. Add nuts.

This wonderful candy recipe is from my aunt, Mildred Ashby, and came to me in a collection of her favorite recipes as a wedding gift — still treasured after 30 years!

Heavenly Hash Squares

- 1 12-ounce package (2 cups) semi-sweet chocolate chips
- 1 14-ounce can sweetened condensed milk
- 2 teaspoons vanilla
- 1 package coconut pecan frosting mix
- 2½ cups miniature marshmallows

Lightly butter a foil-lined 9-inch square pan. In large heavy saucepan, melt chips in milk over low heat. Remove from heat. Stir in vanilla, frosting mix and marshmallows. Spread mixture evenly in prepared pan. Chill until firm. Cut into squares. Store candy in tightly covered container in refrigerator.

64 pieces

Brandied Cherries

- 1 pound canned, pitted Bing cherries, drained
- 4 ounces red currant jelly
- 1 ounce brandy

Mix cherries and currant jelly. Refrigerate overnight. Add brandy when ready to serve. Use picks to serve.

Make five times this amount to serve 200.

Serves 15 to 20.

Fruitcake Bars

6 tablespoons margarine or butter, melted
1½ cups graham cracker crumbs
1 cup shredded coconut
1½ cups mixed candied fruit
1 cup chopped pitted dates
1 cup chopped walnuts
1 14-ounce can sweetened condensed milk

Heat oven to 350°. Pour melted margarine in 15×10-inch jelly roll pan. Sprinkle graham cracker crumbs over margarine, shaking pan to distribute crumbs evenly. Layer in coconut, candied fruit, dates and walnuts. Press mixture gently, to level. Pour sweetened condensed milk evenly on top. Bake at 350° for 25 to 30 minutes or until set and lightly browned. Cool in pan on wire rack. Cut into bars or squares.

Yield: 60 cookies

These are excellent. Gayle's aunt, Nell Childs, gave me the recipe at a family reunion many years ago.

Cookie Logs

Cookies

¾ cup sugar
1 cup butter, softened
2 teaspoons vanilla
2 teaspoons rum extract
1 egg
3 cups all-purpose flour
1 teaspoon nutmeg

Frosting

2½ cups powdered sugar
3 tablespoons butter, softened
2 to 3 tablespoons half-and-half or milk
1 teaspoon rum extract
½ teaspoon vanilla

Heat oven to 350°. In large bowl, combine all ingredients except flour and nutmeg. Beat on medium speed until light and fluffy. Lightly spoon flour into measuring cup; level off. Stir in flour and nutmeg; mix well. Divide dough into 6 parts. On lightly floured surface, shape each part into long rope ½ inch in diameter. Cut into 3-inch lengths; place on ungreased cookie sheets.

Bake at 350° for 12 to 15 minutes or until light golden brown. Cool. In small bowl, combine frosting ingredients; spread on cooled cookies. If desired, mark frosting with tines of fork to resemble bark. Sprinkle lightly with nutmeg.

Yield: 42 to 48 cookies

Brandied Wreaths

Cookies

- 2/3 cup butter, softened
- 1/3 cup sugar
- 1 egg
- 2 tablespoons brandy
- 2 tablespoons grated orange peel
- 1 teaspoon nutmeg
- 1/4 teaspoon salt
- 2 1/4 cups all-purpose flour
- 1/4 cup chopped red maraschino cherries, drained
- 1/4 cup chopped green maraschino cherries, drained

Glaze

- 1 1/4 cups powdered sugar
- 1 tablespoon milk
- 1 tablespoon brandy
- 1/8 teaspoon nutmeg
- Red and green maraschino cherries, drained and chopped (for decorating)

Heat oven to 350°. Grease cookie sheets. In large bowl, combine butter, sugar, egg, brandy and orange peel. Mix well. Stir in salt and flour. Blend in cherries. Shape rounded teaspoonfuls of dough into 5-inch long strips. Shape strips into wreath shapes. Place 2 inches apart on prepared cookie sheets. Bake at 350° for 8 to 12 minutes, or until edges are lightly browned. Cool.

In small bowl, combine glaze ingredients; blend until smooth. Frost warm cookie wreaths with glaze. Decorate with chopped cherries.

Yield: 36 cookies

Ginger Strips

- 3/4 cup butter, softened
- 1 cup sugar
- 1 egg
- 1/4 cup molasses
- 2 teaspoons soda
- 1/2 teaspoon salt
- 1/2 teaspoon cinnamon
- 1/2 teaspoon ginger
- 1/2 teaspoon cloves
- 2 1/2 cups all-purpose flour

Glaze

- 3/4 cup powdered sugar
- 1 tablespoon butter, softened
- 1 tablespoon milk
- 1/2 teaspoon vanilla

Heat oven to 350°. Grease cookie sheets. In large bowl, combine butter, sugar, egg and molasses. Mix thoroughly. Blend in remaining ingredients. Divide dough into 6 portions. Shape each part into a 12-inch roll on prepared cookie sheet; flatten slightly. Brush roll tops with water; sprinkle lightly with sugar. Bake at 350° for 12 to 15 minutes, or until golden brown. Cool 5 minutes. Cut diagonally into 3/4-inch bars. Do not separate. Cool completely.

In small bowl, combine glaze ingredients until smooth. If needed, add a few more drops of milk to make glaze consistency. Spoon over bars. Allow glaze to set. Separate into bars.

Yield: 64 bars

Toffee Squares

Graham crackers
1 cup brown sugar
1 cup butter
1 (11¾-ounce) package milk chocolate chips
1 cup ground pecans

Line a pan (at least 10×15 inches) with foil on bottom and sides. Line this with separated rectangular graham crackers (not crumbs) placed side by side. Simmer together for 3 minutes the sugar and butter. Pour mixture quickly over crackers and bake in preheated 400° oven 5 minutes. Remove from oven. Sprinkle chocolate chips over all, spreading to cover as they melt. Sprinkle pecans over top. Cool and cut into squares. Makes about 75 squares.

Variation: Add finely chopped nuts and 1 teaspoon vanilla to simmered sugar-butter mixture. Pour over crackers. Bake at 350° 10 to 12 minutes. Delete chocolate. Almonds can be used.

Wanda Harder shared this delicious recipe. It is equally good without the chocolate chips and older children enjoy making them.

Eggnog Tarts

2 tablespoons sugar
1 envelope unflavored gelatin
⅛ teaspoon ground nutmeg
1 cup milk
3 slightly beaten egg yolks
¼ cup rum or brandy
3 egg whites
¼ cup sugar
½ cup whipping cream
10 Tart Shells
Whole candied cherries (optional)

In medium saucepan combine the 2 tablespoons sugar, gelatin, nutmeg, and ¼ teaspoon salt; stir in milk and yolks. Cook and stir till slightly thickened and bubbly. Cook and stir 2 minutes longer. Cool; stir in rum or brandy. Pour into a large bowl; chill till partially set, stirring occasionally.

In small mixer bowl beat egg whites till soft peaks form; gradually add the ¼ cup sugar. Beat till stiff peaks form. Fold the beaten egg whites into the gelatin mixture.

Whip cream till soft peaks form; fold into gelatin-egg white mixture. Chill till mixture mounds. Spoon into Tart Shells. If desired, top with whole candied cherries. Chill till firm.

Makes 10.

Tart Shells

2 cups all-purpose flour
1 teaspoon salt
⅔ cup shortening
6 to 7 tablespoons cold water

In a medium bowl stir together the flour and the salt. Cut in the shortening till the pieces are the size of small peas. Sprinkle 1 tablespoon of the water over part of the flour mixture; gently toss with a fork. Push to the side of the bowl. Repeat till all of the dough is moistened. Form the dough into 2 balls.

On a lightly floured surface roll 1 ball at a time to ⅛-inch thickness. Cut each into five 5-inch circles (reroll scraps, if necessary). Fit the dough circles into fluted tart pans. Trim edges. Prick bottom and sides with a fork. Bake tart shells in a 450° oven for 10 to 12 minutes or till golden brown. Cool thoroughly.

Makes 10 tart shells.

These are especially popular, so make plenty. The baked tart shells can be made ahead and frozen, either baked or unbaked.

Rum Cake

- 2 sticks butter
- 2 cups sugar
- 6 eggs
- 2 cups plus 3 tablespoons sifted flour
- ⅛ teaspoon salt
- ¼ cup rum

Rum Sauce

- 1½ cups sugar
- ¼ cup water
- 2 tablespoons white corn syrup
- ½ cup rum

Cream butter then blend in sugar. Add eggs one at a time, beating well after each addition. Add flour and salt all at once. Blend in rum. Bake in tube pan for 1 hour and 45 minutes at 300°.

Sauce

Bring sugar, water and syrup to a boil. Remove from heat and add rum. Pour over cake while still warm.

Make 4 cakes to serve 200. Will keep or will freeze.

Bourbon Pound Cake

- 1 pound butter
- 3 cups sugar
- 8 eggs, separated
- 3 cups flour, sifted
- 2 teaspoons vanilla
- 1 teaspoon butter flavoring
- 2 teaspoons almond flavoring
- 4 tablespoons bourbon
- 1 cup nuts, chopped

Cream butter and sugar together until fluffy. Add egg yolks and beat well. Mix in sifted flour, flavorings and bourbon. Beat egg whites until stiff. Fold into batter. Prepare a tube pan. Do not use bundt pan. Grease well the bottom of the pan. Cut a circle of wax paper and fit into bottom. Grease wax paper. Sprinkle bottom of pan with ½ cup nuts, add batter and sprinkle remaining ½ cup of nuts on top. Bake at 325° 1½ to 2 hours or until brown. To prevent top of cake from cracking open, cover with foil the last 30 minutes of cooking.

My family doesn't care for fruitcake so this has been a good holiday cake for us. Make it ahead and wrap in bourbon-soaked cheesecloth, tightly wrapped in foil, for added flavor.

CHRISTMAS MORNING

SERVES SIX

Brandy Milk Punch

Cranberry Juice

Holiday Scrambled Eggs

Mama's Butter Roll

Strawberry Bread

Baked Oranges

Coffee

Christmas Morning

This menu and the suggested centerpiece can vary from completely informal to a very elegant breakfast, depending on your family's preference. Using silk ribbons, red, green and a combination (or use the colors you have used throughout the season) tie pine cones with bows. Pile into a basket to set an informal mood or a large silver bowl for more formality. Nice quality red and green plastic-coated plates and cups are available or go all-out with china, crystal and silver. Mark each place with a small surprise package—ranging from the simple to the sublime—remembering that thoughtfulness and surprise are the more important elements.

Another suggestion for a beautiful centerpiece is to place a fresh pineapple upright on a tray—brass or silver—and create a della Robbia wreath effect with fruits, frosted grapes, and nuts. To frost grapes; beat egg whites just until foamy; with a pastry brush, "paint" clusters of grapes, being certain that each grape is covered. Let dry slightly until sticky to the touch but not dripping. Sprinkle with sugar. Set on waxed paper and let dry completely. (The heavier the sugar coating the prettier.)

Brandy-Milk Punch

2 cups milk
¾ cup brandy
¼ cup powdered sugar
1 egg white
3 tablespoons anisette
½ teaspoon freshly grated nutmeg
½ teaspoon vanilla
4 ice cubes

In a blender container combine milk, brandy, powdered sugar, egg white, anisette, ½ teaspoon freshly grated nutmeg, vanilla, and the ice cubes. Cover and blend till frothy. To serve, pour into tall glasses; garnish with freshly grated nutmeg, if desired. Serves 6.

Holiday Scrambled Eggs

8 to 10 eggs, scrambled soft
Currant jelly
Sharp Cheddar cheese, grated

Soft scramble eggs; place in Pyrex dish. Spoon currant jelly over eggs and top with grated cheese. Bake at 350° 3 to 5 minutes.

Serves 6.

These are truly delicious and different.

Mama's Butter Roll

1½ cups flour
½ cup shortening
½ teaspoon salt
¼ cup water
1 stick butter
1 cup sugar
1½ teaspoons cinnamon
1 cup half-and-half
½ cup sugar
1 teaspoon vanilla

Mix flour and salt in a bowl. Cut in shortening with pastry blender or two knives, as for pie crust. With a fork, mix in water, stirring until dough holds together. Turn out onto floured surface and knead lightly for two or three turns. Roll dough out to ⅛-inch thickness. Melt butter. Add sugar and cinnamon, mixing until well blended. Spread mixture over dough. Roll in jelly roll fashion and cut into 1½-inch slices. Place in a well-greased pan. Bake at 375° for 20 minutes. While rolls are baking, make a sauce of the half-and-half and sugar, mixed together in a saucepan. Cook over low heat, stirring, for 10 minutes. Remove from heat, add vanilla. After rolls have baked for 20 minutes, remove from oven, pour sauce over, and return to a 400° oven for an additional 10 minutes.

My grandmother Ashby made these for me when I was a little girl and the recipe was given to me by my aunt, Loura Robertson.

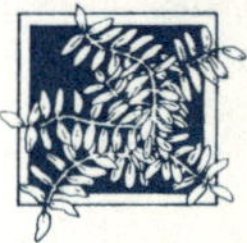

Strawberry Bread

1 cup butter
1½ cups sugar
4 eggs
3 cups flour
1 teaspoon salt
1 teaspoon cream of tartar
½ teaspoon soda
1 cup strawberry jam
½ cup sour cream
1 cup chopped nuts

Cream butter, sugar until fluffy. Add eggs, one at a time, beating well after each addition. Combine jam and sour cream and add alternately with sifted dry ingredients. Mix until blended and stir in nuts. Bake in 2 greased and floured loaf pans or 5 of the small 4½×2½ pans at 350° for 50 to 60 minutes or until done. Freezes well.

This is a combination of several strawberry bread recipes that I've had through the years. It stays moist several days, makes wonderful toast and is delicious spread with cream cheese mixed with mashed strawberries and cut into finger sandwiches.

Baked Oranges

6 oranges
Whole Cloves
Butter
Sugar
Salt
Water

Soak oranges 12 hours in water to cover. (Weigh down oranges to keep under water.) Remove from water. Slice in halves and place in flat Pyrex dish. Sprinkle with sugar and salt. Stick 2 to 3 whole cloves on top of each half and dot with butter. Pour 1 inch water in bottom of casserole. Cover tightly with foil. Bake at 300° for 2 hours. May be made day ahead.

Serves 6.

(Be sure to eat rind, too!)

TEXAS CHRISTMAS DINNER

SERVES EIGHT TO TEN

Buttered Christmas Cheer

Fruit Punch

Sherry Cheese Puffs

Glazed Brie with Apple Slices

Small Dishes of Cranberry Ice

Turkey-in-the Sack or Roast Turkey (See Index)

Cornbread Dressing or Madeira Dressing

Giblet Gravy

Cranberry Relish

Green Beans

Creamed Onions

Brandied Sweet Potatoes

Daiquiri Fruit Salad

Refrigerator Rolls (See Index)

Mincemeat Pie

Pumpkin Pie

Cherry Spice Cake

Coffee

Next-Day-Turkey, too!

Texas Christmas Dinner

Memories should be the golden thread that ties your Christmas Dinner firmly in place for each guest—be they family or friends.

For the centerpiece, cover a box with a removable lid inside and out (lid, too) with Christmas wrapping. Fill the box with toys of the past. (If there are to be children present these toys could be new and each child might be allowed to choose one after dinner to keep.) Some of the toys can be propped on the outside of the box and the lid, complete with a beautiful bow, can be laid at an angle to the box, with toys on it, or propped against the box. Keep height and table proportions in mind as you arrange this. (If you don't want to use toys, the box is an excellent container for fresh Christmas greenery, tied with small bows or tiny silver bells.) Use small boxes, wrapped in the same or in coordinating paper, a bow and Christmas tag with each guest's name as place cards.

Early in the year, buy large, unpainted wooden letters to form MERRY CHRISTMAS. Paint each letter in a different Christmas motif (some solid colors, red, green; some with candy-cane effect; holly leaves, etc.). This could be a good rainy summer afternoon project for older children.

It's no fun for one or two people to be left with the clean-up after a large holiday meal, so turn it into a "spirit of sharing" event.

Fill a small wastebasket with brightly wrapped "gifts", such as new rubber gloves, a new dish towel, small whisk broom; directions to the storage places for china, crystal, silver or whatever special serving pieces will be used could contain a piece of candy, package of gum or some other small treat. Enclose the instructions for how each of these "gifts" is to be used in the joint clean-up and also remind everyone that they may keep their "surprises". (The one who gets the wastebasket will take out all the trash!) Announce before anyone opens the packages that trades may be made—but, after they are opened, the job is yours! Be sure to include some chores that will involve children, too.

Buttered Christmas Cheer

1 cup butter, softened
½ cup packed brown sugar
½ cup sifted powdered sugar
1 teaspoon ground nutmeg
1 teaspoon ground cinnamon
1 pint vanilla ice cream, softened
Rum or brandy
Boiling water
Cinnamon sticks (optional)

In a small mixer bowl cream together the butter, the brown sugar, the powdered sugar, the nutmeg, and the cinnamon at medium speed of electric mixer. Blend in the softened ice cream. Turn the ice cream mixture into a 4-cup freezer container. Seal and freeze. (Ice cream mixture will not freeze solid.)

At serving time, for each serving, spoon 2 to 4 tablespoons of the ice cream mixture into each mug. Add about 3 tablespoons rum or brandy and about ½ cup boiler water to each mug. Stir well. Garnish each mug with a cinnamon stick stirrer, if desired. Makes 12 to 24)

Fruit Punch

2 6-ounce cans frozen orange juice
1 6-ounce can frozen lemonade
1 cup pineapple juice
¼ cup cherry juice (optional)
2 quarts pale dry ginger ale

Mix fruit juices; cover and let stand 12 hours or more in refrigerator. Add cold ginger ale to juices just before serving. Serve over crushed ice or freeze half the ginger ale in refrigerator trays.

Serves 24.

Sherry Cheese Puffs

½ cup water
¼ teaspoon salt
¼ cup butter
1 tablespoon sherry
½ cup flour
2 eggs
1 5-ounce jar Old English sharp cheese spread, softened

Filling

1 3-ounce package cream cheese, softened
1 tablespoon chopped stuffed green olives
2 teaspoons sherry

Heat oven to 400°. Grease cookie sheet. In medium saucepan, heat water, salt and butter to boiling. Add flour and sherry, stirring constantly, until mixture forms ball and leaves sides of pan. Remove from heat; blend in ¼ cup cheese spread. Add eggs, one at a time, beating well after each addition. Mixture will be smooth and glossy. Drop dough by teaspoonfuls onto prepared cookie sheet. Bake at 400° 15 to 20 minutes until puffed and golden brown. Remove from cookie sheets. Cool slightly; make small slit in side of puffs to release steam and prevent sogginess. Cool completely.

In small bowl, combine remaining cheese spread, cream cheese, olives and sherry; blend until smooth and fluffy. Slit puffs; remove any soft filaments of dough. Fill with scant teaspoonful of cheese mixture.

Yield: 18 puffs

Glazed Brie

1 small wheel of Brie, room temperature
2 tablespoons powdered sugar
½ cup sliced almonds
Red grapes for garnish
Apple slices

Scrape rind from top of cheese. Sift 1 tablespoon powdered sugar over top. Arrange sliced almonds over, pressing firmly into place. (May be refrigerated for 2 to 3 days, tightly wrapped, at this point.) Return to room temperature if chilled. Place brie on baking sheet. Sift remaining 2 tablespoons powdered sugar over almonds. Brown under pre-heated broiler, turning as necessary, until top is evenly browned. Watch carefully, sugar caramelizes quickly! Transfer to serving platter and garnish with small bunches of red grapes. Serve with apple slices.

Cranberry Ice

2 1-pound cans jellied cranberry sauce
2 cups lemon-lime soda
Mint leaves (optional)

Beat cranberry sauce on high speed in large bowl of electric mixer until smooth, about 5 minutes. Gently fold in lemon-lime soda. Divide mixture between 2 plastic ice cube trays and freeze until firm.

Transfer cubes to food processor and mix until frothy. Turn into 1-quart container, cover and freeze until ready to use. Let stand at room temperature about 30 minutes before serving. Garnish with mint leaves.

Turkey-In-The-Sack

1 teaspoon pepper
2 teaspoons salt
3 teaspoons paprika
4 teaspoons hot water
1 cup peanut oil
1 turkey, 14 to 16 pounds

Combine pepper, salt, paprika, and hot water. Let stand at least 10 minutes. Add peanut oil and mix thoroughly. Select turkey carefully. It should not exceed 14 to 16 pounds. Wash and dry. Rub peanut oil mixutre into inside and outside of turkey. Pour remaining oil into large paper sack (type used in grocery stores). Rub oil inside sack until every pore in every inch of the sack is sealed. Add additional oil if needed.

Place turkey in sack, breast up. Fold over end of sack and tie securely with string. Bake at 325 ° approximately 10 minutes per pound. Since the sack is airtight, the turkey is cooked by live steam; therefore, when the sack is opened, be careful! With no basting, no careful watching, the turkey comes out tender to the bone and golden brown!

Creamed Onions

3 pounds small white onions
1 teaspoon salt, divided
4 tablespoons butter
5 tablespoons flour
2 cups milk
⅛ teaspoon Tabasco sauce
Almonds and Parmesan cheese

Peel onions; place in saucepan. Add ½ teaspoon of the salt and enough water to cover. Bring to a boil; cover and cook 20 to 25 minutes. While onions are cooking, melt butter in saucepan; blend in flour and remaining ½ teaspoon salt. Gradually add milk; cook, stirring constantly, until mixture thickens and comes to a boil. Stir in Tabasco. Add drained onions; heat to serving temperature. Sprinkle with toasted almonds and Parmesan cheese.

Cornbread

½ to ¾ cup bacon drippings
1½ cups white or yellow cornmeal
½ cup flour
1 teaspoon salt
1 teaspoon baking powder
½ teaspoon baking soda
1 egg, beaten
1½ cups buttermilk

Place 2 to 3 tablespoons bacon drippings in each of 1½ to 2 muffin pans (or use black cast iron skillet and put about ½ cup drippings in it). Place in a 350° oven while mixing cornbread, watch to prevent burning. Mix all dry ingredients. Make a well in center. Add the egg to the buttermilk; mix well. Stir into dry ingredients only until blended. (Never overmix muffins!) Spoon batter into hot grease; increase heat to 400° and bake 12 to 15 minutes or until bottom is crusty and browned. Serve hot with butter.

1½ to 2 dozen muffins.

This is my mother's recipe and everyone agreed that hers was the best ever!

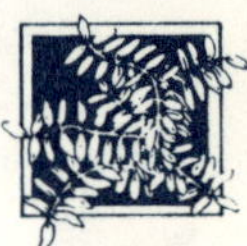

Cornbread Dressing

3½ cups cornbread crumbs
1½ cups white breadcrumbs, toasted
1½ cups butter, melted
1½ cups biscuit crumbs
3 tablespoons minced onion
1 cup chopped celery
2 teaspoons salt
½ teaspoon pepper
½ teaspoon savory seasoning
2 or 3 teaspoons sage
4 eggs beaten slightly
2 cups hot chicken broth

Crumble bread in large bowl. Melt butter and lightly sauté onion and celery. Add to crumb mixture; add other ingredients and mix well. If dressing seems too dry, add more broth. Bake in shallow pans at 400° about 30 to 40 minutes. Dressing should be firm but never cook until it is dry.

Serves 8.

Madeira Dressing

½ cup butter
1¼ cups diced onion
1 cup diced celery
½ cup chopped celery tops
1½ teaspoons thyme
1 pound bulk sausage, lightly browned
1 tablespoon salt
1½ teaspoons black pepper
6 to 8 cups coarse breadcrumbs (part white bread; part cornbread)
¾ cup Madeira wine

Melt butter; add onion, celery, celery tops, and thyme; cook until onion and celery are tender. Add to sausage; add salt, pepper, and breadcrumbs. Add Madeira and mix lightly. Stuff the turkey lightly.

Yield: enough for a 10-pound turkey

Giblet Gravy

1 cup butter
½ cup flour
Turkey giblets (neck, liver, gizzard) cooked and diced, discard neck
4 to 5 cups broth, heated
Turkey drippings from pan (if desired)
Salt and pepper to taste
3 to 4 hard cooked eggs, chopped

Melt butter; with whisk, stir in flour. Cook over medium heat until flour is lightly browned. Slowly whisk in broth and cook, stirring often, until thickened. Add chopped liver and gizzard, drippings from roasting pan, salt, pepper and chopped eggs. Heat thoroughly. Serve hot.

Note: Cook neck, liver, and gizzard in salted water to cover, boiling gently 30 minutes or until liver and gizzard are done. Discard neck. Chop liver and gizzard. Broth may be used as part of liquid for gravy.

Cranberry Relish

4 cups fresh cranberries, ground
4 oranges, unpeeled, seeded, and ground
4 apples, unpeeled, cored and ground
3 lemons, unpeeled, seeded and ground
4 cups sugar

Combine all ingredients in large bowl. Mix well. Chill. Store in airtight container in refrigerator several weeks.

Brandied Sweet Potatoes

6 large sweet potatoes, unpeeled
2 teaspoons cornstarch
½ teaspoon ground nutmeg
2 teaspoons salt
½ cup granulated sugar
1 cup water
1 tablespoon lemon juice
⅓ cup brandy
Miniature marshmallows

Put unpeeled sweet potatoes in boiling salted water to cover. Cover pan and cook about 25 minutes or until tender; drain and cool. In 1-quart saucepan, mix cornstarch, nutmeg, salt, and sugar. Gradually stir in water; cook over low heat, stirring constantly until clear. Stir in lemon juice and brandy.

Peel potatoes; slice crosswise, ¼ to ½ inch thick, into buttered shallow baking dish. Pour on sauce; cover and bake at 375° for 30 minutes or until glazed, basting occasionally. When glazed, sprinkle a few miniature marshmallows over potatoes and broil just until golden.

Serves 8.

Daiquiri Fruit Salad

2 cans (20 ounces each) crushed pineapple, drained (reserve syrup)
2¾ cups liquid (reserved syrup plus water)
3 packages (4-serving size) lime or lemon-flavored gelatin
2 can (6 ounces each) frozen limeade concentrate
1 cup mayonnaise or salad dressing
¼ cup light rum, if desired
1 cup whipping cream, whipped or 2 cups frozen whipped topping, thawed
4 medium bananas, sliced, if desired

In large saucepan, bring liquid to boiling; stir in gelatin to dissolve. Remove from heat; stir in limeade concentrate and rum. Using wire whisk or electric mixer, blend in mayonnaise. Chill until thickened but not set. Fold in pineapple, whipped cream and bananas. Spoon into 12-cup fluted tube pan. Chill until firm.

Serves 10 to 12.

Mincemeat Pie

1 10-inch pie shell, unbaked
1⅔ cups mincemeat
¾ cup chopped apples
¾ cup raisins
1 cup whole cherry preserves
4 tablespoons lemon juice
⅔ cup sugar
½ stick butter, cut up
Whipped cream
Sherry

Prepare pie shell (see Index). Set aside.

Combine all ingredients, pour into the unbaked pie shell, top with crust; bake at 400° for 40 to 50 minutes. Serve with whipped cream flavored with sherry. Makes two 8-inch pies or 1 deep 10-inch pie.

My daddy, Reagon Ashby, loves mincemeat pie and this is always for him.

Pumpkin Pie

1 10-inch pie shell, unbaked
3 eggs, slightly beaten
1 cup evaporated milk
1 cup sugar
1 cup pumpkin
⅛ teaspoon salt
1 stick butter, melted
½ teaspoon cinnamon
½ teaspoon nutmeg
½ teaspoon allspice
½ pint heavy cream
Walnuts, chopped

Prepare pie shell (see Index); set aside.

Cream eggs, milk and sugar. Add remaining ingredients, and mix in well. Pour into an unbaked 10-inch pie shell and bake at 400° for 40 minutes or until a silver knife inserted in the center comes out clean. Cool. Have edge of crust crimped high, as this is a very generous filling. Whip cream and spread over the cooled pie. Sprinkle walnuts over top.

Pecan Pie

1 stick butter
1 cup light Karo
1 cup sugar
3 large eggs, beaten
1 teaspoon vanilla
1 dash of salt
1 cup chopped pecans
9-inch unbaked pie shell

Prepare pie shell (see Index); set aside.

Brown butter in saucepan until it is golden brown, do not burn; let cool. In separate bowl, add ingredients in order listed; stir. Blend in browned butter well. Pour in unbaked pie shell and bake at 425° for 10 minutes, then lower to 325° for 40 minutes.

Burgundy Pudding

6 egg yolks
1 cup sugar
1 cup Burgundy or port wine
1 cup vanilla wafer crumbs
1 tablespoon gelatin softened in ½ cool water
6 stiffly beaten egg whites
1 cup chopped pecans

In saucepan, mix together egg yolks and sugar, stirring until well blended. Slowly whisk in wine (add slowly to avoid cooking the yolks). Cook over low heat, stirring constantly until thickened. Cool slightly and stir in softened gelatin. Stir until well blended. Add vanilla wafer crumbs and nuts. Fold in stiffly beaten egg whites. Mixture may be divided into individual serving dishes at this point or turned into a pretty crystal serving bowl. Refrigerate at least several hours before serving and may be made several days ahead. Flavor improves with age. When ready to serve, top with sweetened whipped cream and a stemmed maraschino cherry.

This, from my aunt, Alma Miller, is another childhood memory. It is a beautiful dessert served from a cut glass bowl and for holidays a sprig of holly is a nice touch that Aunt Alma usually added.

Cherry Spice Cake

2 cups sugar
3 cups flour
1 teaspoon baking powder
1 teaspoon cinnamon
½ teaspoon cloves
¼ teaspoon allspice
1 cup nuts, chopped
Dash of salt
3 eggs
1 cup butter
1 teaspoon soda
1 scant cup buttermilk
1 cup stewed, cooked apples, sweetened to taste
1 teaspoon vanilla
1 medium bottle maraschino cherries, cut

Cook dried apples, sweetened to taste, set aside. In mixing bowl, cream butter and sugar. Add vanilla and eggs, 1 at a time, beating well after each addition. Add soda to buttermilk. Sift flour, salt, baking powder and spices. Add to cream mixture alternating with buttermilk. Sift flour, salt, baking powder and spices. Add to cream mixture alternating with buttermilk. Mix until well blended, fold in stewed apples, cut cherries and nuts. Pour batter into 3 greased and floured 8-inch cake pans. Bake at 350°, 20 to 25 minutes until done. Frost with Penuche Icing.

Penuche Icing

3 cups brown sugar
1 cup sugar
1½ cups milk
6 tablespoons butter
2 teaspoons vanilla

Combine sugars, milk and butter. Cook over medium heat, stirring, to 242°. Remove from heat, add vanilla, beat until mixture is of spreading consistency. (Add cream if hardens too fast.)

I have only seen one other recipe even close to this one. It was our Christmas cake and I've never missed a single year having it. It is from my great-grandmother Bounds and the ones my mother made each year were wonderful.

Next-Day Turkey

2 tablespoons butter
½ pound fresh mushrooms, sliced
¼ cup butter
3 tablespoons flour
Dash cayenne pepper
½ teasoon dry mustard
¾ cup turkey or chicken broth
¾ cup light cream
½ cup dry white wine
1 (3-ounce) can pimento, drained and chopped
1 cup shredded sharp Cheddar cheese, divided
About 5 cups sliced, cooked turkey

Melt the 2 tablespoons butter in saucepan; add mushrooms and sauté over medium heat for 10 minutes. Set aside.

In another pan melt the ¼ cup butter and stir in flour, cayenne and dry mustard; stir until blended. Stir in broth, light cream, and wine. Add pimento and ½ cup shredded cheese. Cook over low heat until cheese is melted.

Butter a 2-quart casserole and in bottom arrange a layer of sliced, cooked turkey, using about 2½ cups meat. Top turkey layer with half of the mushrooms; pour half the sauce over the top. Top with second half of turkey, mushrooms, and remaining sauce. Sprinkle with ½ cup shredded cheese and bake at 300° for about 1 hour. Serve over hot buttered cornbread.

Yield: 6 to 8 servings.

INDEX

B

D

J

K

L

M

N

O

P

Q

R

S

W

Y

Z